I0868328

TWO CIVIL WARS

TWO CIVIL WARS

The CURIOUS SHARED JOURNAL *of a* BATON ROUGE SCHOOLGIRL *and a* UNION SAILOR *on the* USS *ESSEX*

EDITED AND ANNOTATED BY

Katherine Bentley Jeffrey

Louisiana State University Press

Baton Rouge

Published by Louisiana State University Press
Copyright © 2016 by Louisiana State University Press
All rights reserved
Manufactured in the United States of America
First printing

Designer: Barbara Neely Bourgoyne
Typeface: Arno Pro
Printer and binder: Maple Press

Library of Congress Cataloging-in-Publication Data
Names: Repp, Celeste, 1846–1914. | Park, William Little, 1836–1909. | Jeffrey, Katherine Bentley.
Title: Two civil wars : the curious shared journal of a Baton Rouge schoolgirl and a Union sailor on the USS *Essex* / edited and annotated by Katherine Bentley Jeffrey.
Description: Baton Rouge : Louisiana State University Press, 2016. | Includes bibliographical references and index.
Identifiers: LCCN 2015035403| ISBN 978-0-8071-6224-8 (cloth : alkaline paper) | ISBN 978-0-8071-6226-2 (PDF) | ISBN 978-0-8071-6225-5 (ePub) | ISBN 978-0-8071-6227-9 (MOBI)
Subjects: LCSH: Repp, Celeste, 1846–1914—Diaries. | Park, William Little, 1836–1909—Diaries. | Schoolgirls—Louisiana—Baton Rouge—Diaries. | Sailors—United States—Diaries. | *Essex* (Ironclad steamer) | United States—History—Civil War, 1861–1865—Personal narratives, Confederate. | United States—History—Civil War, 1861–1865—Personal narratives. | Baton Rouge (La.)—Biography. | Mississippi River Valley—History—Civil War, 1861–1865—Riverine operations. | United States—History—Civil War, 1861–1865—Riverine operations.
Classification: LCC F379.B33 R44 2016 | DDC 973.7/82—dc23
LC record available at http://lccn.loc.gov/2015035403

The paper in this book meets the guidelines for permanence and durability of the Committee on Production Guidelines for Book Longevity of the Council on Library Resources. ♾

For David,
with whom old books and good words
are daily pleasures

Contents

Maps and Illustrations

MAPS

ILLUSTRATIONS

Following page 106

Note: There are no extant photographs of either Celeste Repp or Matilda Victor. At least one photo of Celeste as a Sister of Mercy was at one time displayed in the hallway of St. Francis Xavier School in Vicksburg, but it has been lost. In Matilda Victor's case, any photographs left in her home or school in Baton Rouge were destroyed under Union occupation. She had no descendants, and her personal effects were apparently dispersed or disposed of at the time of her death in 1891.

Preface and Acknowledgments

Nearly twenty-five years ago, family friends in rural Quebec, Westburn and Gladys Hamilton, asked if my husband and I were interested in seeing a family curiosity, an "old book" that had been passed down to them several decades earlier. The book's principal author, William L. Park, was related to them, though not a direct ancestor. They knew very little about him except that he was kin (possibly a brother or cousin) to Walter Park, Gladys's maternal grandfather, a Scottish stonemason who had immigrated to Canada in the mid-1850s and settled in Clarendon Township. There were vague family stories of William Park visiting the Quebec farm after the American Civil War from his home in Chicago; it was assumed that the volume came to them on such an occasion. Walter's youngest daughter Anna (b. 1874) had been the book's guardian for many years before handing it on to her daughter Gladys.

The "old book" turned out to be the personal journal of a three-year tour of duty aboard USS *Essex,* one of the ironclad gunboats that patrolled the Lower Mississippi during the War Between the States. A contemporary account, not a retrospect, it captures in striking detail both the mundane happenstance of daily life—crew counts, river levels, weather, chores such as coaling, and routine maintenance—as well as the shattering intensity and brutality of battle, the ethical vagaries of shore raids and plunder of Confederate homes, and ambivalent interactions with black "contrabands."

I did not know then how unusual a shipboard document like this was, only that I had never seen anything like it; the Hamiltons allowed me to borrow and transcribe it, though it would be many years before I had time and opportunity to immerse myself in researching its contents.

As intrinsically fascinating as the naval diary is, the context in which one finds it is at least as fascinating. William Park documented his life aboard

Essex in a hardcover notebook that had previously belonged to a Louisiana schoolgirl, Celeste Repp, a student at a small private Catholic academy in Baton Rouge. Her signed "Compositions françaises par M'lle Celeste Repp, 1859, Academie St. Marie, Baton Rouge, La.," which fill the first pages of the notebook, mention both her headmistress, "Mademoiselle Victor," and a revered priest and teacher, "Pere Hubert." To these brief exercises are added three French poems, two of which are in an apparently different hand. They include a Marian devotional hymn, "Je vous Salue Auguste et Sainte Reine"; a love song by Émile Barateau (1792–1870), "Ange à la voix tendre," slightly adapted; and well-known melancholic lines from "Ode imitée de plusieurs psaumes" by Nicolas Gilbert (1750–1780):

> Au banquet de la vie, infortuné convive,
> J'apparus un jour, et je meurs.
> Je meurs, et sur la tombe, où lentement j'arrive,
> Nul ne viendra verser des pleurs.
>
> [An ill-fated guest at the banquet of life
> I appeared for a day, and now die.
> I die, and at the tomb where at last I rest
> None will come to shed a tear.]

The last page of poetry is dated March 20, 1861.[1] On the following page, and without any comment about how he acquired this little schoolbook, William Park launches into his "Abstract Journal kept by William L. Park of the U.S. Gunboat *Essex* during the American Rebellion, Commencing Sept. 25, 1861." It was on that date that Park and his friend Andrew Waterman enlisted in Chicago for service in the Western Flotilla "for three years or during [for the duration of] the war."

How a school scribbler from a private academy in Baton Rouge found its way into the hands of a Union gunboat sailor is, of course, the central

1. While two of these lyrical pieces seem to have been written as French *dictées,* the other was likely memorized for one of St. Mary's popular annual commencement exercises. Despite secession and the beginning of hostilities, St. Mary's stayed open until early 1862, albeit under considerable duress. For the fate of the school and its headmistress during and after the war, see the afterword. For further discussion of the poems and their connection to Celeste's compositions, see the commentary on Celeste's diary, below.

conundrum of this unassuming little volume. That question, and a possible explanation, are addressed at some length in the introduction. But if the "how" is perplexing, the "what" is extraordinary. Between two covers one finds, side by side, two distinct, emphatically different versions of the American experience in the middle of the nineteenth century. Self-evident contrasts (female/male; Confederate/Union; child/adult; native-born/foreign-born) are immediately apparent, but others emerge more organically in the course of reading.

In the first pages of this shared journal, we find ourselves in a Southern river port, in a Catholic subculture whose working language has historically been French, in the presence of a devout and precocious orphaned teenager, her indefatigable teacher, and a remarkable priest who will in 1861 exchange cassock for military garb and accompany the First Louisiana Infantry as chaplain through some of the most harrowing engagements of the Civil War. Celeste herself is happily innocent of the upheavals just around the corner, which lends extraordinary poignancy to her compositions; her life revolves contentedly around those whose faith she trusts and whose virtues she admires. She will herself, after the war, imitate their devotion, self-sacrifice, and idealism when she enters the convent of the Sisters of Mercy in Vicksburg, Mississippi.

In the remainder of the diary, we find ourselves among the pragmatic warriors of the Mississippi gunboats, many of whom, like William Park himself, are foreign-born and lack any patriotic impulse with respect to the Union cause or any tender feelings toward the plight of African American slaves. They are working-class "tars," irreverent, boisterous, generally irreligious, fiercely loyal to each other, and capable of their own forms of heroism under withering fire and in the face of hideous carnage, but they are very much outliers in the dominant narrative of Mr. Lincoln's War. Park and his colleagues who survive their three-year tour will muster out when it expires and not a day later, if they can help it. They will not become legislators or city fathers or culture changers; having done their duty and collected their pay, they will go back to working-class life, marry and settle down, turn the page. Many will suffer from crippling ill health related to their wartime service. Some will attend veterans' reunions as the years go by, but few will seek to tell their stories outside of a small circle of family and friends.

Historical research about a document as personal as this was to both of its authors, about whom little external information is known, is painstakingly slow. One follows innumerable fruitless leads in search of bits of corroborating information. A name as common as William Park presents particular challenges, especially when census records are often unreliable and inconsistent. As for thirteen-year-old Celeste Repp, historians and archivists in Baton Rouge seemed to have no record or recollection of this particular St. Mary's Academy or its long-suffering headmistress, or even of "Pere Hubert," who features prominently and affectionately in Celeste's writing.

As is so often the case in historical detective work, the discovered key to one door lent access to countless others. Learning that Father Hubert was a Jesuit, and that his first name was Darius, allowed me to begin to piece together his extraordinary history through myriad sources. A harried and beloved French-born priest and educator in Baton Rouge and New Orleans before the war, he became one of the most renowned and revered of all Southern chaplains:[2] he prayed a benediction over the Pelican Flag at the Louisiana secession convention, accompanied his regiment of Louisiana volunteers in the Northern Virginia campaign until surrender, was wounded at Gettysburg, tended to the spiritual needs of the crew of *Virginia* (*Merrimack*) at Hampton Roads, was well known to Robert E. Lee, Stonewall Jackson, and Jefferson Davis, and was so eloquent of thought and speech—even in his adopted language of English[3]—that he was after the war regularly called on

2. The role of Catholic chaplains in the South is largely ignored by contemporary historians of the Civil War. The religious character of the Confederacy has been described almost exclusively in terms of evangelical and revivalist piety, from John William Jones's *Christ in the Camp* (1887) and William W. Bennett's *The Great Revival in the Southern Armies* (1876) forward. In Martin Marty's brief summation, "Roman Catholicism plays little part in this history, for Catholics were rare in the South, and to this day their community there is dwarfed by a Baptist-Methodist-Presbyterian-Church of Christ culture with an Episcopalian underlay" (foreword to Donald G. Mathews, *Religion in the Old* South [Chicago: University of Chicago Press, 1977], xi). That it could be said of Fr. Darius Hubert that he was "known and dear to every man in the Army of Northern Virginia" (Clement Anselm Evans, *Confederate Military History* [Atlanta: Confederate Publishing, 1899], 10:234) and that after the war he was regularly asked to offer prayers at veterans' gatherings and events commemorating Confederate leaders both complicates and enriches the story of religion in the Southern army. See the afterword.

3. Unlike many of his fellow Jesuits, notably Hippolyte Gache, whose wartime correspondence as a Confederate chaplain has been translated and edited by Cornelius Buckley, S.J. (*Frenchman, Chaplain, Rebel: The Civil War Letters of Pierre Louis-Hippolyte Gache, S.J., 10th Louisiana Infantry* [Tuscaloosa: University of Alabama Press, 1981]), Hubert wrote and spoke comfortably, even elegantly, in English. This is only one of the ways he transcended traditional

to recount and celebrate the dignity of those who had fought and died in the Lost Cause. His passing in 1893, in his seventieth year, was noted in the *New York Times,* which described him as "one of the most widely-known priests of the South."

It was in researching Fr. Hubert and his tenure as priest at St. Joseph Catholic Church in Baton Rouge that I was able eventually to find young Celeste herself in parish records—to learn that she was orphaned by her midteens (her mother, Amelina, died in 1855 at the age of forty-four, likely of yellow fever; her father, John, died five years later, of unknown causes, at fifty). The children were taken in by Celeste's maternal grandmother, Augustine Mears, twice-widowed and operating a hotel in East Baton Rouge, on the corner of Lafayette and Florida Streets. Although this is their home of record in the census of 1860, Celeste and her sister Alice were boarders at St. Mary's Academy when she wrote her "Compositions françaises" for Fr. Hubert, the academy's French instructor.

Hubert, in his role as teacher, also provided the introduction to Matilda Victor, headmistress of St. Mary's Academy (the third school so-named in Baton Rouge), a Catholic convert from Ohio whose fitness to run a young ladies' academy was constantly questioned, but who persisted in offering a quality liberal arts education to students like Celeste as poverty and plague, occupation and war, religious squabbles and petty jealousies conspired against her. It turns out, in fact, that the cast of characters associated with Celeste's childhood in Baton Rouge is every bit as colorful and worthy of attention as that of the sailors toiling aboard the Mississippi gunboats.

About William Park, the Union quarter gunner, federal pension and service records yielded some important details of his life as a veteran—his place of residence, marriage, children's names, chronic war-related infirmities, and date of death. For additional information about life aboard *Essex* and about the important battles and memorable incidents of Park's three-year tenure, I am, of course, indebted to the *Official Records of the Union and Confederate Navies in the War of the Rebellion* as well as numerous popular and scholarly books—including the recent volume by Michael J. Bennett, *Union Jacks:*

divides. Matilda Victor wrote of him that he was revered in Baton Rouge by Protestants as well as Catholics—a rare commendation in the highly factionalized religious environment of the time. In this respect also, Hubert was unlike Gache, whose antipathy toward Protestants was reflexive and often virulent.

Yankee Sailors in the Civil War. It was Bennett who first led me, in his notes and bibliography, to another unpublished journal from USS *Essex*—that of James Henneberry, who joined the service the same week as Park and, like him, mustered out in the autumn of 1864 to Chicago.[4] Henneberry's "chum," William H. ("Hank") Ruger, who talked Henneberry into enlisting against his mother's wishes, is mentioned by name in the Park diary, and Park and Ruger kept up regularly after the war.[5] I have used the Henneberry text, which is complementary rather than merely supplementary or duplicative of Park's journal, to fill out some of the details that Park omits, particularly the names of sailors involved in various calamities or notable actions, or those who were killed while in service. The existence of two other *Essex* memoirs came to light in the final stages of my research—those of Edward Galligan and of Charles J. Drew.[6] I have been able to consult the Galligan text, which, though a good deal more cryptic than the other diaries, contains some unique sidelights and adds yet more personal names to the ship's roster.

The most important and surprising late addition to my research, however, emerged in a fruitful correspondence with Tom Baskett, County Historian of Volusia, Florida, who has long been collecting materials on the *Essex* officers and crew. Hearing that I was annotating the journal of William Park, he mentioned having intended to look at it himself at the Newberry Library in Chicago. I consulted the Newberry and learned that in 2006, a decade and a half after I first saw and transcribed the Canadian-held journal, a second memoir was donated to the library by the estate of William Park's granddaughter and last living descendant, Virginia A. Park, who died in Chicago (at ninety-seven years of age) in 2005. My assumption was that this would be a verbatim transcription, perhaps made for or by one of William's four children. It turns

4. The James E. Henneberry Papers (comprising photostats of the original handwritten *Essex* journal) are held in the Chicago History Museum Research Center.

5. Ruger, who was a surgeon's assistant on *Essex,* and who also served alongside Park on *Pittsburg* during the eventful spring of 1862, acted as a witness and advocate for Park in several of his appeals for disability compensation after the war. In a deposition recorded by a notary public in Cook County, Illinois, and dated 1890, Ruger indicates that "for five or six years after the service I saw him [Park] on an average of twice a week. . . . From 1870–1882 [after Park was married and had a young family, and prior to his move to South Dakota] I saw him several times a year, and then again frequently since 88." Park had moved back to Chicago in 1888 and lived out his life there. For more on Park's postwar life, see the afterword.

6. The Galligan text is held in the Montana Historical Society in Helena.

out, however, to be a considerably later and more expansive text, composed in the light of official published records and journalistic accounts of the war, as well as conversation with Park's Chicago shipmates. I have, courtesy of the Newberry Library, read that version of Park's memoir entire and have occasionally included a note from it where it added pertinent detail. A more detailed description of that volume, and its divergences from the "ur-text" that appears in Celeste's notebook, is provided in appendix 3.

During a visit to St. Louis in January 2012 to see a Civil War exhibit in the Missouri History Museum, I came face to face with "W. L. Park"—the diary's William—for the first time. A black-and-white photograph entitled *Gunners of the* Essex was on display in a small room devoted to the War on Western Waters. This was not only my own first encounter with an image of Park; it was the first likeness that the Hamilton and Park families in Quebec had ever seen. The same image appears in Francis Trevelyan Miller's *The Navies,* volume 6 of *The Photographic History of the Civil War.* I am grateful to the Missouri History Museum for permission to reproduce it here (figure 5).

Among those who assisted in locating relevant archival materials, I would like particularly to thank Judy Bolton, Head of Public Services in Special Collections, LSU Libraries, Baton Rouge; Katie Oubre, Assistant Archivist for the Diocese of Baton Rouge; Willam Kevin Cawley, Archivist at the University of Notre Dame Archives, where many nineteenth-century records from the Diocese of New Orleans are held; Joan Gaulene, Archivist for the New Orleans Province of the Society of Jesus, Loyola University; Dorenda Dupont, at the Office of Archives and Records of the Archdiocese of New Orleans; Richard Anthony Lewis, Curator of Visual Arts for Louisiana State Museum; Sister Louanna Orth, Archivist for the Ohio Unit, Sisters of Notre Dame de Namur; Grant Gerlich, Archivist at Mercy Heritage House in Belmont, North Carolina (Archives for the Sisters of Mercy in the Americas); Christopher Viscardi and Richard Weaver at Spring Hill College in Mobile, Alabama; Jeff Meyer and Jaime Bourassa at the Missouri History Museum in St. Louis; Marianna Oller, Associate Curator, Special Collections at Wellesley College, Massachusetts; Mark McCallon, Librarian at Abilene Christian University in Abilene, Texas; Lesley Martin, Research Specialist at the Chicago History Museum Research Center; Lisa Shoblatsky, Special Collections Services Librarian at the Newberry Library, Chicago; Evangeline Cessna, Local History Librarian at the Warren County-Vicksburg Public Library;

Cassandra Fedrick and Lee Bareford, Genealogy Librarians at the East Baton Rouge Public Library; Becky Hill, Head Librarian at the Rutherford B. Hayes Presidential Center, Fremont, Ohio; Sean Benjamin, Public Services Librarian at the Louisiana Research Collection, Howard-Tilton Memorial Library, Tulane University; Brian Shovers and Zoe Ann Stoltz at the Montana Research Center in Helena, Montana; Ron Davidson, Special Collections Librarian at the Sandusky Library, Sandusky, Ohio; Joe Ricci and Patricia Ricci at the Confederate Memorial Hall Museum in New Orleans; and the staff of the Pontiac Archives in Shawville, Quebec.

Sister Mary Paulinus Oakes, R.S.M., spent a day with me in Vicksburg in early 2014, showing me the convent and school in which Celeste (Sister Euphrasia) Repp lived and worked after the war, and accompanying me to the Sisters' cemetery; she also provided wonderful background on the Mercy legacy in Mississippi. Drury Wellford, former head of Photo Services at the Museum of the Confederacy in Richmond, Virginia, arranged to photograph the oil portrait of Fr. Darius Hubert in that museum's holdings for me in 2013; she also provided an engaging "rebel tour" of Richmond during a visit in May 2014. Chip Landry, Sexton of the Historic St. Joseph Catholic Cemetery, was unstintingly generous and unfailingly helpful in searching out information about the Repp family gravesites and related funeral records in Baton Rouge.

As an uncredentialed historian whose research has taken me all over the map of Civil War–era America in search of supporting documentation for the persons and events mentioned in this journal, I am indebted to numerous specialists who have shared with me their knowledge and expertise. They were, to a person, encouraging of the work and open-handed with very specific answers to my queries. I shall always be grateful for the assistance of these individuals, many of whose books and articles appear in the notes and bibliography of this volume. In this context I would especially like to acknowledge Fr. Cornelius Buckley, S.J., currently Chaplain at Thomas Aquinas College, Santa Paula, California, and editor of *Frenchman, Chaplain, Rebel: The Civil War Letters of Pere Louis-Hippolyte Gache, S.J.;* Don Beagle and Bryan Giemza, authors of a new biography of Abram Joseph Ryan (*Poet of the Lost Cause: A Life of Father Ryan*); Eric Platt, a historian of Jesuit education in the South (*Sacrifice and Survival: Identity, Mission, and Jesuit Higher Education*); and Steve Mayeux, author of a wonderful book on Fort DeRussy, Louisiana (*Earthen Walls, Men of Iron*). Historian Gary D. Joiner, a specialist on the Mississippi Squadron (*Mr. Lincoln's Brown Water Navy,* as well as several studies of the Red River Campaign), read this book in manuscript and provided a heartening assessment of its merits.

To those in the online genealogical community and to the often unnamed individuals who have toiled in the transcription of census records and local documents, particularly in the parishes of the Acadian Coast, I owe a particular debt. I have had many exhilarating moments stumbling onto family and community connections related to Celeste Repp in the vast web of information now available by this means on the Internet. I have also enjoyed corresponding with individuals who have a personal connection to Celeste's extended family, notably Dick Haines (who married into a family descended from Celeste's brother William) and Kathlene Carr (who descends from Walter Hunter Mears, Celeste's grandmother's second husband); both shared relevant records gleaned while researching different parts of the family tree. Mary McKeough, editor of *Le Baton Rouge* and the *Louisiana Genealogical Register,* kindly sought out local maps for me. Wherever I have discovered information or transcriptions to be in error (e.g., John Junius Burk mistakenly listed as "J. J. Buck" or "I. I. Burke"; Walter Mears as "Walter Means"; and, in one particularly bad census record, Celeste counted as "Silas," Junia as "Julia," Amelina as "Eleonor," etc.), I have silently corrected, knowing that others may find in this volume the basis for further research about their own families and communities. Historical study is a project of continual and shared self-correction. I have endeavored to ensure the accuracy of as many of these details as I could from the sources available to me. For the errors that remain, I ask the forbearance and, indeed, the subsequent amendment of my readers.

My husband, David, with whom I have collaborated on many of his own academic projects, offered unwavering support as I pursued this work off and on for more than a decade. Our son Josh, an avid historian in his own right, created for me Celeste Repp's family tree (see page 2). Indeed, my entire family has cheered me on in what seemed, at first, a rather quixotic project. Having borne patiently my obsessive prattle about nineteenth-century sailors and soldiers, teachers and students, Jesuits and nuns, novelists and suffragists, they now share my joy (and relief) that *Two Civil Wars* has found a wider audience.

LSU Press has been a wonderful partner in this endeavor. I deeply appreciate the courtesy, good judgment, and professionalism of all those associated with the Press who have worked with me to bring this text to published form.

My greatest debt is to the Hamilton family, who first showed me the "old book," and to Wayne Park, its current guardian, who permitted me to digitize it. It has been an inestimable privilege to live in these pages, and to make the acquaintance of four remarkable individuals from often-overlooked communities, whose stories shed new light on this most harrowing, inspiring, and endlessly fascinating chapter of American history.

TWO CIVIL WARS

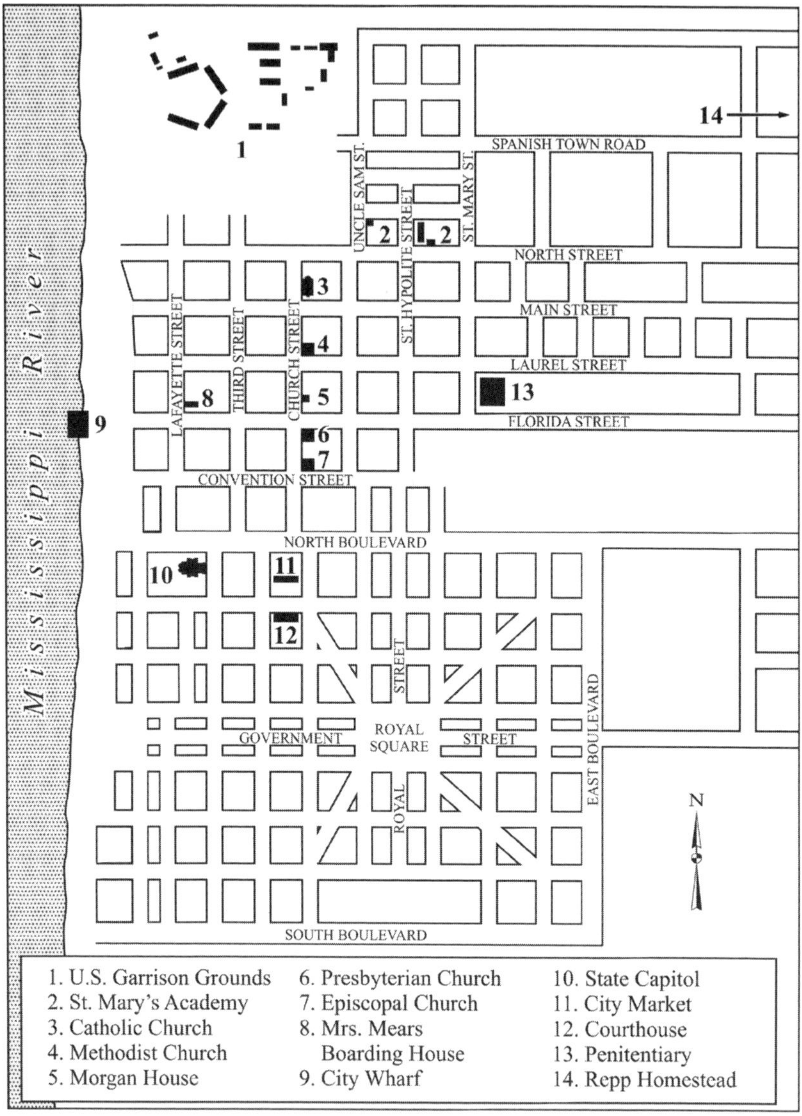

Celeste Repp's Baton Rouge, 1860.

Introduction

THE SCHOOLGIRL: M'LLE CELESTE REPP, L'ACADEMIE ST. MARIE, BATON ROUGE, LOUISIANA

Celeste's Family Circle

Celeste Repp was born in 1846, the fourth of seven children, three of whom died young. Like many Louisiana households of the period, hers reflected a complex multicultural and multilingual character and diverse, even contradictory, social and religious mores; she was heir to both the working-class values of her German immigrant father and the more patrician Southern values of her mother's French and English Catholic family.

Her father was John Diedrich Repp, who worked as a butcher and meat dealer in the Central Market in Baton Rouge several blocks from the river (figures 1 and 2). As such, he would seem to have had little in common with the more settled and prosperous "Pennsylvania Deutsch" community well established on second- and third-generation cotton and sugar plantations in the Highlands district above the Mississippi floodplain. The daughters of some of these prominent and affluent German families (e.g., Klines, Kleinpeters, Garigs) would one day attend school with Celeste,[1] but in her early years their social circles were almost certainly very different.

1. The George Kleinpeter and Family Papers, Louisiana and Lower Mississippi Valley Collection, LSU Libraries, MSS 864 and 1029, include receipts for tuition at St. Mary's Academy for Alice Kleinpeter for the years 1860–62; the *Baton Rouge Gazette,* in publishing its "flattering encomiums" about St. Mary's spring entertainment on April 7, 1858, lists Matilda Kline, Agnes Kline, Emma Kline, Carrie Kleinpeter, and Lucrizia Garig (along with Celeste Repp's sister Alice) among the prominent performers.

THE FAMILY TREE OF CELESTE REPP

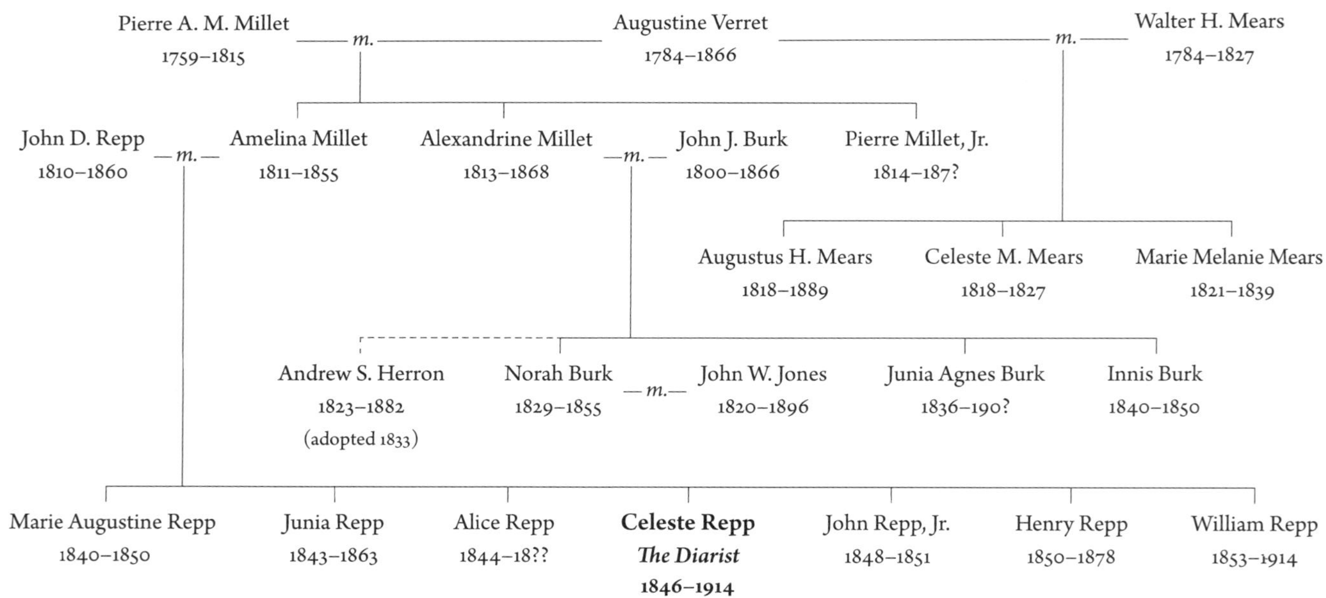

Note: This chart is limited to family members mentioned in order of immediate relevance to Celeste's journal

Celeste's mother was Amelina Millet (sometimes spelled Millette),[2] a Louisianan of French heritage born in 1811 in Plattenville, Assumption Parish. Firstborn daughter of a fifty-two-year-old French immigrant from Bordeaux, Pierre Alexandre Maximilien Millet, and a young Louisiana woman with French-Canadian and Acadian roots, Augustine Françoise Verret,[3] Amelina was soon joined by two siblings, Alexandrine[4] and Pierre,[5] before her father died in 1815, when she was only four.

Amelina's mother, Augustine, remarried a year and a half later (March 10, 1817) to British-born Walter Hunter Mears (b. 1784), whose family immigrated in 1790, initially to Pennsylvania. Walter came to Louisiana as a young man and seems quickly to have found position and influence: he was appointed

2. Amelina's first name is also sometimes given as "Amelia" or "Amelie." (One particularly error-ridden census lists her as "Eleanor.") The form of her name used here is that which appears in baptismal and burial records.

3. Augustine was thirty years younger than her first husband, Pierre. Her great-grandfather, Michel Joseph Verret, was born in Quebec City, moving to Louisiana in the early 1700s. Another branch of Verrets were among the first Acadian settlers in Louisiana; Nicholas Verret established a plantation in the area prior to 1763 and moved with his family by 1766. The family name, still common in the Acadian Coast, is attached to Lake Verret, a popular recreational destination in the lower Atchafalaya Basin.

4. Alexandrine, born February 4, 1813, was to marry John Junius Burk, a second-generation American of Irish stock and a prominent Catholic layman in Baton Rouge, "while she was very young," according to her daughter Junia's memoir (printed in *Some Materials to Serve for a Brief Memoir of John Daly Burk . . . With a Sketch of the Life and Character of His Only Child, Judge John Junius Burk,* ed. Charles Campbell [Albany, NY: Joel Munsell, 1868], 74–87). Burk was possessed of a superb classical education and studied for the bar in Louisiana, thereafter becoming a lawyer and then judge. But he also educated his own children and apparently, for a time, Celeste Repp's oldest sister, Marie Augustine, who was living with the Burks at the time of her death in 1850, at the age of ten. The Burk's own ten-year-old daughter Innis died at the same time, presumably of the same cause (possibly cholera) as little Marie Augustine. Both are buried in St. Joseph Cemetery in Baton Rouge.

5. Pierre Millet Jr., born June 20, 1814, was as an adult better known as Pete; he lived for many years in the boardinghouse of his mother, Augustine, and served as the town wharfmaster, collecting wharfage dues for the city and receiving steamboat freight. According to a reminiscence in the *Baton Rouge State Times Advocate* (February 19, 1915), Pete Millet "from earliest boyhood to a good old age spent his days at the landing and . . . was known by every steamboat officer and roustabout plying the Mississippi." After John Repp died in 1860 and Augustine Mears (the Repp children's grandmother and guardian) in 1866, Pete Millet took in his teenage nephews, Celeste's brothers, Henry and William, until they were ready to strike out on their own.

the first sheriff of Ascension Parish in 1811, serving in that role in Donaldsonville until 1816.[6] The 1820 census finds the Mears family living comfortably in Plaquemine, Iberville Parish. In addition to the three children Augustine brought into the marriage (Amelina, Alexandrine, and Pierre), she and Walter had three children together—two daughters, Celeste Millet Mears (our diarist's namesake),[7] who lived only until 1827, and Marie Melanie Mears, who died in 1839 in her teens,[8] and one son, Augustus Hunter Mears.[9] Two other (unnamed) young adults shared their household in 1820, possibly siblings to Walter or Augustine; the family held seven slaves—two mature women and five children or young adults.

The year 1827 was a tumultuous one in Amelina's blended household. A few months after the death of her half sister Celeste, her stepfather, Walter Mears, then serving as coroner of Baton Rouge, died at the age of forty-three. The cause of his death is not recorded, but one suspects it was one of the many insect-borne diseases that plagued the South and that seemed to take an especially heavy toll in the summer and early fall:[10] the same edition of

6. Walter (whose middle initial is frequently transcribed incorrectly as "N") immigrated as a child to America. His father was a physician, a vocation Walter's son Augustus Hunter Mears would take up in his turn. Walter evidently had a good education and a judicious administrative temperament, filling the role of sheriff and then coroner in adjacent parishes. Though medical training was not required for coroners in this period, Walter's family history likely prepared and predisposed him for such work. In local records, reflecting an oral French culture, his name is sometime misspelled as "Meurs," "Moeurs," or even "Mirz."

7. She is listed in a death notice in June 1827 as "daughter of A. H. Mears," which clearly should be "daughter of W. H. Mears"; "A. H." would have been her ten-year-old brother, Augustus Hunter.

8. Inscribed on Melanie's gravestone in the historic St. Joseph Catholic Cemetery of Baton Rouge is a two-stanza poem, the last lines of which read: "Leave to Heaven its own; wild flowers will shed / Their fragrance, and dews will nightly weep / To hallow the sacred spot, the bed / Where a child of heaven takes her sleep."

9. Augustus Mears, Celeste's uncle, married Marguerite Pamelia Comeaux in 1844; their church records, from both St. Gabriel and Assumption parishes, are tidily complete. They had eleven children, including five daughters, all of whom had variants of "Mary" or "Marie" as baptismal names.

10. Federal forces, both army and navy, referred to the summer months along the Mississippi and its tributaries as "the sickly season." So many crew and officers of the inland navy came down with one or more kinds of fever or illness during June, July, and August that a small steamer was employed exclusively for the transport of the sick to and from hospitals—principally at Mound City, Illinois, and (after the summer of 1862) Memphis, Tennessee.

the *Baton Rouge Gazette* that reported Mears's death published a statement by the town magistrate Bartholomew T. Beauregard refuting rumors that yellow fever (currently rampant in New Orleans) had appeared locally.[11] Whatever the cause, Augustine Verret Millet Mears was unexpectedly widowed for a second time, with five children still at home.

These straitened circumstances may explain why, in January 1828, Amelina, just shy of her seventeenth birthday, married a man twice her age from Georgia named Russell Wilson; the marriage was recorded at Our Lady of Sorrows Catholic Church (later St. Joseph), Baton Rouge. Whether it was arranged by the families or undertaken on a youthful impulse, it was short-lived and produced no children. It is unclear if the marriage was annulled or the couple simply parted ways; Amelina is never listed with Wilson's last name, and at the time of the 1830 census she was again living with her mother and siblings in Plaquemine.

Sometime in 1838/39, Amelina left home for good, marrying John Diedrich Repp, who had emigrated from Germany in 1832.[12] His port of entry was Baltimore, Maryland, from where he may have moved immediately to Louisiana; he was naturalized as an American citizen in 1840 in Baton Rouge. The census of that year shows John and Amelina Repp living in Ward 12 of East Baton Rouge, on a fourteen-acre homestead just outside the eastern town boundary, with their first child, a daughter named Marie Augustine. Born on March 1, 1840, she was baptized at the Catholic Church in Assumption Parish (Amelina's home parish) as an infant, on June 6.[13] Her baptismal sponsors were Augustus Mears (Amelina's half brother, now twenty-two years of age) and Marie Celeste Verret, Amelina's maternal aunt.

A second daughter, Junia, followed in 1843;[14] Alice was born in 1845; Celeste herself made her appearance in 1846. Junia's baptismal records are missing from the Catholic archives, but we know that, unlike their firstborn

11. Though there were no documented cases of yellow fever in Baton Rouge in 1827, the fear of transmission was very high. Mears was doubtless exposed to disease in his role as coroner; cholera, malaria, typhoid fever, dysentery, and tuberculosis were all frequent and often fatal in this period.

12. There are no extant marriage records for John and Amelina. Given Amelina's former union and the fact that John was not a Catholic, they doubtless had a civil ceremony.

13. Marie Augustine lived only to the age of ten; see note 4 above.

14. Though Junia's baptismal records have been lost, parish records indicate that she died on June 6, 1863, in her twentieth year.

sister, neither Alice nor Celeste was baptized as an infant and neither carried a variant of "Marie" in her name. They were both eventually baptized in St. Joseph Church, Baton Rouge, in 1854, just a year before their mother died.[15] The Repps' first son, John Jr., was born in 1848 but lived only until his third birthday; his baptism was likely performed at the time of death.[16] Two more boys, Henry and William, born in 1850 and 1853 respectively, were baptized together in St. Joseph parish in April 1856.

These records, though sparse, are suggestive. John Repp was not a Catholic when he and Amelina married. Whether he objected to infant baptism or was simply irreligious or indifferent to the Church, it is clear that the children's religious initiation and formation, such as it was, was fostered by their mother's side of the family. In the Repp household, two sets of delayed childhood baptisms—Alice's and Celeste's at nine and seven, and Henry's and William's at six and three—bookended the passing of their mother, Amelina, in the summer of 1855. The children's widowed grandmother, Augustine Mears, despite her advanced years, soon stepped in as guardian for the Repp children and seems to have taken a strong hand in getting her grandchildren properly "churched."

John Diedrich Repp himself died in February 1860 of unknown causes; he was baptized on his deathbed by Fr. Darius Hubert and given a Catholic burial,[17] likely fulfilling Amelina's last wish and answering her family's prayers.

Celeste's Headmistress: Matilda Victor

When, precisely, Celeste and the other surviving Repp children went to live with their maternal grandmother, Augustine Mears, is uncertain, but the girls at least seem to have moved out of their father's home before his death—possibly around the time of their mother's passing in 1855. Augustine's aspirations for

15. The year 1855 was, like 1853, a very bad one for yellow fever in the region. See note 20 below.

16. Both Marie Augustine and little John Jr. are buried together with their mother, Amelina Repp, in the historic Catholic Cemetery of Baton Rouge.

17. The entry in the St. Joseph Catholic Funeral Register (SJO-11, page 150, #10) reads: "On the thirteenth day of February A.D. eighteen hundred and sixty, I performed the funeral rights on the remains of John D. Repp, deceased on the previous day . . . having been previously baptized under conditions and anointed by me. /s/ D. Hubert, S.J." "Conditional" baptism occurs when there has been no formal catechism but an acknowledgment and repentance of sin in the presence of a priest.

her granddaughters clearly included a proper Catholic liberal arts education, and Alice and Celeste were soon enrolled in St. Mary's Academy.[18]

An earlier St. Mary's Select and Free School, "that would teach all branches of a good education," was opened by the Sisters of Charity in Baton Rouge in 1847. It met for a time on Church Street, in "the residence of Mr. T. G. [Thomas Gibbes] Morgan," the father of Baton Rouge's famous diarist Sarah Morgan, when he was temporarily stationed in New Orleans as a customs collector.[19] By 1851, however, the struggling Sisters of Charity school had closed its doors. When the Jesuits took over parish ministry in Baton Rouge in 1849, they built a school for boys called the College of St. Peter and St. Paul and invited another group of religious, the Sisters of the Sacred Heart, to open a parallel school for girls in 1851; it was named, unsurprisingly, St. Mary's Academy. This experiment was also short-lived; the school closed in 1855, in no small part because of decimation of the ranks by yellow fever.[20]

18. It is unclear whether Junia, three years older than Celeste, attended St. Mary's as well, as no school rosters are extant. Alice's presence at the school is attested in a newspaper column about a spring "entertainment" in which she performed in April 1858. The *Baton Rouge Gazette,* April 8, 1858, included a lengthy and laudatory review of "the entertainment of the season" afforded by the St. Mary's students, including Alice Repp, who took the role of "boisterous March" in an original play about the seasons, entitled "Father Time." The Sunday edition of the *Gazette* (April 11, 1858) included a complete program and yet another review, including praise for Alice Repp, among others. The only record of Celeste's attendance uncovered to date is her French "compositions" here published.

19. See Sister M. Veronica Kelly, "A Century of Catholic Education in Baton Rouge, 1847–1947" (master's thesis, Catholic University of America, 1947), 10. The Morgans' sojourn in New Orleans is documented in the introduction to *The Civil War Diary of Sarah Morgan,* ed. Charles East (Athens: University of Georgia Press, 1991; reprinted by Simon and Schuster/Touchstone in 1992 as *Sarah Morgan: The Civil War Diary of a Southern Woman*). The Morgans returned to Baton Rouge in 1850. All subsequent citations of Morgan's work are to the 1992 edition.

20. Yellow fever was virulent in both 1853 and 1855. It took the lives of several Jesuit priests and brothers, devastated a Catholic retreat held at nearby St. Michael's parish in the early autumn of 1855, and caused terrible havoc in religious communities all along the Lower Mississippi. Mother Amelie Jouve observed to Bishop Blanc in a letter dated October 11, 1855, that "foreigners" seemed to be especially vulnerable to the epidemic. "All who have died are from the States or from Europe"; in her own community of Sacred Heart Sisters, a third of the religious were killed. But Louisiana natives also succumbed to the epidemic. Diocesan correspondence in the summer and fall of 1855 comprises a woeful litany of sickness and loss that included not only priests and religious but also the flocks they served. In early November 1855, the Sisters of the Sacred Heart departed their Baton Rouge mission, "despite the pleas of

In 1858, the Sisters of Saint Joseph, a French teaching order, commenced yet another attempt to run a successful Catholic female academy in Baton Rouge, this time calling it St. Joseph's School for Girls.

The school attended by the Repp girls was none of these. It was, in fact, something quite distinctive, owing to the singular personality and unusual background of its founder, Matilda Victor.[21]

Though not a religious herself, Matilda Victor was educated by nuns in the convent school of the Sisters of Notre Dame de Namur in Cincinnati, Ohio. This fact is somewhat surprising given that her family was Protestant—even, according to later family correspondence, rather anti-Catholic. Matilda's father, Henry Clay Victor, one of the early pioneers of Sandusky, Ohio, operated a hotel known as the Mansion House with his wife, Gertrude (Nash) Victor, in the 1820s and 1830s before moving to a farm in Seneca County. When Henry died in 1848, Matilda's mother moved back to Sandusky and remained there the rest of her life. Matilda's brother Orville James Victor, who had a public school education in Sandusky, wrote for a time for the *Sandusky Daily Register* before going on to considerable fame as a biographer, historian, journalist, editor, and writer of many volumes still available in reprint editions—notably books documenting and interpreting the "Southern Rebellion."[22]

parents, students, and several leading citizens of the town" (Kelly, "A Century of Catholic Education in Baton Rouge," 19–20). Matilda Victor arrived in Baton Rouge in the immediate wake of this plague.

21. During her sojourn in Louisiana, Matilda adopted the French form of her name. Correspondence and other documents from this period typically list her as Mathilde Victor.

22. Among Orville James Victor titles still widely read are *Incidents and Anecdotes of the War; The History, Civil, Political, and Military, of the Southern Rebellion; The History of the Southern Rebellion, From Its Incipient Stages to Its Close; History of American Conspiracies: A Record of Treason, Insurrection, Rebellion, etc. in the United States of America; The American Rebellion: Some Facts and Reflections for the Consideration of the English People;* and *Men of the Time: Being Biographies of Generals.* Despite his strong Unionist sentiments and rather bellicose style in defending them, Orville advocated for his sister Matilda during the hardships of the postsecession period in Baton Rouge, writing sympathetically of her Catholic identity and Southern loyalties in a May 21, 1861, letter sent from the offices of *Cosmopolitan Art Journal* in New York to Archbishop Jean-Marie Odin, New Orleans (University of Notre Dame Archives, VI–2–d *A.L.S.* 2, pp. 8vo.5). During the occupation of Baton Rouge by Union forces, however, Matilda declared herself an adherent to the Federal rather than secessionist cause and willingly allowed her buildings to be used by Union personnel. For more on Matilda's experience following occupation, see the afterword.

Another brother, Jacob Nash Victor, was a construction engineer for military railways during the Civil War and then served as general manager of the California Southern Railway (Victorville, California, is named for him). What prompted the family to enroll Matilda as a boarding student with the Notre Dame Sisters in Cincinnati is a mystery. If, as one supposes, they were looking for intellectual outcomes of a high order, they were doubtless unprepared for the spiritual outcome of her formative years in a convent school.

Sister Louise (Josephine van der Schrieck), the American founder of the order and its superior in the Cincinnati house from 1845 until her death in 1886,[23] was responsible for religious instruction during Matilda's time as a student and came to be a great favorite among the girls, Matilda included. Alone among the early sisters, all of whom came, like her, from Europe, Sister Louise "became an American" in sensibility, embracing her adopted culture and language in a way that made her instruction especially winsome.[24] An unnamed student captures the girls' collective admiration nicely: "She was an unusually dignified person, extremely good-looking, and elegant in manner, but so lovable and kind and so absolutely just, that she has always been my ideal of a saint and a lady."[25] Sister's Louise's friendship and guidance, combined with rigorous studies and a calendar stocked with celebratory feast days and consummated each year with polished public performances associated with commencement, proved to be transformative for young Matilda. While she was at the convent school, she departed her family's faith tradition and became a Roman Catholic. It was not an easy road. She was later to write, very feelingly, to the prominent Catholic layman Orestes Brownson, likewise a convert, about the "position of American young ladies who are converts to our holy [Catholic] faith":

> In embracing the faith they are but too often discarded by their friends and driven to self-maintenance, a thing rather difficult in existing circumstances. The Church discourages mixed marriages as endangering faith. There are few Catholic gentlemen, and a well-educated American girl cannot so easily descend the

23. See Sister Helen Louise (Nugent), *Sister Louise: Josephine Van Der Schrieck 1813–1886*, Studies in American Church History, vol. 10 (Washington, DC: Catholic University of America, 1931).

24. Ibid., 195–96. Matilda will later, in lamenting the state of American Catholic education, specifically note the "foreign" sensibilities, and lack of requisite academic training, of most teaching nuns.

25. Ibid., 208–9.

> social ladder. The majority have no vocation for the religious state. Almost the only resource is teaching and for that they seem to be well qualified, but here again is an obstacle—their faith, or rather public bigotry—closes the public schools against them. . . . Under the present arrangements an American girl who has the courage to become a Catholic enters at once upon a life of martyrdom.[26]

Matilda's family being largely unreconciled to her conversion, she departed for the Southern states, to live (in her brother Orville's words) "in the enjoyment of her religion." She settled for a time in Little Rock, Arkansas, where census records show her living in 1850 with five other young women in the precincts of the Cathedral of St. Andrew; Bishop Andrew Byrne, Pastor John Patrick Reilly, rector of the Cathedral, Vicar Frances O'Donohoe, and John Sheridan, a divinity student, were living in the adjacent rectory. Matilda seems to have been part of a nascent Catholic educational establishment that would become yet another St. Mary's Academy (now Mount St. Mary) in Little Rock. When the school opened its doors formally in 1851, it was staffed by Sisters of Mercy who had been personally recruited for the task in Ireland by Bishop Byrne; this was likely the first time that Matilda was to feel the sting of being displaced, despite her evident academic gifts, by less qualified teachers in the religious orders. As she observed in her letter to Orestes Brownson several years later: "Convents, supported by the influence of the Bishops and priests, monopolize almost all the catholic patronage, and will not give employment to secular teachers. The majority of religious in this country are foreigners and in too many cases, rude and illiterate servant girls are, in a few months, transformed into teachers and guides for American ladies. Why is it that our Bishops and priests throw all their influence into the convent cause?"[27] Matilda was never one to mince words. Despite her indisputable devotion to her adopted Church she became an articulate and forceful advocate for Catholic educational reform. Her concerns fell mostly on deaf ears.[28]

26. Mathilde Victor to Orestes A. Brownson, August 22, 1859, University of Notre Dame Archives, I–3–o—*A.L.S.* (3pp.). Published with permission.

27. Ibid. There is a brief discussion of this correspondence between Matilda Victor and Orestes Brownson in *Records of the American Catholic Historical Society of Philadelphia* 62 (1951): 170–71.

28. The exception seems to have been her Jesuit friends, Frs. Lavay and Hubert, who supported her even and perhaps especially when she was being criticized by the religious sisters in Baton Rouge.

The Arkansas diocese was at this time attached to the newly created ecclesiastical province of New Orleans, and Matilda turned next to the archbishop of New Orleans in pursuit of her vocation as an educated Catholic laywoman. In 1854, Sister Louise, Matilda's mentor in Cincinnati, wrote a letter of introduction to Archbishop Anthony Blanc, vouching for Matilda's Catholic fidelity and recommending her for employment as a teacher or governess. Blanc must have suggested her, initially, for a placement in Mississippi; the autumn of 1855 found her in Percy Creek, Wilkinson County, south of Natchez, where she opened a school, only to have it shut down by a yellow fever outbreak as virulent as that occurring simultaneously in Baton Rouge. Quarantined and isolated, she appealed to the bishop for his prayers and expressed her sadness at the departure of several Jesuits, "almost her only friends in the South."

It was the Jesuits in Baton Rouge, tasked with religious and educational oversight in that city, who welcomed Matilda as a teacher later that year. She moved to the river capital on December 2, 1855, announcing the opening of classes for December 10. In the wake of a very dispiriting season of deaths and departures, Matilda's energy and resourcefulness must have seemed a godsend.

The first location of Miss Victor's academy was the "old convent building" left vacant by the Sisters of the Sacred Heart. Correspondence between Matilda and Archbishop Blanc in New Orleans indicates that use of the property was, in a meeting between the Sisters and Victor, "guaranteed for one year on condition that she pay $240, the interest on their share in the building";[29] this sum seems to have been forgiven by Blanc in the interest of helping Victor get her school established. Later the same year there was a flurry of correspondence about an apparent rumor that the nuns intended to sell the house out from under the fledgling academy; the superior, Madame Adine Guidand, wrote to assure Blanc that he was not to worry about "the house occupied by Miss Victor; he alone has the right to dispose of it."[30]

An able but self-important teacher hired by Victor in early 1856, Olympe Delente, left in a huff before the year was out, but not before attempting to stir up dissension with some of the parents and the two parish priests, Frs. Joseph

29. Mathilde Victor to Archbishop Anthony Blanc, May 12, 1856, University of Notre Dame Archives, VI–1–J—*A.L.S.* (2 pp.).

30. The house the Sisters *were* intending to sell was the one they had bought from "Mr. Burk," a commodious home on the outskirts of town (likely that of Judge J. J. Burk, Celeste Repp's uncle and a noted Catholic layman).

Lavay and Darius Hubert. One of the ways Delente sought to undermine Victor was by making "unprincipled use" of confidences Matilda had shared with her when she first arrived, especially about "a deep sorrow" from her youth. Whether this "sorrow" was a failed love affair or an adolescent indiscretion, Delente's gossip apparently reached the archbishop's ears. Victor appealed to him directly, asking him not to heed this faithless tale-telling but to seek out the "whole story" from a dependable third party, Sister Louise in Cincinnati, who knew Matilda's history and would bear her faithful witness.[31]

Despite this rocky start with a member of her staff, Matilda Victor won favor in the community very quickly. Fr. Lavay reported to Blanc five months after the opening of St. Mary's that things looked very promising; although Matilda had arrived well after the beginning of the school term, she had twenty-nine students, including seven boarders. "Her students love her like a mother," he added, and in his opinion the spiritual character of the school compared favorably with that of many a convent.[32] Meanwhile, local newspapers crowed about the closing exercises for the school's inaugural class (July 21, 1856) as a "great event in the life of Baton Rouge."[33] The program, conducted on a canopied stage in the open air on a beautiful moonlit night, consisted of choral singing, solos, poetry recitations in French and English, and several elaborate and original plays.[34] It was nearly midnight before the formal commencement exercise itself got under way; the state governor was present to distribute academic prizes.[35]

31. Mathilde Victor to Archbishop Anthony Blanc, June 25, 1856, University of Notre Dame Archives, VI–1–J—*A.L.S.*

32. May 16, 1856, University of Notre Dame Archives, VI–1–J—*A.L.S.* (French).

33. *Baton Rouge Gazette,* July 23, 1856, quoted in John Mobley, "The Academy Movement in Louisiana," *Louisiana Historical Quarterly* 30 (1947): 781.

34. In one of these, fourteen-year-old Sarah Morgan (whose *Civil War Diary,* begun in 1861, still captivates readers) had the lead. She gave an apparently lively impersonation of the goddess "Fashion" ("exulting in her power and moralizing upon the effect on her giddy followers"). Other classmate belles were her "votaries" from different periods, "from [the time of] King James down [to the present] . . . clad in all that [was] considered beautiful and becoming in the past" (*Baton Rouge Daily Comet,* July 23, 1856). Sarah Morgan's diary does not mention either Matilda Victor or St. Mary's Academy by name, but she and her sister Miriam are both listed in the program notes for the school's 1856 commencement exercises; this is the first time her attendance at any specific local school has been confirmed.

35. The governor in question may have been either Robert Charles Wickliffe or his predecessor, Paul Octave Hebert, whose term had just ended. Hebert was a native of Iberville Parish,

Matilda's early success and dauntless energy prompted her to purchase the buildings once used to house the "priest's college" of St. Peter and St. Paul. With dormitories, chapel, and classroom space, it sat on a four-acre property within walking distance of the old Catholic parish church and the new St. Joseph Church still under construction[36]—just across North Street, between Uncle Sam Street on the west and St. Mary Street on the east. The college had been the first local project of the Jesuits in Baton Rouge and faced stiff opposition from anti-Catholic elements; local Methodists, in a fit of spitefulness, prevailed upon the mayor and town council to extend a street through the middle of the property (cynically named St. Hypolite Street), effectively separating the school and dorms from the gardens and grounds.[37] Partly because of ongoing harassment and partly because of the effects of yellow fever on its teaching and student ranks, the boys' school had been closed for several years. In September 1856 it reopened its doors as the

a decorated military officer, a devout Catholic layman, and a noted educational reformer; in 1861 he was to become a brigadier general in the Confederate army.

36. The cornerstone for St. Joseph Church (now St. Joseph Cathedral), which replaced the smaller parish church built in 1830 on the same block by Fr. Anthony Blanc, was laid by Fr. Lavay in June 1853; construction was slowed by shortness of funds, local opposition, and factional rivalries. In December 1855, Lavay took possession of the new church, hoping to hold a Christmas Mass there despite its being still under construction; in early 1856 the old church building was sold and torn down. Five years later, however, the interior of the new edifice was still unfinished, according to parish correspondence (see note 42, below). Shortly after it was finally completed, it was shelled by Farragut's fleet. This long "sea of troubles" overwhelmed St. Joseph during the postwar years. In 1873, indebtedness caused the church to be seized and sold at a sheriff's sale. Not until 1885 was it bought back; not until 1889 was the church, for the first time in its long and checkered history, finally debt-free.

37. This remarkably nasty episode (which included threats of armed violence) is recounted by Cornelius Buckley, S.J., in the introduction to *Frenchman, Chaplain, Rebel: The Civil War Letters of Pere Louis-Hippolyte Gache, S.J., 10th Louisiana Infantry* (Tuscaloosa: University of Alabama Press, 1981), 21–22; and in Frank M. Uter, *A History of the Catholic Church in Baton Rouge: 1792–1992* (Baton Rouge: St. Joseph Cathedral, 1992), 26. The school's location is confirmed in the congressional records of Matilda Victor's appeal for damages to the property during occupation by Federal troops (e.g., *Congressional Serial Set,* 48th Cong., 2d Sess. [Washington, DC: U.S. Government Printing Office, 1885], "Mathilda Victor," 4.) This was the height of the nativist, Know-Nothing movement, which contended that European immigration and "popish" influence threatened pure Anglo-American (Protestant) values. It was promulgated locally by such publications as the *Plaquemine Southern Sentinel,* which for a few years fanned the flames of anti-Catholic sentiment.

new home of St. Mary's Female Academy under Matilda Victor's tutelage. The roster of teachers included Frs. Lavay and Hubert, both of whom were trusted friends and staunch advocates.

All indications are that St. Mary's continued to be popular and successful, notably welcoming both Protestant and Catholic families and providing what was repeatedly celebrated by the local press as a superb education.[38] A liberal arts curriculum with a strong literary focus (in both French and English) was in 1856 broadened with the addition of German, Spanish, and Italian studies. A full course in mathematics was offered, with special attention to the training of teachers. Extracurricular music lessons in piano and guitar were provided for boarding students, as well as dancing and painting classes, and "all kinds of fancy work taught free of charge." There was a strong emphasis on social comportment and good manners, but this was far more than a finishing school. When St. Mary's was formally incorporated in 1858, its board of directors included some of the notable citizens of Baton Rouge: Philip Hickey,[39] John Kleinpeter, Peter Enders, Joseph Larguier, Andrew Stewart Herron,[40] and Henry Sherbourne.

38. Typical was a comment in the *Baton Rouge Weekly Gazette and Comet,* September 15, 1860, averring that no similar institution in Louisiana took greater care to see that proper instruction was given to its pupils.

39. Colonel Philip Hickey owned several large sugar plantations in the Baton Rouge area, including Hope Estate, where he and his family resided. In an unpublished manuscript by Sarah Morgan entitled "The Hope Estate Ladies" (November 19, 1908), an excerpt of which appears in Leah Wood Jewett, "A Confederate Girl Remembers," *Civil War Book Review* (Winter 2011), www.cwbr.com, Sarah provides an affectionate remembrance of the man she called "Grandpa Hickey" ("not that he bore that relationship, but because his daughter Adele had married my mother's brother, Walter Fowler, and his daughter Caro had married my father's brother, Morris Morgan"). Sarah's brother Philip Hickey Morgan was named for him. Colonel Hickey was also a prominent parishioner at St. Joseph Catholic Church.

40. Andrew Stewart Herron (b. 1823) was the adopted son of Judge John Junius Burk, Celeste Repp's uncle (see note 4, above); he had been taken in by the Burk family after his father was killed in a duel (Judge Burk's own colorful and controversial father, John Daly Burk, had died the same way, doubtless evoking a particular empathy for the orphaned youngster). In addition to being, thus, part of Celeste's extended family, Andrew Herron was also her baptismal sponsor (hence, godparent). Although a Unionist delegate to the secession convention in 1861, he fought for the Confederacy, earning great renown as a captain with Company B, Seventh Louisiana (Baton Rouge Fencibles) in the Virginia campaigns; he returned home to an illustrious career as an attorney and public servant. Elected to the U.S. Congress in 1882, he

Matilda evidently achieved in Baton Rouge what her predecessors in the Sisters of Charity and Sisters of the Sacred Heart had not, and did it with aplomb. But for all the public accolades and community support, her sense of home in the South was rather tenuous, and "the enjoyment of her religion," as her brother Orville called it, centered almost exclusively in her relationship with Frs. Lavay and Hubert, whose intellectual and spiritual companionship she cherished. All of her local attachments were soon to be tested, and then, with the advent of war, shaken to the core.

An early harbinger of these upheavals came in a shocking incident at the Catholic rectory a few days before Christmas in 1857. While Frs. Lavay and Hubert were at dinner, someone fired a revolver at them through the glass of the door and then escaped undetected. Joseph Lavay was hit in the left arm; though the wound was not life-threatening, the bullet could not be extracted. Darius Hubert escaped the gunfire but was sprayed in the face by shards of flying glass. The incident was never resolved: no warning or threat had been received, no motive was ascertained, no culprit found. Matilda Victor wrote to Archbishop Blanc a week later about the pall that the attempted assassination, "the sin and sacrilege of one," had cast over the Christmas season, observing that "all about the church is dark and gloomy." Fr. Lavay seems never to have recovered emotionally from this incident and soon sought and was granted alternate placement. Darius Hubert, more lion than lamb, was undeterred, though indignant about the senseless violence. His superior, Fr. Aloysius Curioz, seemed intent on moving him from Baton Rouge at the time Lavay was withdrawn, but Archbishop Blanc, yielding in part to the entreaties of Matilda Victor, kept him on. Archived correspondence suggests anxiety or disapproval on Curioz's part about Hubert's friendship with Victor, though there was not a whiff of impropriety in it—likely because of her reputation as a tenacious and strong-willed, although devout, woman who was not under the authority of a religious order. In Victor's own words, Curioz was "inimical to her." But she contended with diocesan authorities, reasonably enough, that the chronic failure of Catholic ministry in Baton Rouge owed largely to the

died before being seated. The Confederate monument erected in Baton Rouge in 1886—with its avowed intent of "raising no sectional feelings, sinking all political differences"—is topped with Herron's likeness as "the beau ideal of a patriotic citizen" (fig. 21). At the time St. Mary's Academy was incorporated, Andrew Herron was not only one of its board members but also secretary of state for Louisiana.

frequent turnover of pastors. At least two other priests were briefly considered for service in Baton Rouge after Lavay's departure, Fr. George McMahon and Fr. Richard Hardey, neither of whom proved adequate or suitable to the task. As a result, Darius Hubert stayed on for several more years (apart from a brief stint of teaching at Spring Hill College in Alabama in the fall of 1860),[41] burdened by poor health, inadequate help, chronically insufficient church revenues, and incessant parish bickering,[42] until he exchanged, apparently very willingly, the insoluble troubles of a seemingly "cursed" parish ministry for more decisive battles and a more dangerous form of service.

As for Matilda Victor, six years after beginning her educational project in Baton Rouge, and despite her excellent reputation as a teacher, things were coming apart at the seams. Political and religious tensions, which she had always managed to conciliate in her own institution, became insurmountable. Her support from local Catholic families (for whom boarding privileges were reserved) began to fall off, and she feared that unless she was permitted to take in Protestant boarders the project would fail financially. Additionally, Baton Rouge—like hundreds of other cities in the South—was caught up in rumors of war and arguments over secession.[43] Uncertainty warred against stability. Anxious families withdrew their daughters from the school, funds ran dangerously short, teachers were let go, and Victor had to appeal for a delay in mortgage payment on the property—a severe blow to her pride. She took the threatened removal of Fr. Hubert from Baton Rouge personally, convinced that the reason was that "he was her friend" and ran interference for her both with his distrustful Jesuit superiors and local nuns

41. The 1860 federal census (recorded July 11) finds Fr. Hubert still resident in East Baton Rouge; he apparently taught at Spring Hill in the autumn term before returning to Louisiana.

42. In a letter to Fr. Stephen Rousselon, vicar general of the diocese, written from Baton Rouge in February 1861, he observes pointedly that "if he had the power he would send all the trustees of the world to bathe in the sources of the Nile. They pocket the revenues of the church, paying what they wish and caring very little if their pastor dies of hunger." The church interior was still unfinished nearly a decade after the building project was undertaken (University of Notre Dame Archives, VI–2–d *A.L.S.* [French]).

43. A shrewd firsthand account of debates raging in Baton Rouge at this time, including heated conversations in local cafés and hotels, may be found in William Watson, *Life in the Confederate Army: Being the Observations and Experiences of an Alien in the South during the American Civil War* (London: Chapman and Hall, 1887), esp. chaps. 4, 5, 10, and 12.

who undermined her and enticed students away from St. Mary's.[44] To add to her sorrows, Archbishop Blanc, "an inestimable friend and advisor,"[45] died in June 1860; his successor, Jean-Marie Odin, whose tenure commenced in early 1861, "turned coldly away" from her entreaties for material and spiritual support, which only reinforced her sense of isolation.[46]

But Matilda was also evidently deeply conflicted about secession. She had worked shoulder to shoulder with plantation families and town officials since coming to Louisiana and worshiped with citizens whose Southern blood ran deep and hot. Her brother Orville claimed that she was not an abolitionist.[47] But she was Northern-born and a loyal American. Her hometown of Sandusky, Ohio, had long been a center of antislavery activism,[48] and her brothers were all convinced Federals who, she knew, would serve the Union if war came. Her sister-in-law Metta Victoria Fuller Victor, Orville's wife, was a prolific writer and winsome propagandist for the Union through her immensely popular Beadle novels, notably *The Unionist's Daughter* (1862), an indictment

44. She complains about the Sisters in a letter to Archbishop Blanc on September 27, 1859. Their competitive educational projects, though academically inferior, once again disrupted Matilda Victor's efforts as a Catholic educator.

45. In the words of her brother Orville James Victor, in correspondence with Archbishop Odin. See note 22, above.

46. Letter from Mathilde Victor to Archbishop Odin, April 9, 1862, University of Notre Dame Archives, VI–2–f *A.L.S.* (4 pp.).

47. In his letter to Archbishop Odin; see note 22, above. It is also clear from Matilda's war claims that she had "servants" in her school facility preparing meals and performing other domestic duties.

48. Sandusky was home to free African Americans as early as the1820s and became a magnet for runaway slaves (and their pursuing bounty hunters). The town's Second Baptist Church was a station on the Underground Railroad, from which fugitives were assisted, initially by local African American men, across Lake Erie into Canada. In the 1840s prominent white citizens in the town became involved, with the formation of an antislavery society intent on lending "personal, moral, and religious influence for its [slavery's] suppression" and the creation of additional "safe houses" in local homes, barns, and cellars. In March 1864, Frederick Douglass gave a speech in Sandusky titled "The Mission of the War" at a fund-raiser for local soldiers, defending the Union and supporting the cause of abolition. See, for example, Rush R. Sloane, "The Underground Railroad of the Firelands," *Firelands Pioneer,* n.s., vol. 5 (1888): 28–59; and Wilbur Henry Siebert, *The Underground Railroad: From Slavery to Freedom* (New York: Macmillan, 1898). Also the novel by Sandusky writer Randy Koch, *Eyes Toward the North: A Story of Flight to Freedom Aboard the Underground Railroad* (West Conshohocken, PA: Infinity, 2012).

of secessionist anarchy and violence in Tennessee.[49] More influential still was her best-selling "slave romance," *Maum Guinea and Her Plantation "Children"* (1862),[50] set in Matilda's adopted state of Louisiana. Though Matilda seems not to have taken sides publicly as debates over secession raged, she doubtless hoped against hope that the nation could be spared the trauma of war.

It was not, of course, to happen. On January 26, 1861, an ordinance of secession was voted on and adopted at the state capital in Baton Rouge, and Louisiana was declared a free and sovereign republic. The "glorious Pelican Flag" was borne into the chamber with great solemnity by Captain Henry Watkins Allen,[51] along with Governor Thomas Overton Moore and other dignitaries, including Matilda Victor's friend, confidant, and priest, Darius

49. *The Unionist's Daughter: A Tale of Rebellion in Tennessee* (New York: Beadle and Co., 1862), a double number in Beadle's Dime Novels Series, no. 40. Metta's strong partisan convictions are never in doubt. She says of the events that inspired her melodramatic story: "When the history of this unholy struggle of ambition and jealousy against the fatherly hand of a beneficent Government comes to be written, there will be no chapter more embalmed by the tears of our children than that which does justice to the fidelity and persecution of the Union people of Tennessee" (215)—"bearing a martyrdom which nothing in history excels, since the Christians hid in the catacombs of Rome to hold the faith which heathens denied them" (144). It is striking how the rhetoric here parallels that which will later be used to opposite purpose in many an anti-Reconstruction tract: "the fatherly hand of beneficent overseers" will there be said to have been repudiated in "an unholy struggle of ambition and jealousy" by Yankee agitators; the people of the South will bear their own "martyrdom" at the hands of ruthless and unrelenting "heathens."

50. *Maum Guinea and Her Plantation "Children": or, Holiday-Week on a Louisiana Estate; a Slave Romance* (New York: Beadle and Co., 1861), a double number in Beadle's Dime Novels Series, no. 33. Prepublication advertising and publicity for this novel, termed "Beadle's Christmas Story," was unprecedented: in the days leading up to its strategic mid-December release, the *New York Tribune* enthused that it would be "the most popular and unique book of the year" and should be on everyone's gift list (December 6, 1861). Said to have been praised by President Lincoln, *Maum Guinea* was also extremely popular in Britain. Contemporary accounts suggest that one hundred thousand copies were sold during the war years. It is tempting to speculate whether Metta may have visited her sister-in-law in Baton Rouge while writing her novel.

51. H. W. Allen commanded the Fourth Louisiana and was wounded both at Shiloh and in the Battle of Baton Rouge; he retired from military life at the rank of brigadier general and was elected governor of Louisiana in 1864. His term was short-lived, ending abruptly with the collapse of the Confederacy in 1865. He died in exile in Mexico the following year, at the age of forty-five; his body was returned to Baton Rouge and buried on the grounds of the Old State Capitol.

Hubert. In an act presaging his own dramatic role in the coming conflict, Fr. Hubert pronounced a public benediction on this cherished state symbol—now charged with new and revolutionary meaning:

> I bless this our flag in the name of God. I bless it in the name of the Father, who is all-powerful; I bless it in the name of the Son, who has spread blessings on mankind; I bless it in the name of the Holy Ghost, who is a spirit of fortitude. Oh! Our flag! Let it be the symbol of the purest liberty; let it be the palladium of the imperishable rights of our dear Louisiana. Let us all be willing to stand and die by it. *Benedictio Dei Omnipotentis, Patris et Filii et Spiritus Sancti descendat super te et maneat semper.* Amen.[52]

Celeste's Teacher and Priest: Fr. Darius Hubert, S.J.

Darius Hubert was born in the military port city of Toulon, France, on July 19, 1823, to Jacques Joseph Hubert, a navy quartermaster, and Marie Rose Adelaide Ferrandin. Though a serious and diligent student, he was by all accounts somewhat indifferent to faith as a boy. At twenty, he experienced a profound spiritual conversion and call to religious life. Over his father's objections, he entered the Lyon Province of the Society of Jesus on September 23, 1843, and, after finishing his formal philosophical training and serving several churches in France, volunteered for the Jesuit mission in America. With a group of ten other hardy (some thought foolhardy) compatriots, he embarked on the sailing vessel *St. Ann* in November 1847, arriving in Mobile, Alabama, on December 12. From thence he was sent by his superiors to Louisiana. Hubert's first assignment there was as a teacher at St. Charles College in Grand Coteau, during which time he undertook theological and English-language study on his own. He was ordained in 1850 and arrived shortly thereafter in Baton Rouge to take up a teaching post at the short-lived College of St. Peter and St. Paul and to share ministry duties with Fr. Joseph Lavay. Unlike Lavay, Hubert had by this time acquired excellent fluency in English, which equipped him for ministry to both native and immigrant English-speakers.[53] He was also,

52. Hubert's prayer was delivered in French; the English translation given here was published on the second page of the *Baton Rouge Daily Advocate,* January 29, 1861.

53. Limited facility in English was an Achilles heel of many of the French-born Jesuits in the South. Hippolyte Gache, another of Hubert's sometime colleagues in Baton Rouge and a fellow chaplain in the Confederacy, was notoriously "all but unintelligible" in English all of

despite his lifelong struggle with asthma and other ailments, a generous and extroverted personality with broadly "catholic" and ecumenical affections as well as high Catholic principles and devotion. These qualities made him an especially helpful associate to Matilda Victor as she established her academy for young women in Baton Rouge, and they would win him the ardent loyalty of soldiers, officers, and civilians he encountered during the Civil War and in its aftermath. His physical frailty belied an inner fortitude and force of character that allowed him to meet attempted assassination at the parish rectory and the chaos and carnage of war with remarkable equanimity.

In the sweetly candid "Compositions françaises" of young Celeste Repp, published here for the first time, we see a child's impressions of "Pere Hubert" as he conducted his daily round of priestly duties at St. Joseph's Church and at her school in 1859 and 1860. Whether teaching French in the St. Mary's classroom, accompanying the girls on a field trip to the Louisiana State Fair, or bringing cakes and candies to the boarding students on Christmas Day, he was evidently given to simple acts of fatherly kindness that touched and delighted Celeste. One of her compositions is addressed to him directly; although she uses the formal "vous" form, as befits her relationship as a spiritual daughter, her affectionate devotion is unmistakable: "Cher Père Hubert, je souhaite que vous restiez ici et que vous soyez toujours notre maître de français" [Dear Father Hubert, I would like for you to stay here and for you always to be our French instructor]. In the context of ecclesiastical debate about Hubert's ongoing tenure in Baton Rouge, the vote of this one Catholic child (had anyone asked) was clear.

In the end it was political events that removed Hubert permanently from the river capital. Notwithstanding Matilda Victor's persuasive (and entirely prudent) argument about the need for stability and continuity in the pastoral ranks, the world changed utterly in the spring of 1861—the call to arms

---

his life. Hubert was, because of his facility in English, able to lead retreats and to preach in the preferred language of Louisiana's growing immigrant Catholic population, and to communicate comfortably with military personnel during the Civil War. While Hubert's diocesan correspondence through the 1850s is conducted in French, his wartime records are written in English. Likewise, though his prayer at the secession convention was offered in French, his frequent speeches and public prayers after the war were all given in English. He was not merely functionally bilingual but effortlessly fluent and affecting in his adopted tongue.

affecting church as well as state. As young men prepared to don the gray and defend Dixie from "Northern aggression," many of their priests and pastors undertook duties as chaplains. Darius Hubert, who had prayed at secession that Louisianans would be willing to stand by and to die for the Pelican Flag, and who was sprung of soldierly ancestors in France, was specifically requested by Colonel Albert G. Blanchard to accompany the First Louisiana Infantry as it served in the Army of Northern Virginia.[54] This he did from April 1861 to April 1865—in an officer's uniform rather than his Jesuit cassock, and often on horseback.[55] He was, in the course of four long years "a perfect

54. Blanchard, who was not long in command of the First, evidently depended heavily on Hubert for spiritual counsel and friendship. In a plaintive letter on March 26, 1865 (included in Hubert's service records), he requested that the chaplain seek a transfer to Raleigh, North Carolina, where Blanchard then held an administrative post: "My dear friend. I am going to ask of you a great sacrifice, and yet I hope you will grant my request. . . . There is no Catholic Chaplain [here] . . . and there are many who would be glad to see a priest. It is not necessary to say that I should be delighted to have you with me again. . . . I hope you will come for I need you. I have no news from my family since the fall of Columbia, SC. . . . If you come, please bring a few books." Irrespective of his broken health, Fr. Hubert would not likely have forsaken his charge, even for so good a friend, but the matter was in any event settled for him. Two weeks later, Lee's surrender effectively ended the war, permitting both men to return at last to New Orleans (though Hubert was unable to travel until autumn).

55. Fellow Jesuit Fr. Hippolyte Gache commented derisively on Fr. Hubert's choice of garb in his letters from the front: "I almost had to be told who it was. . . . Imagine, if you will, a young dandy: his hair elegant, his beard splendid; gold-braid festooned upon his blue kepi and embroidered upon the sleeves of his high-collared frock coat; the golden buttons of his waistcoat emblazoned with the Louisiana pelican; his gold-filleted trousers falling neatly into a pair of comely boots. This dazzling sight was none other than Father Hubert himself!" (Gache, *Frenchman, Chaplain, Rebel,* 60). Gache evidently regarded the uniform as a pretentious and unworthy "costume" for a Jesuit priest. For Hubert, though, it was a means of identification with those he served; to wear a uniform but carry no weapon doubtless greatly enhanced his vulnerability on the battlefield, where he was often found ministering to the wounded and dying while missiles flew. As the conflict wore on, Hubert's garb was decidedly less splendid and generally "disguised in Confederate mud," as fellow chaplain Fr. James Sheeran (Fourteenth Louisiana) observed. Hubert was well known for giving away his better garments; his clothes were so tattered when he passed through Fredericksburg, Maryland, after a long march that he was forced to beg new apparel from the people of the town. After the Gettysburg campaign, he marched long miles barefoot. Gache's pettiness and jealousy with respect to the reputation Hubert enjoyed among his men is evident throughout his correspondence.

man, always with his Regiment," according to his service record,[56] a "soldier-priest known and dear to every man in the army of Northern Virginia."[57]

> So kindhearted was he that his better food and clothing were always passed down to the poorly provided men in the ranks. When he [intended] to do the same with his horse, he got a formal order to keep it.[58] President Davis considered him the model chaplain, and General R. E. Lee never met him without a respectful bow.[59]

Fr. Emmanuel de la Morinière, S.J., a friend of Fr. Hubert's in New Orleans, recounted the priest's zealous pastoral care for the soldiers under his charge: "He had shared their exultation in the flitting hours of success. He had cheered their drooping spirits and roused their energies in the brief hours of dark despondency; and whether in closed ambulance, or on open field amid shell, shot, grape, and canister, he had shriven the wounded, spoken of duty's crown to the fallen, and made pure for heaven and the land of unbroken peace the parting spirits of the valorous dead."[60] Among the notable engagements in

56. Darius Hubert's war records are contained in the Compiled Service Records of Confederate General and Staff Officers, and Nonregimental Enlisted Men (M331), Roll 0134, Record Group 109, National Archives and Records Administration.

57. Clement Anselm Evans, *Confederate Military History* (Atlanta: Confederate Publishing, 1899), 10:234.

58. Hubert's last and apparently favorite mount (likely the one mentioned here) was a fine bay horse ridden first into battle by Union Major Andrew Barney of the Twenty-Fourth New York at Second Manassas; when Barney was shot and killed by Confederate sharpshooters, the panicked horse was captured and ridden thereafter by Lieutenant Colonel Michael Nolan of the First Louisiana, a close friend of Fr. Hubert. Nolan himself died at Gettysburg, after which the warhorse was given to Hubert, under whose kindly hand it retired from the front lines (ibid.).

59. From "Letters of Civil War Chaplains," *Woodstock Letters* 43, no. 2 (1914): 170. Hubert himself spoke eloquently of this deference afforded him by Confederate commanders, including Robert E. Lee: "the chieftain whose hands so often grasped mine in friendship . . . even at the heads of charging columns, always paid me, the humblest minister of Christ, the courteous homage of a reverential bow which a king might envy" (see Emmanuel de la Morinière, S.J., "Chivalry," in *The Louisiana Book: Selections from the Literature of the State,* ed. Thomas M'Caleb [New Orleans: R. F. Straughan, 1894; repr., New Orleans: Cornerstone, 2012], 179).

60. "Chivalry," 178–79. This brief tribute to Darius Hubert, which was attached to his own reflection on the chivalrous character of Robert E. Lee, is reprinted also in Michael Kenny, S.J., *Catholic Culture in Alabama: Centenary Story of Spring Hill College 1830–1930* (New York: America Press, 1931), 216–17.

which members of the First Louisiana participated were King's School House (Oak Grove); Malvern Hill, Second Manassas; Chantilly; Harper's Ferry; Sharpsburg (Antietam); Fredericksburg; Chancellorsville; Second Winchester; Gettysburg; Bristoe Station; Payne's Farm (Mine Run); Wilderness; Spotsylvania; Yellow Tavern; Pale Green Church (Ware Bottom Church); Second Mechanicsville (Beaver Dam Creek); Monocacy; Snicker's Gap (Cool Spring); Second Kernstown; Smithfield Crossing; Shepherdstown; Third Winchester; Fisher's Hill; Cedar Creek; and Hatcher's Run. Casualty rates were catastrophic; the regiment lost 37 percent of its combatants at Chancellorsville, 23 percent at Gettysburg, and 25 percent at Payne's Farm. Shriving the wounded and attending the "parting spirits of the valorous dead" was for Fr. Hubert virtually a daily duty.[61]

He himself was fired on at Second Manassas and narrowly escaped injury; an enemy bullet pierced the stirrup of his saddle.[62] He was wounded at Gettysburg, though apparently not severely.[63] At the fateful naval battle of Hampton Roads (March 8–9, 1862), he insisted on boarding the Confederate ironclad *Virginia* (*Merrimack*) to encourage and pray with the men; some of the ship's hastily assembled crew were "his own boys" from the First Louisiana, and

61. When Sarah Morgan's brother Gibbes (Seventh Louisiana) returned home to Baton Rouge, having been wounded at the bloody Battle of Antietam, he recounted a conversation with Fr. Hubert, likely in hospital following the engagement. He had been reassured by the chaplain that his brother George (First Louisiana) had come through the battle safe; Gibbes had not even known until then that they were both in the fight that day (Morgan, *Civil War Diary,* 293). Gibbes returned to the front after he recovered and did not survive the war; he died in Johnson's Island Prison in January 1864; George fell ill and died a week later in the Virginia theater.

62. Hubert kept the bullet as a souvenir. It was, after his death, donated by a fellow Jesuit to the Confederate Memorial Hall in New Orleans, which also houses a portrait of Fr. Hubert.

63. Fr. Terence S. King, S.J., "Letters of Civil War Chaplains," *Woodstock Letters* 3, no. 2 (1914): 170, indicates that Hubert was wounded in the arm at Gettysburg. Hubert himself, in a one-paragraph self-penned obituary that was written during his last illness and, at his request, remained sealed until his death, confirms but does not specify the Gettysburg injury. Sidney J. Romero, in his "Louisiana Clergy and the Confederate Army," *Louisiana History* 2, no. 3 (1961): 290, refers to Hubert's injury "during Pickett's Charge at Gettysburg," citing the eulogy for him by his friend and fellow chaplain Thomas R. Markham, printed in the *New Orleans Times Picayune,* June 23, 1893. Some sources suggest that the bullet Hubert kept and then donated to Memorial Hall was from "his injury at Gettysburg," though the donor of the artifact indicated otherwise.

he had been formally "detailed for duty" as Confederate naval chaplain for *Virginia,* possibly at his own request.[64]

When Fr. Hubert became too ill to accompany his troops in the spring of 1864 and was granted medical furlough, he asked to be assigned to the military hospitals in Richmond, so as to minister to the suffering as he had strength.[65] Despite increasing infirmity and chronic illness, he was to outlive all too many of the officers and soldiers he loved, and to be among the very few remaining members of the First Louisiana still in the Virginia theater when Lee surrendered at Appomattox on April 9, 1865.[66]

64. The incident is recounted in "Letters of Civil War Chaplains," *Woodstock Letters* 43, no. 2 (1914): 170, and in numerous newspapers (e.g., a *Richmond Dispatch* article written at the time of Hubert's death, titled "Chaplain on the Merrimac: The Death of a Priest Who Was a Hero in the Confederate Army," August 5, 1893); several sources include a purported conversation between Admiral Buchanan and the persistent priest. Buchanan, having been severely wounded in the first day's battle, surely could not have "come ashore to give his answer in person," as some accounts have it. It is more likely that Fr. Hubert asked, through an intermediary, to board *Virginia* when it anchored off Sewell's Point on the evening of March 8, and was through firm importunacy granted permission. In the early-morning hours of March 9, along with the other seriously wounded men, Buchanan was landed and taken to the Norfolk naval hospital—before *Virginia* steamed out to meet *Monitor;* it would have been natural for the priest to disembark at that time, in company with the wounded. An alternate scenario would have Hubert coming aboard the ironclad after the inconclusive but history-making battle of March 9. Hubert's chaplaincy with the *Virginia* is confirmed in his self-penned obituary; his boarding of the vessel was referred to in his funeral oration and recounted by those who had the story firsthand. Hubert would surely have known many of the combatants. A complete list of the First Louisiana (Nelligan's) men assigned to duty on CSS *Virginia,* as well as members of the Second, Fifth, Eighth, Tenth, Fourteenth, and Fifteenth Louisiana regiments also aboard the ironclad can be found in John V. Quarstein, *The CSS* Virginia: *Sink Before Surrender* (Charleston, SC: History Press, 2012), appendix VI; see also, by the same author, *C.S.S.* Virginia: *Mistress of Hampton Roads* (Lynchburg, VA: Howard, 2000).

65. "In my opinion, dear Father, you have already exposed yourself too much in persisting to remain in active duty on the field in cold and biting weather of the winter. Hoping that . . . your health will be actively restored and 'ere long grant the men of the old First the presence of their beloved and revered Chaplain" (Major Charles E. Cormier to Fr. Hubert, March 12, 1864). The surgeon who attended Hubert at the Infirmary of St. Francis de Sales described his condition (March 9, 1864) as "phthisis pulmonalis [tuberculosis] attended by constant and harassing cough, severe pain, and frequent hemorrhages and general debility" and asserted that "he is entirely unfit for the active duties of the field."

66. Of the approximately two thousand members of the First Louisiana, only one officer and eighteen men were present at surrender. Though Fr. Hubert's parole was signed on April 14, 1865, he remained in Richmond through the summer, too sick to travel.

THE SAILOR: WILLIAM LITTLE PARK, QUARTER GUNNER, USS *ESSEX*

Prior to his decision to enlist as a sailor with the Union "brown water navy" in September 1861 and thereafter to maintain a detailed three-year account of his wartime service, there is a very modest paper trail on William Park.

He was by his own account born in Scotland in 1836. In the 1841 Scottish census, he is listed as youngest of five children of Edward and Mary Park, resident in Craigielands village, in the parish of Kirkpatrick-Juxta, Northeast Dumfriesshire. Craigielands was a small hamlet adjacent to a wooded estate known as Craigielands Manor, not far from the popular spa town of Moffat. The entire parish had a population of less than a thousand at the time the Parks lived there; the village had less than a hundred. The area was best known for sheep and cattle farming; William Colvin, who owned the manor, was a wealthy sheep breeder and stockman in the second half of the nineteenth century.

At the age of eighteen, William left home to serve with the Royal Navy in the Crimean War. In that complex and bloody conflict, remembered best for the catastrophic Charge of the Light Brigade and the heroism of the Lady with the Lamp, Florence Nightingale—both immortalized in poetry[67]—more than 750,000 combatants died in the course of twenty-seven months. Park was fortunate not to be among them. Serving on the Black Sea until hostilities ended, he returned home with the rank of able seaman and a "Victoria Regina" service medal, seasoned in the art of war but harboring no intention of ever taking up arms again.

It may have been a desire to "put fighting behind him" that prompted William Park to emigrate to Canada, following the lead of his elder brother Walter.[68] The arrival of Walter and his Scottish wife, Janet, in Canada can be dated to 1855 or early 1856; they brought with them their firstborn, Edward (b. 1854), and settled in Clarendon Township, Pontiac County, a largely English-speaking and Protestant farming settlement in rural western Quebec,

67. Alfred, Lord Tennyson's "The Charge of the Light Brigade" (published a few weeks after the event, December 9, 1854) and Henry Wadsworth Longfellow's "Santa Filomena" (1857).

68. In the 1900 American census, William lists his "immigration year" as 1860. Since he was living with his brother in Canada in early 1861, before moving to Oswego, New York, later that year, this may suggest that the immigration he is referring to is from Scotland to Canada. (Or he may merely be "rounding off" his time of immigration from the United Kingdom to North America.)

on the Ottawa River. This is where the 1861 Canadian census finds William, living with Walter's growing family in a log house, helping his brother farm the sloping, wooded acreage near the town of Shawville.[69]

Sometime in the spring or summer of that year, however, William—single and restless—crossed another border and commenced working as a commercial sailor in Oswego, New York, which was at the time a bustling Great Lakes port and a magnet for Irish, Scottish, English, and Canadian immigrants. The docks and shipyards and associated businesses employed hundreds of men and boys. In mid-September, in company with his friend Andrew Waterman, William found himself in Chicago, having made the trip of several weeks aboard the schooner *Surprise.* While they were there, news came of the capture of Lexington, Missouri, and the surrender of Colonel James A. Mulligan and his "Irish Brigade" (the Twenty-Third Illinois Infantry), a regiment raised with great fanfare in Chicago just a few months earlier. Patriotic fever seems to have seized Andrew, who immediately determined to fight for the Union; he convinced William to accompany him to the local naval rendezvous and to enlist with him for service in the Western Gunboat Flotilla. Andrew was evidently the more eager of the two, having all of the excitement and none of the burden of bitter memory associated with wartime naval service; his friend's enthusiasm and the promise of a year-round paycheck evidently prevailed over Park's reluctance.

The two men enlisted for a three-year term, little thinking it would come to that (everyone expected that the "duration of the war" would be very brief). After a last week of civilian R&R with friends, they boarded a train with other Chicago-area recruits for St. Louis, where the Western Flotilla was headquartered.

Andrew Waterman, whose idea it was to sign up in the first place, was never to come home; he died a horrible death at Fort Henry, Tennessee, in

69. The census of 1861 for the province of Quebec (then referred to as "Canada East") was taken in the spring/summer of that year, but the information collected by census takers reflected who was in each household on "census day," March 30, 1861. Both Park brothers were listed on that census as farmers, though Walter was also a stonemason; he built a number of fine stone homes in Clarendon township, still occupied more than a century and a half later. William's sojourn as a farmer and a Canadian resident was short-lived; by the time his nephew and namesake (William W. Park) was born to Walter and Janet in 1862, he was aboard a Union ironclad, fighting for the United States.

one of the first major engagements of the brown water navy (February 6, 1862). William himself, though harried by poor health and partial deafness after a near-fatal bout of typhoid fever, fulfilled his term and mustered out to Chicago three years later, almost to the day, well before the bloody and devastating conflict would at last draw to its close. William seems to have known what many at the time failed to acknowledge: the inland navy, with its unconventional iron vessels that penetrated into the heartland of the South and seized control of the Mississippi waterways, had decisively shaped the war's outcome. His three-year journal forms the bulk of what follows in this volume.

HOW DID CELESTE'S NOTEBOOK FIND ITS WAY INTO WILLIAM PARK'S HANDS (AND WHEN DID HE WRITE HIS JOURNAL)?

There was enormous upheaval in Baton Rouge in the months following secession. In the flush of early partisan optimism, benevolent societies sprang up, funds were gathered for the support of families whose sons were marching off to distant battlefields, and ladies' sewing circles stitched flags and personal items for various regiments preparing to "defend the Southland."[70] Matilda Victor, who was conflicted in her political loyalties and doubtless anxious about her own future as well as that of her adopted community, was attempting to maintain a semblance of normalcy at her school, despite the difficulty of holding quorum and the consequent need to cut back on classes. In January 1862 she, too, offered a forum for patriotic support for the local war effort, hosting a fund-raiser at St. Mary's for the Louisiana Volunteers, of whom, doubtless, she knew quite a few.

70. Celeste Repp's stylish cousin Junia Burk was the spokesperson for "the Young Ladies of Baton Rouge" in a presentation of a hand-sewn flag to the Creole Guards: "Now while the gentle May-breeze comes sighing through these silken folds, arranged by the delicate hands of so many fair maidens, it seems that the spirit of chivalry descends to encourage the task you are prepared to undertake" (*Baton Rouge Daily Gazette and Comet,* May 3, 1861). Newspapers of the day were filled with both appeals for practical assistance (e.g., donations of "lint for the army," old brass and copper for construction of bayonets and howitzers, blankets, canteen covers, socks and uniforms, etc.) and praise for the generosity and patriotism of Southern women: "when the victory is won, and the insolent invader driven from our soil, although they may not have shared in the immediate dangers of the battle field, our fair countrywomen will be entitled to and shall wear a full share of the wreaths distributed to the victors" (Andrew S. Herron [Celeste's adopted cousin], *Baton Rouge Daily Advocate,* June 4, 1861).

Happily, a ticket for that fund-raiser has survived; it was for a time in the holdings of the medical antiquities dealer Alex Peck, who posted its image online before selling it to another collector. The front of the invitation reads: "St. Mary's Academy. Entertainment for the Benefit of the Louisiana Volunteers. January 28th & 29th, 1862. Admit the Bearer, $1." The reverse of the ticket is inscribed in cursive handwriting by an unidentified Union combatant: "you can keep this as a memento of the hospital where I lay sick while at Baton Rouge La." The writer then adds, wryly, "you see that the rebels have had all kinds of aid to help the cause along." Peck, in his online catalogue, surmises that "The writer probably found the ticket on the premises and sent it home in a letter."[71]

This 150-year-old ticket affords the first clue to a plausible connection between St. Mary's Academy and Union combatants such as William Park—affording evidence that Matilda Victor's school became a Federal hospital during the occupation of Baton Rouge in 1862. Though histories of Civil War–era Baton Rouge provide little in the way of corroboration, the fact is borne out in surprising detail in an unlikely source to which few historians have had cause to turn. Only someone who had encountered Matilda Victor and been interested in her educational project in the river capital would have been likely to stumble onto her application to Congress for war reparations.[72] In her petition, which is bolstered by extensive documentation and letters of support, she recounts that she "continued to occupy the . . . property [known as St. Mary's Female Academy] as a school until the 27th day of May, 1862 when the buildings were damaged by shell, and the school broken up by the bombardment of the town by the United States naval forces, commanded by Admiral D. G. Farragut, when she was compelled to leave. . . . [O]n or about the first day of June, 1862, the said property was taken possession of and used as a United States hospital by order of General Williams, and was retained for such purpose until August of that year." The claim goes on to detail other subsequent uses of the property by Federal forces, including as a contraband facility and cavalry outpost. For our purposes here, however, the period of

71. http://antiquescientifica.com/archive9.htm.

72. *Congressional Serial Set,* 48th Cong., 2d Sess., January 28, 1885, "Report [to accompany bill S.2117] . . . for the relief of Mathilda Victor." The claim had been initiated in 1869 and was not finally settled until 1886, just five years before Matilda's death. See the afterword for a detailed account.

June through August 1862 affords the likely time frame when someone acquainted with William Park was hospitalized in the rooms formerly serving as classrooms of St. Mary's Academy—Park himself, according to his later memoir, enjoyed unusually good health through these months—and happened onto a useful school notebook that was largely empty save for some prettily inscribed passages in French "par M'lle Celeste Repp" in the opening pages.[73]

Here, the *Essex* journal of Park's shipmate James Henneberry provides a tantalizing clue. On August 7, 1862, just after the Battle of Baton Rouge and the confrontation of *Essex* with the Confederate ram *Arkansas,* Henneberry came down sick with fever, a version of the ubiquitous illness that had already decimated the ranks of the gunboat crews. Along with Hank Ruger, his own and Park's mutual friend, also sick, he was taken to a hospital facility in Baton Rouge. In his entry for August 9, Henneberry writes: "I was very sick and I believe I should have been worse only for the kind attention of the Lady of this place. She came up at 10 P.M. and stayed with me for about ½ an hour and pressed me to take some gruel the first bite of food I had taken since the day before. The next morning I felt better." "The Lady of this place" is an unusual locution in this context, but would nicely accord with the temporary facility Matilda Victor was overseeing on her school property, only a few blocks from where *Essex* was moored. We know from her own depositions that she not only allowed Union personnel to convalesce in St. Mary's buildings but that she personally nursed and fed them. At any rate, if two of Park's mates—one a close friend—found themselves hospitalized at St. Mary's Academy, as did

73. Scarcity of paper in the South was an early casualty of the Union blockade; most paper mills were concentrated in the North, and the few located in the South were largely shuttered as workers left to fight for the Confederacy. Many Southern newspapers were eventually forced to shut down; the *Vicksburg Daily Citizen* attempted to make do with a creative alternative—producing several "wallpaper editions" during the last weeks of the Federal siege in the summer of 1863; other news outlets, such as the *Opelousas [LA] Courier,* tried the same expedient. Wallpaper was sometimes also torn from the walls of Southern homes to be used as stationery by family members of Confederate soldiers. James Henneberry, in his *Essex* journal (January 22, 1863), writes of his great delight when another ship's yeoman from the Union fleet provides him with foolscap, letter paper, and envelopes—items he could not readily have procured locally. Henneberry, who had clerical duties aboard *Essex,* used a Navy-issue record book for his own war diary; for Park, who had no comparable access to paper, Celeste's notebook proved a great boon.

the soldier or sailor who signed the back of the fund-raiser ticket,[74] Celeste's notebook could surely have been carried back onto *Essex* with one of them, and thus into Park's hands.[75]

Since Park's chronological record of his three-year tour of duty commences on September 25, 1861—at least eight months prior to the occupation of Baton Rouge by Federal forces and ten months prior to his own arrival on the scene as part of the naval support for the defense of the city from Confederate attempts to retake it—it is clear that the entries recorded during the initial period of his service must have been recopied from earlier notes into Celeste's journal once he acquired it. Park was an assiduous record keeper: the details of his early weeks and months aboard *Essex* (e.g., the boiler explosion at Fort Henry that disabled the ironclad and killed or injured many of his mates, prompting his temporary reassignment to the *Pittsburg,* as well as his near-fatal bout of typhoid fever in late 1861) have a strong sense of immediacy and do not appear to be have been "recollected in tranquility" or assembled retrospectively from naval records. One assumes, therefore, that he may have recopied earlier entries verbatim during a lull in fighting sometime after the hostilities off Baton Rouge and then simply continued on with his contemporary account. There is a significant gap in the early autumn of 1862, between the mid-September promotion and departure of Captain William Porter and the mid-November resumption of *Essex*'s river reconnaissance under its new captain, Charles H. B. Caldwell. Indeed, this is the longest single hiatus in Park's three-year journal record. "Nothing of any importance has occurred since the last date [i.e., September 15]," he says on November 12, 1862; "we have been laying at New Orleans . . . first getting repaired and the Ship calked [caulked]." This would have been an entirely natural time for Park to transcribe his earlier notes into the newly acquired notebook.

74. The handwriting on the back of the St. Mary's ticket in no way resembles that in Henneberry's journal. It closely enough resembles Ruger's writing, however (as found in his 1888 affidavit on Park's disability application), to prompt speculation that he may, indeed, have been the anonymous individual who sent the ticket home.

75. Evidence that Union personnel helped themselves to other books from St. Mary's may be found in Special Collections at Hill Memorial Library, LSU—specifically, a volume of French poetry by Jean-Baptiste Rousseau, which includes a bookplate from "St. Mary's Female Academy, Baton Rouge" and a flyleaf notation by Colonel. Volney S. Fullam of the Seventh Vermont: "this book was left in my tent by someone at Baton Rouge, La. after the battle Aug. 5th 1862 while I was the commander of the 7th VO Infantry."

It is possible, of course, that Park did not use Celeste's journal until after he mustered out in 1864—that he took the notebook with him and used it as a place to rewrite a clean copy from an earlier shipboard draft. We know from postwar records that Park went back to commercial sailing on the Great Lakes for several years immediately following his wartime service; during the winter months, when the Lakes were iced in, he was unemployed.[76] This would have been another natural period for him to recopy an earlier draft of his naval journal. It is evident that he appended, during this period, hand-copied accounts of published official naval correspondence relevant to his time of service[77]—especially his first year under Captain William D. Porter—as well as the rousing farewell speech Porter gave when he departed from *Essex* in September 1862.[78] One factor that might tend to support this time frame is the relative clarity and consistency of the penmanship, and the lack of strikethroughs and corrections.[79] One that might tell against it is the lack of editorial comment or retrospective revision, even of known errors, that would have been natural in a document recopied in its entirety after the war. (Park did later revisit and expand upon his wartime service in a more reflective memoir that was passed down to his children and then donated to the Newberry Library in 2006, following the death of his last living descendant. In that document he does correct several details and add a good deal of commentary; see appendix 3.)

We are left, then, with a mystery still, but a mystery somewhat resolved by the little-known fact that Matilda Victor's school was occupied by Federal forces in the summer of 1862 and used as a hospital for several months (during which time two of Park's mates may well have convalesced there), and the

76. These details occur in his application for a disability pension (see the afterword).

77. There are letters from Captain William D. Porter, Flag Officer Andrew Foote, Navy Secretary Gideon Welles, Rear Admiral David Farragut, and Robert K. Riley, executive officer of *Essex* under William Porter (see appendix 2).

78. The same speech, word for word, was kept in the James Henneberry diary (see appendix 1).

79. William gives his address, in the first page of the notebook, opposite the title page of Celeste Repp's "Compositions françaises," as "77 Throop Street, Chacago [*sic*]." The Chicago City Directory shows "William L. Park, sailor" at that address in 1867; he had married Agnes Gillespie that spring and moved in alongside her family. The address does nothing to clarify the time of composition, except to indicate that our journal was written "not later than" 1867; he may simply have inserted an address lest the volume, possibly being passed around among local crewmates, became lost.

much better-known fact that confiscation by Union personnel of any "rebel" property that was deemed useful or valuable (from furniture to paintings to silver tea services) was ubiquitous. The lifting of an unknown Southern student's notebook from the shelves of St. Mary's Academy while it served as a makeshift hospital would have been entirely unremarkable in the context of the occupation of Baton Rouge. At this distance, one cannot but regard this petty theft as fortuitous; Celeste's notebook, had it *not* been confiscated and then retained by William Park for his own wartime journal, would have been very unlikely to survive the chaos that befell the Academy property.[80] With it, a remarkably concise and unaffected introduction to some of the unsung heroes of antebellum Baton Rouge and indeed of the nation—during and after the war—would have been forever lost.

CHARACTER OF THE WRITING AND EDITORIAL PRINCIPLES

Both Celeste Repp and William Park employ clear—and by today's standards beautiful—cursive handwriting that is readily legible to a nonspecialist. (Celeste's charming doodles and elaborate calligraphy are unusually elegant and striking.) The inconsistent and often inaccurate spelling, capitalization, and punctuation in Park's diary may reflect not only the harried and difficult conditions in which he was writing but also literacy levels consistent with those of many of his working-class peers aboard the *Essex*. He was likely without much in the way of a formal education even in his native Scotland. He was quite evidently, however, a curious and engaging mind and an avid reader; he regularly mentions the arrival of "the Mail" (though never any of his own correspondents) and recounts what he learns about progress of the war from newspapers of the day. It is especially telling that the one pillaging expedition in which he describes himself as participating at Bayou Sara has

80. The utter destruction of all personal property in the Academy buildings and on its grounds following upon Federal occupation is thoroughly documented in Matilda Victor's claims for compensation. Sadly, this ensured the obliteration of all on-site records from her rather remarkable educational project, which had during its brief existence "larger patronage than any other school in Baton Rouge" (Mobley, "Academy Movement in Louisiana," 782; see note 33, above). It is unsurprising then that, even in the 1940s, "none of the old residents in Baton Rouge today ever heard of this school" (ibid.), and that what little information has been previously published has been riddled with inaccuracies.

him lifting "a good number of valuable books" rather than more obvious and more lucrative treasures from Confederate homes (August 24, 1862).

I have chosen not to correct Park's spelling or to regularize his capitalization or punctuation, except to insert missing periods where sentences obviously end. The reader will encounter many versions of terms such as "skedaddle," "reconnoiter," or "underway/weigh" and will frequently see "quite" when "quiet" is intended or "follied" for "followed," "surrended" for "surrendered," "of" for "off," "two" for "tow" (or vice versa), or "their" for "there." Sometimes, simple errors creep in: "Rebs" becomes "Bebs"; "skirmishes" become "skrimmages." The Union gunboat *Anglo-American* is typically spelled *Angelo-American* by Park; *Sumter* is spelled *Sumpter* and *Tyler* becomes *Taylor.* In his notation for May 18, 1863, "with loosing a man" is clearly intended to read "without losing a man." The only alterations I have made to the text are (1) to separate the four years during which Park served into chapters (his own diary is continuous from the day of enlistment to the day of his "sign off"); (2) to remove Park's pagination, which is unnecessary (and cluttering) in a dated journal; and (3) to italicize the names of ships, which allows for greater clarity and readability, especially since vessels on the western waters were typically named for towns or cities; we have, thus, in Park's entry for July 1, 1862: "The Gun Boat Cairo came up to relieve us so as that we could go up to Cairo to get repaired."

Park's diary is filled with colloquialism and gallows humor of a kind featured in many war journals; the term "skedaddle" itself, indicating a hasty, disorganized, and inglorious retreat—made famous at the outset of the Civil War in what was called "the Great Skedaddle" of Union troops after the First Battle of Bull Run (Manassas)—is used frequently here. He and his men frequently prepare "a warm reception" for their Confederate counterparts; after recovering and dismantling a particularly dangerous mine from the river, he says that courtesy demands that they "return" the powder at the earliest opportunity. In recounting a potentially deadly incident in which he went overboard trying to get into a landing boat, Park notes with self-deprecating humor that he "made a hole in the water." Such lingo, while a far cry from the rhetoric of the *Official Records of the Union and Confederate Navies* or even of officers' correspondence and ships' logs, brings us much closer to the culture of the gunboat crews and the quotidian rounds of shipboard life. I have occasionally glossed expressions whose meaning may be unclear.

Park's racial terminology has not been altered, despite its offensiveness to modern readers. In this as in other ways, his own voice has been retained—historically and culturally bound as it is. (His Chicago-born crewmate, James Henneberry, a more self-conscious writer, who pens sentimental poems for those back home and sees himself as somewhat above the ordinary tars, uses similarly charged language and expresses much more harshly racist views.)[81] If there is an irony in the specific dramatis personae in this double journal, it is that no one in the household or intimate acquaintance of our Confederate schoolgirl, Celeste Repp, can be imagined to hold blacks in comparable contempt, or to use such racially charged language.[82]

81. For more on the racial views of the Union sailors, see Michael J. Bennett, *Union Jacks: Yankee Sailors in the Civil War* (Chapel Hill: University of North Carolina Press, 2004), esp. chap. 7. Henneberry's diary entry for April 11, 1864, following his visit to several contraband camps near Vicksburg is especially disparaging. But he also denounced the Emancipation Proclamation as treachery (January 1, 1863). See also appendix 3, containing William Park's later reflections on the views of his fellow sailors on abolition.

82. The intellectual and spiritual disposition of Celeste's family, at least as it can be determined from public records, suggests benevolent and protective concern for blacks, as well as conscientious obligations of charity. Celeste's uncle J. J. Burk, a philanthropist with a refined and generous temperament, was a benefactor to many in Baton Rouge, including, apparently, a middle-aged black woman named Matilda (sometimes listed as Matilda Crossword), illiterate and disabled, who was part of his extended household. After Judge Burk's death, she lived with Burk's daughter Norah (Celeste's godmother) and her husband, John Warren Cadwallader Jones. Listed in the 1870 and 1880 census as a domestic servant, she remained with the family until her death. She is buried, as Matilda Jones, in the family plot in the historic St. Joseph Catholic Cemetery, not far from Celeste's parents and siblings.

The Celeste Repp Journal (1859–1861)

COMMENTARY

The French Compositions

Celeste Repp's brief original French compositions, appearing in her notebook under the title "Compositions françaises," were all written during the academic year 1859–60 at St. Mary's Academy in Baton Rouge. The first is dated by her September 4, 1859, and another provides a reflection on the beginning of the year 1860. No other pieces bear a date, but the final entry, about a visit to the Louisiana State Fair, was likely written shortly after the event, which took place in Baton Rouge in mid-March 1860. These simple exercises are arranged chronologically and several are seasonal, marking major events in the calendar year (Thanksgiving, Christmas, and New Year).

Baptismal and census records indicate that Celeste was born in the first half of 1846,[1] so she was thirteen at the time she opened her plain black school notebook and created an elaborately ornamented title page for her French exercises. She was especially fond of filigreed lettering with a vine or floral motif, which she uses both in titling her compositions and in heading her little essay "Mensonge" (Lying), but she also experiments with a variety of calligraphic and cursive flourishes throughout her text. Like many a thirteen-year-old girl, she was evidently as concerned with artistic presentation as with content. Perhaps such decoration was part of the assignment, perhaps

1. The Sisters of Mercy, on her member information card, have her birth date penciled in as 1836, evidently a simple clerical error, as her age at the time of her death in 1914 is correctly given as sixty-eight.

not. Penmanship would almost certainly have been evaluated, along with the accuracy of French vocabulary and grammar. Here, Celeste seems to have been adept and comfortable—though in her letter to Fr. Hubert she is modest about her skills and expresses appreciation for his patience with her occasional difficulties in comprehension and reading.

The range of subjects Celeste addresses is unremarkable for a student of her age. What is memorable in her writing is not dazzling or unusual content but a winsome innocence combined with moral seriousness and unaffected faith. The analogy of spring flowering with the Resurrection ("Descriptione d'une Jardin en Printemps") is conventional, but here sweetly and feelingly rendered. Though she does not mention it, Celeste had suffered a great deal of personal loss in her young life, including the death of her mother and at least two siblings. The hope of the Resurrection, central to her Catholic faith, was evidently a touchstone for her. "Mensonge," her essay on lying—specifically tale-telling, lying about others—addresses the dire social and spiritual consequences of such behavior but also the benefit of God-given "time to repent." A later piece about respect for teachers ("Reconnaissance envers nos Maîtresses") mentions lying again, this time in the broader sense of willful deception, as a betrayal of gratitude and an offense against ordained authority.

Gratitude is a feature of several pieces, notably "Action de Graces," which commends making appreciation for God's blessings the centerpiece of the Thanksgiving holiday. Celeste sees worship as an appropriate way to celebrate Thanksgiving; dancing until midnight less so. Lest one think her simply dour or sanctimonious, though, her two mentions of Christmas—in "La Fête de Noël" and her letter to Fr. Hubert—express both unaffected piety in her imagination of the Virgin's joy at the birth of Jesus and delight in the kindness and generosity of her headmistress and priest/mentor in sharing seasonal treats with the girls.[2] "Christmas was for me the happiest time of my life," she effuses to Fr. Hubert, adding that she couldn't help wishing it lasted a whole week.

2. Celeste's use of the term "Noël dernier" in the first of these undated compositions indicates that she is, in the midst of her overall joy in the Christmas season, reflecting on the previous year (December 1858) with reference to the kindnesses of Miss Victor and Fr. Hubert. (In her later letter to Fr. Hubert, she is clearly referring to the current Christmas season, 1859.) This confirms her tenure as a boarding student at St. Mary's for at least one previous academic year from the time of writing; there are records of her older sister Alice attending St. Mary's in the 1857–58 school year (see the introduction). They may have enrolled at the same time.

Following upon her Christmas reflections, she offers a self-examining consideration of the way one should respond to the plight of the poor and unemployed in winter. The seasonal reference suggests her contemplation of what it must be like to be turned away thoughtlessly by those enjoying their holiday plenty; having no personal experience of deprivation, they lack empathy for those in reduced circumstances. There is here something of the pathos of Hans Christian Andersen's "The Little Match Girl," which Celeste may well have read in one of its popular early English-language editions.[3] The bottom line for her is not mere sentiment, however, but a statement of Christian obligation: God loves the poor and expects us to be merciful to them.

Celeste's New Year's essay, written in early 1860, expresses her resolve to be more diligent in her studies in the coming year—indeed, to out-achieve all of her classmates—as well as the simple hope of enjoyment of time "with those I love." There is special poignancy in these words for the reader who knows that her only living parent, John Repp, died on February 12, 1860, very shortly after these lines were written. Baptized on his deathbed by Fr. Hubert, Celeste's father was given a Catholic burial, doubtless a consolation to his devout child.[4]

Celeste's affection for her priest and mentor, Darius Hubert, is one of the tenderest aspects of this short school diary. We know from her note written to him in the spring of 1860 that he was her French instructor at St. Mary's and, in her words, a gentle and patient teacher. From other records we know that Fr. Hubert was a polished speaker in his native tongue; his French tutorials were likely especially valued by students and their parents. In a local newspaper advertisement for St. Mary's Academy in 1860, Matilda Victor calls special attention to "the great facilities for acquiring a thorough and speaking knowledge of the French language afforded by that department of the Academy. It could not be more ably superintended."[5] But it was for his special acts of kindness—bringing Christmas treats to her and the other boarders, taking her with a group of classmates to the State Fair—that Fr. Hubert was especially cherished as a pastoral and paternal presence in Celeste's life. That

3. For the American publishing history of Andersen's works, see Herbert Rowland, *More Than Meets the Eye: Hans Christian Andersen and Nineteenth-Century American Criticism* (Madison, NJ: Fairleigh Dickinson University Press, 2006), 11.

4. For more on the religious character of Celeste's family, see the introduction.

5. *Baton Rouge Weekly Gazette and Comet,* September 15, 1860.

she wished for him to stay on in Baton Rouge and to be "always her French teacher" is unsurprising. Perhaps she already knew, when she wrote these words, that both were unlikely.

The Poems

Immediately following Celeste's "Compositions françaises" are three French poems, the second and third of which—both secular rather than religious in character—are in a decidedly different (and less elegant) hand.

The Marian hymn, which begins on the page immediately after Celeste's brief account of her visit to the State Fair, is clearly in her own hand, though it may have been written several months later. The slant and formation of the letters is consistent, and the attractive capitals are virtually identical to those in her compositions. She seems to be experimenting with a more mature Spencerian cursive style,[6] as the shading of uprights is highlighted, giving a sophisticated texture to the whole.[7] Perhaps she chose the script to accord with the elevated content of the poem, a traditional hymn to the Virgin from the Ignatian liturgy. The hymn's five stanzas are marked off with numbered headings, which may suggest that Celeste was memorizing them for recitation for the summer commencement. The annual recitals that capped the Academy school year typically contained both religious and secular performance pieces, probably according to the tastes and preferences of the girls.

Celeste did not title the hymn. Someone else later added a heading above it, simply using the first line, "Je vous Salue Auguste et Sainte Reine," in more upright and less self-consciously stylized handwriting. This same writer then penned the second and third (secular) poems on two subsequent pages, as well as a dateline on the final page of the St. Mary's portion of the diary: "Baton Rouge Mars 20 1861." Both of these poems lack line punctuation and

6. Platt Rogers Spencer (1800–1864) was an American educator and "the father of American handwriting." His *Spencerian Key to Practical Penmanship* (New York: Ivison, Phinney, Blakeman and Co., 1866) set the standard for cursive penmanship until the twentieth century. This newly published and very popular primer would have been the instructional text at St. Mary's during Celeste's tenure. Chapter 9 introduces the subject of shading, to be learned after "correctness of form" has been achieved, and models precisely what Celeste uses in this poem.

7. Celeste's penmanship is surprisingly refined, even when compared to that of Fr. Hubert and Matilda Victor, several of whose handwritten letters may be found in the University of Notre Dame Archives.

many accents, and the margins, so careful and exact in Celeste's compositions, are, by contrast, very uneven. Capitalization is sometimes added where it is not called for. All these factors suggest that these are dictation exercises by another Academy student who was using Celeste's notebook sometime after she penned the last of her own *compositions françaises.*[8]

The final poem, a simple but oft-quoted quatrain by Nicolas Gilbert, is unchanged from the original, apart from the aforementioned missing punctuation. Its easy vocabulary and straightforward grammar would have made it an excellent *dictée* exercise.

The other, a three-stanza love poem, is a slightly modified version of a French art song by Émile Barateau, "Ange à la voix tendre." It, too, features short lines and simple vocabulary. The changes are inconsequential as to content, with two notable exceptions. First, they remove any possibility that the "angel" who is at last wittily identified as the addressee of the poem could be masculine. Second, they provide a name for the "angel" when none is given in the Barateau text. The final lines in this version, read: "Et l'ange qui j'aime / Dorceline, c'est vous."

Who is Dorceline? The name is uncommon. There is, however, a small cluster of Dorcelines in Louisiana census records (specifically from the heart of Acadian Louisiana) who were born within a few years of Celeste. The possibility that one of these might have attended St. Mary's Academy in Baton Rouge as a boarding student is far from remote.[9] It would seem that whoever was giving the dictation exercise in this instance deliberately inserted the young student's name in the last line as a bit of affectionate whimsy.

A delightful, almost invisible witness to who might have done just that can be found in a superimposed penciled comment, in English, written lightly across the page, perpendicular to the *dictée,* and within a distinctive oval

8. Since Celeste was a boarding student, the notebook would have stayed in the school, and likely in the classroom used for French instruction. It is impossible to know the circumstances leading to it being used, fleetingly, by a different student a year later, or to determine whether Celeste was herself still in residence at St. Mary's in 1861.

9. The likeliest candidates in currently available census records may be Marie Dorceline Janise, born in Opelousas in 1849; Dorceline Doris Trahan, born in or near Lafayette in 1850; or Dorceline Fuselier, born in St. Landry ca. 1848. The name Dorceline (a compound of Greek "doron," meaning gift, and "celine," which—like "celeste"—means "heavenly") is still extremely rare, occurring almost exclusively in Louisiana, or in families of Louisianan heritage.

flourish. It reads: "So far, So Good." The handwriting in this instance can be identified with certainty; it is clearly that of Fr. Darius Hubert.[10]

THE TEXT

"Compositions françaises"

Descriptione d'une Jardin en Printemps

La première chose à faire lors qu'on veut avoir un jardin, c'est de bêcher la terre et de semer les graines; quand les graines sont restées enfouies un certain temps, il en sort de jolies fleurs; c'est l'image de la ressurection; car nos corps, après quelques jours qu'ils sont enfouis, se décomposent, mais au dernier jour ils ressusciteront plus beaux que jamais.

September 4th 1859
Celeste Repp

Description of a Garden in Springtime

The first thing to do when one wants to have a garden is to till the earth and to sow the seeds; after the seeds have been buried a certain time, lovely flowers emerge. This is the image of the Resurrection; for our bodies, after they have been buried for a few days, decompose, but on the last day they will be raised, more beautiful than ever.

Mensonge

Le mensonge est une très mauvaise habitude, car ceux qui disent des mensonges sont toujours haïs de toute le monde. Il ya bien des personnes qui sont habituées à dire des mensonges sur le compte des autres; mais elles seront punies soit dans ce monde, soit dans l'autre. Dieu ne laissera jamais rien de

10. The capital letters and especially the enclosing oval, with flourishes, accord perfectly with those in the handwritten correspondence of Fr. Hubert held in the University of Notre Dame Archives and in documents bearing his signature in his service records. Among other things, this "signature" in a St. Mary's schoolbook confirms that Fr. Hubert was teaching there, at least part-time, in the spring of 1961, very shortly before Albert Blanchard called him into the service of the Confederacy.

bien sans être récompensé, et nonplus rien de mal sans être puni. Il est si bon de donner le temps de se repentir à ceux qui ont parlé mal de leurs prochains!

Celeste Repp

Lying

Lying is a very bad habit; those who tell lies are always reviled by everyone. There are people who routinely lie about others, but they are punished, either in this world or in the next. God will never allow any good to go unrewarded, nor will he allow any wrong to go unpunished. He is so gracious to give time to repent to those who have spoken ill of their neighbors!

Action de Grâces

Le jour d'action de grâces devrait être gardé comme le dimanche; il fait droit remercier Dieu des bienfaits qu'il a répondus sur nous. Cette fête a été d'abord célebrée en Angleterre, mais elle est à présent observée dans tout les Etats-Unis. Le matin, on va à l'Eglise, et le soir on donne des festins, on danse jusqu'à minuit. Ce ne devrait pas être de cette manière qu'il faudrait finir ce jour là.

Celeste Repp

Thanksgiving

Thanksgiving Day should be treated like a Sunday; one should thank God for the blessings he has bestowed upon us. This feast was first celebrated in England, but at present it is observed all over the United States. In the morning, we go to church, and in the evening we host feasts and dance until midnight. This is not the manner in which we ought to end this day.

Reconnaissance envers nos Maîtresses

Nous devons beaucoup aimer nos Maîtresses,[11] et leur obèir fidèlement; c'est le moyen de leur témoigner la reconnaissance qu'elles ont droit d'attendre de nous.

11. The feminine form here suggests that all of Celeste's instructors, save Fr. Hubert, were women.

Quand nos Maîtresses nous parlent, ne soyons jamais de mauvaise humeur, ne répondons pas avec impertinence. Dieu n'aime pas cela. Il ya surtout une chose que nous ne devons jamais faire, c'est de dire des mensonges à nos Maitresses, parce qu'elles remplacent Dieu et que nous ne devons pas mentir à Dieu.

Celeste Repp

Appreciation for Our Teachers

We owe great love to our teachers and should faithfully obey them; this is the way we bear witness to the gratitude that they rightly expect from us. When our teachers address us, we must never behave moodily or respond with impertinence: God does not like that. There is one thing especially that we must never do, and that is to lie to our teachers, because they stand in place of God and we should not lie to God.

La Fête de Noël

Noël est la naissance de Notre Sauveur. C'est en pareil jour qu'il vint au monde tout petit enfant, ne pouvant ni marcher ni parler. Oh! Quel heureux jour dut être le jour de Noel pour la Sainte Vierge, quand elle se vit la Mère de son Redempteur! Noël dernier nous avons en la Messe à minuit, et après la messe Mademoiselle Victor nous a fait aller dans sa chamber pour nous chauffee, et nous a donné du café et des gâteaux, et ensuite nous sommes allées nous coucher, mais nous n'avais pas pu dormir. Le lendemain nous avant visite notre bon ami Pere Hubert, qui nous a régalés avec des gâteaux, du vin, et des bonbons.

Celeste Repp

The Feast of Christmas

Christmas is the birth of Our Savior. It is the same day he came to the world as a little child, unable either to walk or to talk. Oh, what a joyful day Christmas Day must have been for the Holy Virgin, when she saw herself the Mother of her Redeemer! Last Christmas we went to Mass at midnight, and after the Mass, Mademoiselle Victor invited us to her room to warm up, and for coffee and pastries; then we all went to bed, but we were unable to sleep. The next day our good friend Fr. Hubert came to visit, who delighted us with cakes, wine, and sweets.

Les Souffrances des Pauvres en Hiver

Il ya beaucoup de pauvres en ce monde qui ne peuvent pas trouver du travail pour gagner leur vie; ils sont obliges d'aller demander la charité de maison en maison et ils sont très souvent repoussés par des personnes qui ne savent pas a que c'est que d'être pauvres.

Nous devrions toujours être charitables envers le pauvres parce que Dieu les aime et qu'il récompensera soit dans ce monde soit dans l'autre tous ceux qui font l'aumone aux malheureux.

The Sufferings of the Poor in Winter

There are many poor people in this world who cannot find work to earn their living; they are obliged to beg for charity from house to house and they are very often rebuffed by people who do not know what it is to be poor.

We should always be charitable toward the poor because God loves them and because he will recompense either in this world or in the next all those who give alms to the destitute.

Réflexions au commencement de l'année 1860

Mil huit cent soixante est donc enfin arrivé et mil huit cent cinquante-neuf est passé avec toutes ses espérances, ses joies et ses évènements. Mes souhaits pour cette brillante année qui commence sont que le temps se passé agréablement avec ceux que j'aime et mes resolutions touchant mes devoirs sont que j'étudie bien et que je soie [soit] à la tête de toutes mes compagnes. Oh! Combien je desire faire beaucoup plus de progrès cette année que l'année passée et remporter tous les prix de ma classe!

Celeste Repp

Reflections on the beginning of the year 1860

Eighteen sixty has finally arrived and eighteen fifty-nine has passed along with all of its hopes, its joys, and its milestones. My desires for this splendid year just beginning are that the time passes pleasantly with those I love, and my resolutions concerning my schoolwork are that I study well and that I be at the head of all of my classmates. Oh, how I desire to make much more progress this year than the last, and to win all the prizes in my class!

Cher Père Hubert,

C'est la première fois que je vous écris; j'aurais dû l'avoir déjà fait car vous êtes si bon pour moi, si indulgent lorsque j'ai quelque difficulté à savoir mes leçons ou à lire. Je tâcherai de faire beaucoup de progrès afin de vous plaire.

Noel a été pour moi le temps le plus heureux de ma vie; j'aurais voulu que cette fête pût durer une semaine.

Cher Père Hubert, je souhaite que vous restiez ici et que vous soyez toujours notre maître de français.

Votre élève,
Celeste

Dear Father Hubert,

This is the first time that I have written to you; I should already have done so: for you are so kind to me, so indulgent when I find it difficult to learn my lessons or to read; I will try to make great progress so as to please you.

Christmas was for me the happiest time of my life; I wished that this celebration could last a whole week.

Dear Father Hubert, I would like for you to stay here and for you always to be our French instructor.

Your student,
Celeste

La Faire de l'Etat

Nous sommes allées à la faire pour voir toutes les belles choses qui y étaient exposées. La foule était si grande que nous pouvions à peine trouver une place. Le Père Hubert a en la bonté de nous offrir de fruits et plusieurs autre bonnes choses. J'ai été enchantée de tout ce que j'ai vu.

The State Fair

We went to the fair to see all of the lovely things that were being exhibited there.[12] The crowd was so large that we could hardly find a place. Father Hubert was generous enough to offer us some fruit and many other good things. I was enchanted by everything that I saw.

Three French Poems

Je vous Salue Auguste et Sainte Reine

1st

Je vous salue auguste et sainte Reine,
Dont la beauté ravit les immortels.
Mère de grâce, aimable souveraine,
Je me prosterne au pied de vos autels.[13]

2d

Je vous salue, ô divine Marie!
Vous méritez l'hommage de nos coeurs:

12. The first ever Louisiana State Fair took place March 12–17, 1860, on the garrison grounds in Baton Rouge. It was a festive and colorful event that drew huge crowds; schoolchildren like Celeste enjoyed time off from their studies, and many local planters gave their slaves a holiday to attend the exhibition, according to a reminiscence by William Watson (*Life in the Confederate Army: Being the Observations and Experiences of an Alien in the South during the Civil War* [London: Chapman and Hall, 1887], 60–61). A description in the weekly *West Baton Rouge Sugar Planter,* March 24, 1860, affords some sense of the "enchanting" displays Celeste enjoyed: "articles of female workmanship and the fine arts . . . a large quantity of worsted and needle work, specimens of wax flowers and . . . pickles, preserves and peaches . . . photographs by J. H. Clark, of New Orleans . . . a finely executed full length painting of the Iron Duke of Wellington, a sleeping child exquisitely carved in marble, and several portraits painted on glass. . . . beautiful specimens of jewelry furnished by Gregor & Co., of New Orleans . . . a Knitting machine of J. B. Aiken, an *engine* that can make a pair of socks in 16 minutes . . . [and] a beautifully shaped powder horn, set in silver and gold." Of industrial and agricultural implements, with which Celeste was likely less enthralled, there was also a vast display.

13. This French Marian hymn is included among the *Cantiques spirituels à l'usage du diocese d'Amiens* (1807) and reprinted in the Hymnbook (*Recueil de cantiques*) section of the *Manuel des ouvriers de Saint-Francois Xavier et de la Sainte-Famille* (Paris: Poussielgue-Rusand, 1859), 58. The rhymed quatrain stanzas are not numbered in either edition, but a musical setting is specified.

Après Jésus, vous êtes et la vie,
Et le refuge et l'espoir des pécheurs.

3d

Fils malheureux d'une coupable mère,
Bannis du ciel, les yeux baignés de pleurs,
Nous vous faisons, de ce lieu de misère,
Par nos soupirs entendre nos douleurs.

4th

Ecoutez-nous, puissante protectrice;
Tournez sur nous vos yeux compatissans,
Et montrez-nous qu'à nos malheurs propice
Du haut des cieux vous aimez vos enfans.

5th

O douce, ô tendre, ô pieuse Marie!
O vous de qui Jésus reçut le jour;
Faites qu'après l'exil de cette vie
Nous le voyions dans l'éternel séjour.

[I salute you, exalted and holy Queen,
Whose beauty delights the angels—
Mother of mercy, gracious sovereign,
I prostrate myself at the foot of your altars.

I salute you, o divine Mary!
You merit the homage of our hearts.
After Jesus, you are the life
And the refuge and the hope of sinners.

Unfortunate sons of a guilty mother,
Banished from heaven, eyes bathed in tears,
We [beseech] you, from this place of misery,
By our sighs, attend to our sorrows.

Hear us, powerful protector;
Turn your eyes of compassion toward us
And show yourself favorable to our afflictions,
From the heights of heaven, that you love your children.

O gentle, o tender, o loving Mary!
O you who welcomed Jesus that day;
Let it be that after the exile of this life
We see him in the eternal dwelling.]

["Ange à la voix tendre"]

1er Couplet
Ange a la voix tendre[14]
Ange aux blonds cheveux
Puissiez vous comprendre
Mes chants et mes voeux [Mes chants et mes pleurs]
Lorsque brille l'Etoile [Quand brille une etoile]
Sous un ciel si doux [Dans un ciel plus doux]
Mon regard se voile
Et je pense à vous

2d Couplet
Du bosquet l'ombrage
Sombre et silencieux [Si mystérieux]
Et l'eau du rivage [Les flots du rivage]

14. Poem, slightly adapted, by Émile Barateau (1792–1870), published with the title "Vous" in *Bigarrures* (Paris: Librairie D'Abel Ledoux, 1834), 188–90. Rossini included this poem, with a musical setting by Ferdinand Paër, in a manuscript he gave to Mademoiselle Louise Carlier, daughter of a Paris impresario, in 1835. A 1941 recording of Suzanne Danco singing all of the songs in the Rossini manuscript, including "Ange à la voix tendre," is available on iTunes. A musical score, with piano accompaniment, was widely available by the 1840s (*Vous!: Romance* [Paris: A. Meissonnier et J. L. Heugel]). Bracketed words indicate the original text.

Bleu comme vos yeux
L'onde qui murmure
Sur ses blancs cailloux
Tout dans la nature
Me parle de vous

3me Couplet
Lorsque je Sommeille
Mon ange apparait
Tout bas à l'oreille [Tout bas son oreille]
Recoit mon Secret
Je lui dis je taime
Je t'aime a genoux
Et l'ange qui j'aime [Car l'ange lui-même]
Dorceline cest vous. [Lovely . . . c'est vous!]

[Angel with gentle voice,
Angel with blond tresses
Can you understand
My songs and my wishes?
When the star shines
So sweetly in the sky
My gaze is veiled
And I think of you.

The shady grove,
Somber and hushed;
The water at the shoreline,
Blue like your eyes;
The wave murmuring
On the white pebbles:
Everything in nature
Speaks to me of you.

When I am asleep
My angel appears,

Whispers in ear,
Receives my secret.
I tell her "I love you,"
I kneel in love.
And the angel I love,
Dorceline, is you.]

["Au banquet de la vie"]

Au banquet de la vie infortuné Convive
J'apparus un jour et je meurs
Je meurs et sur la tombe où lentement j'arrive
Nul ne viendra verser des pleurs[15]

[An ill-fated guest at the banquet of life
I appeared for a day, and now die.
I die, and at the tomb where at last I rest
None will come to shed a tear.]

15. Nicolas Joseph Laurent Gilbert (1750–80), seventh stanza of a nine-stanza poem entitled "Ode imitée de plusieurs psaumes" (1778), but better known as "Adieux à la vie." The tragic circumstances of Gilbert's death prompted curious (or morbid) fascination with these lines. In 1858, the quatrain was introduced to American readers by Oliver Wendell Holmes in *The Autocrat of the Breakfast-table* (Boston: Phillips, Sampson and Co., 1858), 185, along with Holmes's rhymed translation: "At life's gay banquet placed, a poor, unhappy guest, / One day I pass, then disappear; / I die, and on the tomb where I at length shall rest / No friend shall come to shed a tear."

The William Park Journal (1861–1864)

COMMENTARY ON THE "ABSTRACT JOURNAL KEPT BY WILLIAM L. PARK OF THE U.S. GUNBOAT *ESSEX* DURING THE AMERICAN REBELLION"

The idea of controlling the Mississippi River system as a means of severing the Confederacy and strangling its supply routes was somewhat controversial at the outset of the Civil War. It was central to Winfield Scott's proposed strategy that became known, derisively at first, as the Anaconda Plan, or "Scott's Great Snake." A Federal blockade would be maintained along the Atlantic and Gulf coasts and a squadron of gunboats (the snake's "head") would subdue the riverways from Cairo, Illinois, to New Orleans. Scott believed that such an approach would ensure the capitulation of the Southern states with less loss of life than an aggressive military campaign into the heart of "Secessia."

Though the overall plan was unpopular with many of President Lincoln's military advisers, the case for an inland, or "brown water," navy was pressed by Edward Bates of St. Louis, Lincoln's first attorney general and the first American cabinet member from west of the Mississippi. Bates's friend James Eads, a brilliant and tireless entrepreneur with profound knowledge of the Mississippi River and strong Union sympathies, went to Washington in April 1861 and laid out his vision for an ironclad gunboat fleet; when the U.S. Army requested bids for their manufacture, Eads himself won the contract, though he had never built such a vessel in his life. He promised to deliver seven gunboats in sixty-five days; despite having no shipyard, foundry, machine shop, or skilled labor when he started out, and despite government delays in keeping up with contractual payments, Eads managed to deliver eight boats in a little more than one hundred days, the original Western Gunboat Flotilla. He would build twenty-five vessels for Federal use during the war.[1]

The Flotilla was formally attached to the army for the first year of the war; the navy initially wanted nothing to do with the inland waterways or their peculiar rivercraft—squat, flat-bottomed, steam-powered vessels that bore a striking resemblance to "gigantic turtles wallowing slowly along in their native element."[2] William Park's shipmate James Henneberry recounted the disparagement and ridicule of the sailors from Farragut's oceangoing fleet when the *Essex* was anchored off New Orleans in late 1862. For the purpose for which they were designed, however, better vessels than the Eads ironclads can scarcely be imagined—a fact that the Union navy ultimately acknowledged when it reluctantly adopted the ugly stepchildren of marine forces in October 1862, renaming them the Mississippi Squadron.

No one in the United States was better acquainted with "this immense, writhing snake of a river, this Mississippi"[3] than James Buchanan Eads. He well understood that his vessels would need not only to withstand enemy fire from forts and batteries along the high cliffs and swampy bayous of Confederate territory but also to navigate snag-infested shoals, complex and fierce currents, serpentine bends, channels so narrow that crews could reach out and touch trees along the riverbanks, rapids, violent whirling eddies, and broad, swift straightaways. The Mississippi also carries a massive sediment load and would sometimes deposit a "sand," as Park calls it (e.g., November 29, 1861), where no chart warned of it. The whole river system was prone to dramatic

1. The seven original "Pook turtles," designed by S. M. Pook and built by Eads, were *Cairo, Carondelet, Cincinnati, Louisville, Mound City, Pittsburg,* and *St. Louis* (later renamed *Baron De Kalb*); they are known officially as "city class gunboats." *New Era*—renamed *Essex* by William Porter—and *Benton* are sometimes referred to simply as "Eads ironclads"; they were both converted (*Essex* from a ferry boat; *Benton* from a snag-boat) for use in the Gunboat Flotilla in 1861. Eads later built the ironclads *Choctaw* and *Lafayette* on a design proposed by William Porter, as well as several river monitors and other vessels. For a detailed account of the vessels of the brown water navy, see the appendix to Fletcher Pratt's *Civil War on Western Waters* (New York: Holt, 1956), 227–46.

2. Alfred Thayer Mahan, *The Gulf and Inland Waters: The Navy in the Civil War* (New York: Scribner's, 1883), 14.

3. The words are those of John M. Barry, whose *Rising Tide: The Great Mississippi Flood of 1927 and How It Changed America* (New York: Simon and Schuster, 1997) provides the best introduction to Eads currently in print (see esp. pt. 1, "The Engineers").

seasonable variability in water levels (as much as seventy feet between high water and low water) and velocity, and it could change from a languorous calm to a turbulent torrent in a matter of hours. For a vessel like *Essex,* steaming upriver against a heavy current was often out of the question; the boat would need to be "taken in tow." Park frequently comments on river levels, with good reason. They were to affect dramatically the outcome of a number of military engagements during the war. Unprecedented high water below New Orleans in April 1862, according to Confederate General Mansfield Lovell, rendered useless his best-laid plans—strategic obstructions across the river between Forts Jackson and St. Philip—allowing Farragut's Federal fleet safely to pass the forts and to capture the city. Unprecedented low water in the Red River in the spring of 1864 doomed Union General Nathaniel Banks's military campaign to capture Shreveport and advance into Texas, nearly forcing him to abandon his entire fleet above the falls at Alexandria.

But this vast, unpredictable waterway—which Mark Twain called the longest and crookedest in the world[4]—was the highway into the very heart of "secesh" territory. It allowed a Federal presence to penetrate deep into the unprotected front yards of the Confederacy, along the edges of plantations whose owners and young men were gone under arms to the eastern theater of the war, and into shallow bayous and streams where nothing larger or less benign than flat-bottomed fishing boats had ever ventured. As the "turtles" prowled Southern waters, slaves began to appear on the riverbanks seeking safe passage to Union-held contraband camps or offering themselves for service aboard the boats; increasingly, as the war churned on, and as Northern crews were decimated by sickness, blacks were accepted onto the gunboats and given an active role in fighting for their freedom. Park was, like his fellow tars, dubious about sharing crowded quarters and life-and-death engagements with contrabands, especially when, despite their inexperience, they were called on to man the guns (see August 5, 1862); he nevertheless shows a degree of sympathy toward their plight, and seems less burdened with ingrained racial prejudice than many of his mates (see, e.g., September 6, 1862). James Henneberry, by contrast, on January 1, 1863, writes of the Emancipation Proclamation as a betrayal of those who had heretofore died in service of the Union, and of Lincoln, if indeed he has signed such a proclamation,

4. *Life on the Mississippi* (New York: Harper, 1911), 15.

as a "traitor to his country and traitor to his God." Park confirms in his later memoir that such views were near universal among his fellow sailors on the ironclad fleet.[5]

For the largely unarmed local civilian population,[6] with the enemy at their door and their community structure in tatters, the emancipation and flight of slaves only intensified anxiety. Whatever the generals and their troops might be accomplishing in the Army of Northern Virginia, those left behind on the home front felt incredibly vulnerable, especially after the fall of New Orleans and the occupation of Baton Rouge.[7]

To counter the presence of the Federal gunboats, self-appointed militias—to whom the term "guerillas" was generally attached—sprang up along the river. They were not always, or even often, local; many came from considerable distance to pursue an unconventional campaign against the Yankees. Having neither professional training nor an established military chain of command, they fought the gunboats with a commando mentality and with ingenuous and often ruthless tactics; they devised and launched homemade riverine mines ("torpedoes," in contemporary parlance) in the murky rivers

5. At the very least, such statements give evidence of a simple truth often overlooked: the common Union soldier or sailor did not see himself as fighting against slavery—any more than the common Confederate soldier or sailor saw himself as fighting to defend it (see appendix 3). For a valuable contemporary witness to the slavery question as viewed by both Northern and Southern combatants, see William Watson, *Life in the Confederate Army* (London: Chapman and Hall, 1887), 44, 395–98. Watson was a native Scot living in Baton Rouge when war broke out; despite strong Federal sympathies, he enlisted with the Third Louisiana regiment to fight for the Confederacy. His memoir recounts in considerable detail, and with sophistication and evenhandedness, the cultural milieu in Louisiana before and during the war.

6. Women who had been left with firearms for self-defense by their departing husbands and sons routinely had them confiscated by Union personnel; see, for example, the memoir written by the daughter of John Hampden Randolph, master of Nottoway Plantation, south of Baton Rouge: M. R. Ailenroc, *The White Castle of Louisiana* (Little Rock: Morton, 1903), 58–59.

7. Their apprehension was fueled by the reckless threats of Union officials such as General Benjamin Butler to "arm every negro in the South, and make them cut the throat of every man, woman and child in it! I'll make them lay the whole country waste with fire and sword, and leave it desolate!" This tirade, directed at Baton Rouge resident Solomon Benjamin (brother of Judah Benjamin, Confederate secretary of war), is recounted by Sarah Morgan, who adds that those who heard it "believe him fully equal to carry it in execution, and some even believe it will be done" (Morgan, *The Civil War Diary of a Southern Woman,* ed. Charles East [New York: Simon and Schuster/Touchstone, 1992], 145).

and built clever obstructions using chains, timbers, or even sunken vessels to disrupt travel. They employed black men and women as bait to draw gunboats or their landing boats ashore, and then ambushed the ship's crew (e.g., December 13, 1862). They picked off unlucky sailors who were thrown into the river or jumped from burning ships in the chaos of battle. They lay in wait for foraging parties from the gunboats and often killed and sometimes tortured and mutilated their captives.[8] After they had done these things, they would simply vanish into the countryside. And if one ever imagined them to be decisively beaten back, they would rise "phoenix-like . . . up out of the ashes of defeat again to menace us."[9]

Their presence actually hurt more than it helped the civilian population living along the rivers. It incensed the captains of individual Federal vessels and their superiors. Rear Admiral David Farragut bombarded Baton Rouge after a guerilla incident on May 28, 1862—an attack that damaged Celeste Repp's church and school, displaced families, killed or injured several civilians, and prompted a scathing passage in Sarah Morgan's diary concerning "illustrious Farragut, the Woman Killer!!!"[10] Acting Rear Admiral David Dixon Porter, in his General Order No. 4 (October 18, 1862), formally mandated retribution against those huddled on plantations and in largely unguarded towns along the rivers for guerilla attacks against the boats. By that point, precedents were already well established: *Essex* and its crew had reduced Bayou Sara, Louisiana, to rubble in late summer (see Park's entry for August 24, 1862) after guerillas set fire to the ship's coal heap, and severely damaged Natchez, Mississippi, a little over a week later (Park, September 2, 1862). In mid-December, having taken continuous musket fire from guerillas on shore for several hours, *Essex* "replied by shelling every piece of Bush, House and Plantation to within 7 miles of Baton Rouge" (Park, December 14, 1862).[11]

8. See Michael J. Bennett, *Union Jacks: Yankee Sailors in the Civil War* (Chapel Hill: University of North Carolina Press, 2004), 87–92.

9. *Warfare along the Mississippi: The Letters of Lieutenant Colonel George E. Currie*, ed. Norman E. Clarke Sr. (Mount Pleasant: Central Michigan University, 1923), 101.

10. "It seems the only thing that saved the town was two gentlemen who rowed out to the ships and informed the illustrious commander that there were no men there to be hurt, and he was only killing women and children" (Morgan, *Civil War Diary*, 94–95).

11. Sarah Morgan, breezily determining to "have a gallop and a peep at the gunboats from the levee" a few days after the Battle of Baton Rouge, was warned by her mother that "it was well known they fired at every horse or vehicle they saw in the road, seeing a thousand guerillas

The Federal rationale was explicable, given the guerillas' tactics, but directing big guns at soft targets, especially when the victims bore no necessary connection to the militias and had negligible influence over them, came to be openly questioned in even Northern newspapers. Thus the *New York Times,* on February 24, 1863, editorialized:

> We have an announcement now and then from the West that the gunboats . . . have destroyed this or that town or landing on the Mississippi River "in retaliation for the firing of guerrillas." This sort of news is more or less gratifying to the public, because it conveys the idea of prompt punishment for a very foolish and cruel style of warfare frequently adopted by the rebels. . . . [But] the guerrillas that depredate in the Southwest are rarely citizens of the locality where their evil deeds are committed. Their acts are those of unrestrained brigandage, and those who follow the lawless pursuit find it easier to prey on strangers than upon the people with whom they have ties of acquaintance and consanguinity. Hence the guerrilla bands . . . care nothing for the "retaliation" that follows their acts. . . . If the miscreants cannot be followed and chastised, in *propria persona,* it is a poor satisfaction to burn houses that shelter women and children.

Guerilla activity also served to embolden and rationalize reckless, undisciplined, and even brazenly criminal behavior on the part of Federal soldiers and sailors in rebel territory. Shore raids and "foraging expeditions" that were fairly benign in the first months of the war—Park recounts bagging chickens and turkeys and nabbing a heavy "bee gum" laden with honey on October 31, 1861—became more transparent looting ventures (as at Bayou Sara, where Park helped himself to some "valuable books" in a plantation house before the town was burned). Sometimes they would turn into incidents of wholesale vandalism, arson, and violence, fueled by confiscated liquor (see note 68 under Park's entry for August 24, 1862). Northern journalists who witnessed these events were sometimes candid enough to report them, though such accounts were greatly at odds with the version of Union operations normally heralded in Federal newspapers and magazines. As one embedded reporter observed: "A spirit of destruction and wanton ferocity seems to have seized upon many of [our troops]. . . . There is danger of our whole noble army degenerating into

---

in every puff of dust." To satisfy her, Sarah "took the road about a mile from the river, in full view, however," and lived to tell the tale (ibid., 203).

a band of cut-throats and robbers."[12] Despite the fact that such behavior was formally prohibited, it routinely went unpunished; psychologically demoralizing and personally devastating to the families it affected, it also enflamed anti-Yankee sentiment and remained one of the greatest sources of prolonged Southern bitterness (especially on the part of women) after the war.[13]

As troublesome and potentially deadly as ubiquitous guerillas were to the Federal crews, a still-greater threat actually lay in the environment itself—in the regiments of mosquitoes that served as something of a "third army" in the South,[14] imparting malarial fevers of several kinds, dengue ("break-bone") fever, and yellow fever to thousands of sailors and soldiers. The Federals called mosquito season the "sickly season" since so many in the ranks succumbed to one form of infection or another. But conditions faced by the brown water navy and the armies that accompanied them were conducive to the spread of many and varied ailments—typhoid fever (from which William Park was very fortunate to recover), dysentery, measles, smallpox, cholera, tuberculosis, and pneumonia being only a few of the most prevalent. Many illnesses were spread by contaminated food and water; others simply preyed opportunistically on

12. Frank Moore, ed., *The Rebellion Record: A Diary of American Events,* vol. 8 (New York: Van Nostrand, 1867), 430, quoted in Steven M. Mayeux, *Earthen Walls, Iron Men* (Knoxville: University of Tennessee Press, 2007), 149.

13. In a recent volume about the experience of Southern women on the home front, Lisa Tendrich Frank describes the particular sense of violation experienced by women whose bedrooms were ransacked by Federal soldiers. The invasion of and rummaging in these intimate spaces, off-limits to all but one's most trusted family members, constituted an unforgivable violation of decency and honor, and intensified women's hatred of the enemy (see *Occupied Women: Gender, Military Occupation, and the American Civil War,* ed. LeeAnn Whites and Alecia P. Long [Baton Rouge: Louisiana State University Press, 2009], chap. 3, "Bedrooms as Battlefields"). The postwar role of Southern women in not only memorializing fallen Confederates but resisting reconciliation with the North has been documented by Caroline E. Janney in *Remembering the Civil War: Reunion and the Limits of Reconciliation* (Chapel Hill: University of North Carolina Press, 2013); Jefferson Davis famously remarked in 1873 that he had never met a reconstructed Southern woman (cited ibid., 238).

14. See especially Andrew McIlwaine Bell, *Mosquito Soldiers: Malaria, Yellow Fever, and the Course of the American Civil War* (Baton Rouge: Louisiana State University Press, 2010). Philadelphia-born surgeon John H. Brinton, assigned to establish the Mound City Hospital at the outset of the war, spent his evenings killing mosquitoes, the like of which he had never seen: "very powerful and bloodthirsty . . . grey-backed, huge, and insatiate" (*Personal Memoirs of John H. Brinton: Civil War Surgeon, 1861–1865* [New York: Neale, 1914; Carbondale: Southern Illinois University Press, 1996], 52).

weakened, fatigued, and undernourished men sharing close quarters and giving little or no attention to what we would think of as basic sanitation. Showers were virtually nonexistent; hand washing occurred to no one. Food was consumed off plates and utensils half-cleaned at best in muddy river water. Shore latrines were carelessly dug near waterways or cooking quarters; they were often inadequate and not, in any case, universally used. Refuse of all kinds and even dead animals were thrown into the river; Park's shipmate James Henneberry comments with disgust on the bloated bodies of horses and mules (and occasionally human remains) floating downriver from Vicksburg past *Essex*'s moorage at Profit Island during the summer of 1863 "with a stench strong enough to knock a man down" (May 4, 1863; June 16, 1863; July 2, 1863); a similar grisly flotilla of animal carcasses and some dead soldiers was seen off Memphis following the notorious Battle of Fort Pillow (marginalia to Henneberry's entry for May 15, 1864).

Death was everywhere. Death from illness, death from artillery fire, death from infected wounds, death from botched surgery, death from exposure, death from weapons malfunctioning and boilers exploding, death by drowning, death from guerilla snipers, death by suicide. If war is hell, then the American Civil War was surely a particularly bleak corner of hell. The chances of surviving this particular conflict were poor; of the 3 million men who served on both sides, 750,000 or more died.[15] The chances of surviving with all four limbs and a modicum of health were vastly poorer yet. Those who signed up for service aboard the gunboat flotilla as a bit of a lark in 1861 were irrevocably changed within the first few months of service. They had seen friends scalded to death; they had swabbed blood and collected mangled body parts from the ship's decks and timbers; they had tended to shipmates horribly wounded and then loaded them onto hospital boats unsure of ever seeing them again; they had buried some and been prevented from burying others—helplessly watching them swirl away in the river. And as Michael Bennett trenchantly observes, "unlike soldiers who could march away from the sites of their nightmares, sailors had to continue to live amid the reminder" of the carnage.[16]

15. The long-held estimate of 620,00 dead has recently been revised upward by J. David Hacker, historian at Binghamton University, based on a reevaluation of postwar census and other records. His findings, which have been widely affirmed, are published in "A Census-Based Count of the Civil War Dead," *Civil War History* 57, no. 4 (2011): 307–48. According to Hacker, this new estimate may still sorely underestimate the actual numbers.

16. Bennett, *Union Jacks,* 206.

Sailor Edward W. Bacon, aboard the sloop USS *Iroquois* with Farragut's fleet off Vicksburg in the summer of 1862, wrote a candid note home about "the intense fatigue, the horrible prostration" he felt after a battle and which he came to dread "almost as much as the falling shells." His words doubtless capture the feelings of men aboard the ironclads as well:

> The tension of one's nerves and the work of the mind is dreadful. You have to force yourself to be cool. You see the flash of a gun and in a second hear the shriek of shell—yet in the intervening period my mind goes thro this—This shell may hit me. If I get below, if I fall down, run under cover, I may save my life (and my body starts to do so). But I can't permit this. My duty is here—on deck—ready, ready to jump forward in a minute—I must assist my captain—tell him when I see Batteries, where the following vessels are. I am sworn to do this duty. I can't save myself. Perhaps God will protect me. Every time I see that the guns in the hills flash, comes that irresistible impulse to run, to dissolve, which exhausts itself in a dodge of the head.[17]

Sailors found various means of surviving the chaos and enduring the relentless, withering assault on their sense of human dignity. Many sought various forms of anesthesia—alcohol chief among them. Others withdrew into silence, immersed themselves in work, and sleeplessly relived the events each night until the horror subsided. Some few who came to the ships with a sturdy faith managed, through informal prayer gatherings and services with mates, to retain spiritual ballast through dark times. The inland navy was not well served with chaplains; there was, in fact, one only, and he was stationed at Cairo, Illinois. Although Andrew Foote, the first flag officer of the Western Gunboat Flotilla, himself a devoutly religious man and an able preacher, encouraged "divine service" on all Union vessels, William Porter, the first captain of *Essex,* showed no inclination toward religious practice of any kind. When Charles Caldwell replaced him in the autumn of 1862, he experimented with church—one of the officers reading a few chapters of the New Testament to about half the ship's company on the quarterdeck at 10:00 a.m. on November 28, apparently in observance of Thanksgiving.[18] Such gatherings

17. Edward W. Bacon, *The Letters of Sailor and Soldier Edward W. Bacon,* ed. George S. Burkhardt (Carbondale: Southern Illinois University Press, 2009), 49.

18. Though the annual day of National Thanksgiving was not officially fixed to the last Thursday of November until President Lincoln's "Proclamation of Thanksgiving" on October 3, 1863,

seem thereafter to have been irregular at best on *Essex*. (On the ironclad *Carondelet,* by contrast, divine service was held weekly, almost without fail, and often led by Captain Henry Walke himself.)[19] On May 15, 1864, as *Essex* was anchored off the Union-held but largely Confederate city of Memphis, the crew was treated to the "first sermon ever given on this boat," according to James Henneberry. He styles the preacher a "bishop," though he was likely the Episcopalian rector of Calvary Church, Memphis, Rev. George White, whose Federal sympathies prompted part of his flock to leave and establish a new congregation after the war; his obscure but pertinent text for the morning was Ezekiel 20:38: "And I'll purge out the Rebels from among ye."[20]

As months turned into years, sailors became of necessity seasoned and battle-hardy, and they also sought amusements and recreation to distract them from the memories of their last engagement and apprehension of the next. In some ways, idle time was the worst enemy not only of ship discipline but also of the psychological well-being of the sailors. So they wrote letters home or kept journals or played cards or made music or engaged in various forms of skylarking. They looked forward to any opportunity for "liberty" from the claustrophobic, poorly ventilated, and often insufferably hot "federal bake ovens" on which they served.[21] When *Essex* was moored for several weeks off Port Hudson in the spring of 1863, the crew formed baseball teams

---

Thanksgiving had long been celebrated in many states, following the precedent of George Washington's original Thanksgiving Proclamation of October 3, 1789, specifying Thursday, November 26 of that year as a day to "acknowledge the providence of Almighty God" and to offer thanks, prayers, and supplications to "the great Lord and Ruler of Nations." Matilda Victor had evidently put Thanksgiving on the calendar of St. Mary's (see Celeste's third *composition,* above).

19. See "The Civil War Diary of John G. Morrison, 1861–1865," available online at http://dmna.ny.gov/historic/reghist/civil/infantry/30thInf/30thInf_Diary_Morrison.htm. Morrison was a soldier with the Thirtieth New York Infantry who volunteered for service in the west on the gunboat *Carondelet* in February 1862. He received the Medal of Honor for exceptional bravery in the Union navy's first encounter with the Confederate ram *Arkansas,* July 15, 1862.

20. The breakaway "Confederate" church on Madison Avenue in downtown Memphis was named St. Lazarus (because, like the poor man of that name in Jesus's parable in Luke 16, "we were licked by the dogs," according to caustic parishioners). St. Lazarus was attended by Jefferson Davis during his sojourn in that city in the early 1870s and was the site of his daughter Margaret's marriage on New Year's Day 1876.

21. Temperatures belowdecks in the heat of a Southern summer could reach 150°F.

and played almost every day (the foreigners, like Park, mostly sitting out). When the vessel was anchored off Donaldsonville in the late summer of 1863, the gunners engaged in target practice with the ship's guns—using barrels as targets. Such recreation was also, of course, purposeful and could prove crucial to success or failure in the heat of battle. A handful of Confederate soldiers guarding Fort Griffin in Texas, with nothing but time on their hands, placed range markers in the Sabine River and engaged in competitive artillery practice to break the monotony; when a large Union fleet finally showed up on September 8, 1863, expecting an easy victory, the marksmen proved their worth—their well-practiced, accurate firing causing a complete skedaddle by a Federal force that outnumbered them a hundred to one.

Sailors, like soldiers, also enjoyed taunting the enemy, often in humorous ways. On March 20, 1863, the Federal sloop-of-war *Monongahela* fired at a rebel transport near Port Hudson, making "very wild shooting," according to Park. "The Rebels hoisted a flag on the stern of their boat in derision." The steamer *Genesee* then moved in and managed a good deal better, causing the Confederate boats to leave "for a cooler climate."

It was not uncommon for "unofficial" and often witty communications to be sent down the river—either in a bottle or attached to a bit of wood. On April 3, 1863, off Port Hudson, Park reports that "we picked up a letter that the rebels had stuck in a piece of drift wood and sent down from the Fort. They wished to know why Mr. Banks and his Yankees did not attack the Batteries, also an invitation for the Fleet to attack them, promising not to sink more than half of the Fleet and four of the Mortar Boats." On May 24, in the same location, another rebel message came down with the current: "Farragutt you renegade what is the good of throwing away so many shells. That does no harm. If you want Port Hudson come and take it. You will find plenty of Cotton." It was signed "Stonewall" (the writer was obviously unaware that General Jackson had died earlier that month). Another, less whimsical message was found by James Henneberry while he was looking for souvenirs among the abandoned belongings of Confederate soldiers who had evacuated Baton Rouge (December 17, 1862); he came across a playing card, the back of which read: "You D——d Yankee Son a b——s only for your Gun boats we would see you in h—ll before we would give up this place."

There is a very human side to all of this, of course—not all that different from the playground bravado of men and boys engaged in lesser games. And as in those fields, one also finds betimes a peculiar etiquette operating between sworn enemies. Since all men need to eat, hostilities routinely paused for meals. Thus Park, on June 13, 1863: "The Rebels opened from two other batteries and kept up a steady fire until 4 O'clock when we went to supper." Likewise, on June 27: "We fired until supper time and as soon as supper was over we commenced fireing again until dark." Breaks in fighting also occurred under "flags of truce" for various reasons, sometimes so that the dead could be buried and the field cleared before combat was resumed. There is a particularly striking instance of an agreed-upon truce at Port Hudson, in the midst of a long siege. Union pickets and Confederates working the shore battery consented to cease fire for a matter of several days (Park, June 18, 1863). While rebel soldiers watched new emplacements being constructed by Federals right in front of them, they held their fire: "they say they will not be the first to break the agreement and our Sharpshooters wont fire until the battery is completed." During the lull, officers from both sides met to discuss the long Port Hudson fight, events on other battlefields, and their respective prospects for victory; Confederate officers opined that their dug-in troops could hold the fort indefinitely, while some of the privates more candidly acknowledged that they might soon be "obliged to surrender for the want of Provision." In recounting all this, Park makes the strangely affecting observation: "There is good feeling between both parties."

TIMELINE OF ENGAGEMENTS AND LOCATION OF PARK'S VESSELS

William Park, though attached to USS *Essex* for his full three-year term, spent five months aboard USS *Pittsburg*[22] while *Essex* was being repaired and rebuilt following the Fort Henry disaster.

USS Essex *(William D. Porter commanding)*

October–December 1861: reconnaissance along the Mississippi, Ohio, and Cumberland Rivers; *New Era* refurbished and renamed *Essex.*

22. Though the ship's name was spelled inconsistently throughout the Civil War, it is spelled without the final "h" in the *Official Records of the Union and Confederate Navies.* That convention will be followed in this volume, though Park himself typically adds an "h." (His preference for the "Scottish" form is reflected also in his addition of a final "h" to Pittsburg Landing.)

January 1862: "running battles" with Confederate gunboats near Columbus, Kentucky
February 5–6, 1862: Battle of Fort Henry, Tennessee

USS Pittsburg *(Egbert Thompson commanding)*

February 14, 1862: Battle of Fort Donelson, Tennessee
March 14–April 7, 1862: Battle of Island No. 10, near New Madrid, Missouri
April 13–June 4, 1862: Naval Battle of Fort Pillow, near Henning, Tennessee
June 4–30, 1862: guarding Fort Pillow

USS Essex *(William D. Porter commanding)*

July 13–24, 1862: with the Gulf fleet, off Vicksburg, Mississippi
July 26–August 23, 1862: off Baton Rouge, Louisiana
August 5, 1862: Battle of Baton Rouge
August 6, 1862: confrontation with Confederate ram *Arkansas*
August 23–24, 1862: burning of Bayou Sara, Louisiana
August 28, 1862: off Port Hudson, Louisiana
September 2, 1862: shelling of Natchez, Mississippi
September 7, 1862: running the batteries of Port Hudson
September 8–November 12, 1862: repairs at New Orleans, Louisiana

USS Essex *(Charles H. B. Caldwell commanding)*

November 18, 1862–early March 1863: reconnaissance between Port Hudson, and New Orleans, stationed for the most part at Baton Rouge
March 13–early July 1863: in the vicinity of "Prophet's Island" and Port Hudson
May 22–July 9, 1863: bombardment and siege of Port Hudson

USS Essex *(Robert Townsend commanding)*

July 12, 1863–March 6, 1864: reconnaissance, based at Donaldsonville, Louisiana
March12, 1864: commencement of Red River Campaign
March 14–April 17, 1864: off Fort DeRussy, Louisiana
April 17–30, 1864: reconnaissance along the Mississippi and White Rivers (Vicksburg, Natchez, Fort Pillow, etc.)
May–September, 1864: off Memphis, Tennessee

AN ABSTRACT JOURNAL KEPT BY

William L. Park

OF THE U.S. GUNBOAT *ESSEX*

DURING THE AMERICAN REBELLION

COMMENCING SEPT. 25TH 1861

William Park's Civil War, 1861–1864.

1861

September 25th

I arrived in Chicago from Oswego in the Schooner *Surprise.* had some words with Captain and left. My Friend Andrew Waterman going with me. He determined to Join the Western Flotilla of Gunboats and fight for the Union, and he persuaded me to go with him. So we both went down Town and Joined for three years or during the War. I accompanied him on a short visit to his friends in Kane County before we left.

October 1st

Left Chicago in Company with nineteen others in the Railway Cars bound for St. Louis. we arrived their at 10 P.M. went on board the receving ship *Nebraska*[1] where we got Supper, which consisted of Hard Crackers and *harder Coffee,* and then to bed where every man had to take his knife and feel for the softest *Plank.*[2]

1. A privately owned riverboat by this name was placed under contract with the War Department under the Anaconda Plan. In a dispatch dated October 12, 1861, the first mention occurs in an order of Commander A. H. Kilty to Lieutenant S. L. Phelps that men should "on their arrival be immediately transferred to the squadron at Cairo or to the receiving ship *Nebraska,* here [St. Louis]" (*Official Records of the Union and Confederate Navies in the War of the Rebellion* [Washington, DC: U.S. Government Printing Office, 1894–1922], 1.22.367). Subsequent references to the *Official Records* will be cited as *ORN.*

2. James Henneberry (who admits to retrospective reconstruction of the first part of his journal) has a suggestively similar note here, mentioning "hard biscuit and harder Coffee" and retiring to bed "on the soft side of a plank." Edward Galligan, another shipmate who came aboard *Nebraska* at the same time, details being supplied by the purser with "1 Blanket, 1 Matress, 1 Tin Cup, 1 Plate, and 1 Spoon amounting to $6.04."

October 4th

We was all sent on board the Gunboat *New Era* Commanded by Cap. W. D. Porter.[3] the *New Era* was an old Ferry Boat which the government bought and put heavy Breastworks round her to protect her Boilers and Machinery. She mounts 5 nine inch Dalghren Guns and a Crew of 70 Men and Officers.[4]

October 6th

We left the Levee this morning for Cairo.[5] Nothing of much importance has occured up to this date, excepting taking the Oath of alligence.[6] Commodore

3. William David Porter (figure 4) was the son of Commodore David Porter (1780–1843), who saw distinguished service in the War of 1812, brother to Admiral David Dixon Porter, and foster brother to Admiral David Farragut. In the summer of 1861, having had a somewhat checkered career (he was widely known as "Dirty Bill"), he was assigned to help establish the Western Flotilla. *New Era,* which he renamed *Essex* after it was refitted later in the year (see below, November 17) in honor of his father's famous frigate, was under his command until September 1862 when he was promoted to the rank of commodore and moved to New York. Though Porter was something of a maverick and was often a thorn in the side to his superiors (a common Porter trait), Park and the crew were deeply devoted to him and greatly regretted his departure. See notation for September 13, 1862, and appendices 1 and 3. Porter died of heart disease before the war ended.

4. Later in the war this number doubles, to more than 140 on board the rebuilt *Essex.*

5. Cairo, Illinois, strategically located at the confluence of the Mississippi and Ohio Rivers and served by the Great Central Railway of Illinois (completed in 1856), was a bustling steamboat port and important Union supply base during the Civil War. It was James Eads who first argued in a letter to Secretary of the Navy Gideon Welles, dated April 29, 1861, that the key to control of the Upper Mississippi was control of the town of Cairo. Historian Gary D. Joiner argues that it was early in the war "the most strategically important real estate on the North American continent, excluding the District of Columbia" (*Mr. Lincoln's Brown Water Navy* [Lanham, MD: Rowman and Littlefield, 2007], 15). Cairo is described unflatteringly by John G. Morrison, a soldier turned seaman, as a "dirty, swampy hole, no sidewalks, and mud knee-deep. Poor accommodations. No hammocks, no mess traps, nor no regulations whatever" (*The Civil War Diary of John G. Morrison, 1861–1865,* https://dmna.ny.gov/historic/reghist/civil/infantry/30thInf/30thInf_Diary Morrison.htm, Feb. 21, 1862). John H. Brinton, who established a hospital at Cairo, characterized it as rat-infested, "a pestilential hole fraught with all malarial poisonous influence" (*Personal Memoirs of John H. Brinton: Civil War Surgeon, 1861–1865* [New York: Neale, 1914; Carbondale: Southern Illinois University Press, 1996], 67).

6. "The Oath of Allegiance to the United States Government," recorded in St. Louis, Missouri, in 1861, read: "I solemnly swear that I will bear true allegiance to the United States and support and sustain the Constitution and laws thereof; that I will maintain the national

Foote[7] came on board yesterday and adminstered the oath to both Officers and Crew.

October 8th

Arrived at Cairo this morning and anchored in the River. found the *Conestoga, Lexington,* and *Taylor*[8] Gunboats laying here. these compose the whole of the Western Flotilla. in the mean time their is 5 New Iron Clad's building at St. Louis and 3 Building at Mound City, a small place about 7 miles above here on the Ohio River.

October 14th

The Rebel Steamer *Grampus*[9] came up from Colombus with a Flag of truce. all hands was called to Quarters expecting she was a Rebel Gunboat.

---

sovereignty paramount to that of all state, country or confederate powers; that I will discourage, discountenance and forever oppose secession, rebellion and disintegration of the Federal Union; that I disclaim and denounce all faith and fellowship with the so-called Confederate armies and pledge my honor, my property and my life to the sacred performance of this my solemn oath of allegiance to the Government of the United States of America."

7. Andrew Hull Foote, a career naval officer, had been active in suppressing the slave trade off the African coast prior to the Civil War. A noted abolitionist and supporter of the Federal cause, he was named commander of the Western Gunboat Flotilla in August 1861. He forged a strong relationship with Ulysses S. Grant, with whom he shared several significant Union victories. Shortly after his promotion to rear admiral for his exploits on the western waters he died unexpectedly from "albuminuria," a complicated disorder of the liver and kidneys. According to a *New York Times* editorial: "He was with his ship what Stonewall Jackson was with his division, and his mode of attack, his style of maneuver, his dash and daring, resembled greatly those of the rebel General. . . . Admiral Foote was distinguished for his devotion to his principles as a consistent Christian and total abstainer from intoxicating drinks, being the first to introduce total abstinence in the navy." A more concise contemporary assessment described him as an officer who "prays like a saint and fights like hell."

8. *Conestoga* was a side-wheeler converted into a timberclad gunboat in the summer of 1861. *Lexington* and *Tyler* were the other two earliest Federal timberclads. See "Gun-Boats Fitting Out at Cincinnati, Ohio, for Government Service on the Mississippi," *Harper's Weekly,* July 13, 1861, for an image of all three vessels. (Park misnames *Tyler* as *Taylor* throughout his journal, even in copied official correspondence.)

9. CSS *Grampus* was a fortified stern-wheeler steamboat based in Columbus, Kentucky. When she spied Union gunboats coming down the Mississippi, she would blow her steam whistle to warn Confederates on shore. Porter once asked for a naval duel (January 18, 1862),

October 16th

This evening the Steamboat *Aleck Scott*[10] came alongside with a Regement of Soldiers on board. We immeadeatly got under weigh and accompanied her up the Mississippi to Chester where Jeff Thomson and his Band[11] was commiting depredations. On the passage up the *Scott* took us in tow and nearly towed us under water. we had obliged to tie up to the bank and Pump out as there was two feet of water in the hold.

October 17th

We arrived at Chester this morning where we captured several Prisoners also a large quantity of grain. started down the River and arrived at Cairo on the next morning.

October 20th

Got under weigh and proceded up to Mound City to go on the ways[12] to be Corked.[13]

---

to which Captain Marsh Miller replied, "Sir: The ironclad steamer *Grampus* will meet the *Essex* at any point and time your Honor might appoint, and show you that the power is in our hands." The showdown never took place. *Grampus* was trapped and scuttled during the Union assault on Island No. 10 on April 7, 1862.

10. *Aleck Scott* was a side-wheel steamer converted to an ironclad ram in St. Louis in September 1862 and renamed *Lafayette*. Here, Park uses the old name; later in the diary (e.g., April, 1864) he refers to the same vessel as *Lafayette*. Accompanying transports up and down the river with army regiments and carrying officers and soldiers on board (e.g., October 29, 1861) kept the gunboat sailors in regular contact with infantry and cavalry, with whom they cooperated militarily throughout the war.

11. Jeff Thomson = Meriwether Jeff Thompson, a flamboyant Confederate cavalry commander, the wily "Swamp Fox of the Confederacy." On October 15, at the Big River Bridge, "Thompson succeeded in capturing some 66 much needed guns and some not so needed prisoners" (Carolyn Bartel, *The Civil War in Missouri Day by Day 1861–1865* [Independence, MO: Two Trails, 1992]). See also Doris Land Mueller, *M. Jeff Thompson: Missouri's Swamp Fox of the Confederacy* (Columbia: University of Missouri Press, 2007).

12. "The ways" = the slipway where ships can be repaired and then returned to the water. The shipyard itself was called the Mound City Marine Ways. At its busiest, it employed 1,500 men working around the clock to keep the inland navy afloat.

13. Cork was used for both buoyancy and stability in the ironclads and also served to keep the interior of ships dry in warm and moist climates. Although that makes the term "corked" plausible here, Galligan has "caulked," as does Park's later memoir.

October 24th

We got of the ways this morning and proceded up the Ohio River to Paducah,[14] where we arrived on the 25th. General Smith[15] has command here. he has about 6000 troops with him. they are very busy fortifing the Town and getting a Ponton Bridge accross the River.[16]

October 26th

The Gunboat *Conestoga* arrived here this evening from the Tenessee River where she had been on a reconnisance. she Captured 60 Prisoners a large number of Horses and wagons & small arms.

October 29th

Got under weigh and proceded up the Ohio to Smithland where we took 40 Soldiers on board and then went up the Cumberland River on a reconnicence.

October 31st

This morning we came to a stand still as the Rebels had Blocaded the river by filling Flat Boats with Stones and sinking them across the River. we Fired a few shells into the bush on both sides on the River and then went in one of the Boats to sound and see if their was no passage but found none. we then landed at a farm house to see if we could get any information but the People had left and every thing in confusion. They had left in the middle of breakfast as the dishes was on the table and some of the cups full of coffee. We had a very sharp engagement with the turkey's, chickens &c. which resulted in a complete victory to our arms. we baged the whole lot. I found a fine old Kentucky Rifle in a wheat Bin covered over with Wheat. She was loaded and caped all ready for action. when we got on board I told the captain about some

14. Paducah, Kentucky, at the confluence of the Ohio and Tennessee Rivers, had been captured on September 6 by forces under Ulysses S. Grant and became a major supply depot for the Union fleet.

15. Charles Ferguson Smith, division commander in the Department of the Missouri under Grant, was later involved in the assault and capture of Fort Donelson; Grant attributed that success "emphatically to him."

16. The longest floating bridge constructed during the Civil War was built at Paducah, Kentucky, in 1861 to facilitate Union troop movement across the Ohio River.

bee gums that was on shore. He ordered me on shore and I was not to come off without some honey. I soon found out that they stood fire better than the Chickens. I tried to smoke them out but found itt was of no use. They still showed fight. At last, I got hold of something that was never meant for such a purpose. (itt was some Young Ladies Petticoat.) I hope she will forgive me. I tied up the head of it and then slipped itt over the Gum and sholdered itt run for the Boat. some of the Bees still following me. It was a pretty heavey lift as it was full of honey. as soon as I got on board we started down the river again. when we arrived at Paducah we took in coal and started for St. Louis.[17]

November 4th

At Anchor of Chester. last night one of the Crew fell overboard and was drowned. his name was James Edwards. he belonged to Cleveland Ohio.[18]

November 6th

Arrived at St. Louis, where we was all sent on board the receiving ship *Emerald,*[19] and our boat was put on the Dock to have false sides put on and thourly[20] repaired.

17. This is the first place in Park's diary that his sense of humor and gift as a raconteur emerges. Evidently he was quite pleased with his ingenuity and tenacity in "bagging" honey (despite the bees "standing fire" rather well) and with his good fortune in locating a hidden Kentucky rifle. Though this incident seems relatively benign, shore raids of this kind would become increasingly frequent—and increasingly reckless and vandalistic—over the course of the war.

18. This is a rare instance of Park naming a crewmate, and the first recorded fatality of one of his colleagues. James Henneberry records that while he was on watch "I heard a splatter in the water and soon after a drownding man cry." Running for a lifeboat, Henneberry found that one had already been taken; despite the efforts of his mates, however, Edwards could not be recovered. Henneberry also identifies him by name, calling him "a sailing man from Ohio."

19. Revisiting his journal in later years, Park adds here, "I cannot proceed further until I have had a good growl by abusing receiving ships in general and those on the Mississippi in particular. They are the dirtyest, most dissagreable, and without exception the most uncomfortable vessels I ever had the misfortune to put my foot in. After enduring with Christian resignation twenty days misery, twenty-five of us had the good luck to be chosen from amongst our crew to be sent on board the new gunboat *Pittsburgh* to take her down to Cairo" (see appendix 3).

20. "Thoroughly." This was only one of several refurbishments and repairs of the gunboat during the course of Park's tenure. This one is noteworthy because it accompanies the name change from *New Era* to *Essex*. The next major refitting—actually more of a reconstruction—would come after the tragedy off Fort Henry, Tennessee (see notations for February 6–7, 1862).

November 17th

Since the last date nothing of importance has occurred. only changing the Boats name from the *New Era* to the *Essex*. to day we put on board a slide and carriage for a 10 inch Gun.

November 25th

25 of us sent on board the new iron Clad Gunboat *Pittsburgh* to take her down to Cairo.[21]

November 29th

We arrived at Cairo to day. we struck a sand on the passage down which detained us one day.[22] yesterday theire was 500 Sailors arrived here from Washington. they was put on board the *Maria Denning.*[23]

December 1st

We arrived in St. Louis this morning from Cairo by the Cars.[24] Busily employed all day getting the stores and a ten inch gun on board the *Essex.*

December 3rd

We started this morning from Cairo in the *Essex*. she has got 2 ½ inches of

21. Flag Officer Foote to Lieutenant James W. Shirk, November 22, 1861: "Sir: You will repair on board the new gunboat *Pittsburg* with a file of 25 men from the receiving ship *Emerald,* and proceed in that vessel to Cairo, Ill., in company with Commander John A. Winslow of the gunboat *St. Louis,* who will give you further instructions." Park was later to serve on the *Pittsburg* for five momentous months in 1862 while *Essex* was out of commission and being rebuilt in St. Louis.

22. Winslow, who obviously continued on to Cairo when *Pittsburg* grounded, sent a telegram on November 28 to Flag Officer Foote reporting that "*Pittsburg,* while alongside of *Lexington,* got ashore 12 miles above Cape Girardeau by carelessness. *Lexington* and *Brown* [i.e., USS *William H. Brown*] will probably get her off to-day."

23. The Western Flotilla was initially under oversight of the U.S. Army. Gideon Welles supplied naval officers to the fleet but suggested soldiers be recruited for these awkward hybrid rivercraft. Here, under pressure from Foote, a supply of sailors was sent from the eastern front to help man the growing ironclad fleet.

24. According to contemporary sources, Cairo was an easy day's journey from St. Louis by water, considerably less by rail.

Iron on her forward Case-Mates. the Carpenters & Ironers are hard at work fixen her up and puting ¾ Iron on her sides and Stern.[25]

December 7th

We arrived at Cairo to day. we had a very tedious job getting down the river as itt was so shallow on the Bars. we struck 4 times and had to get Boats to tow us off each time.[26]

December 16th

This evening we received an addition of 40 men to our old Crew from the receiveing Ship *Maria Denning*.[27]

25. Henneberry's entry for December 3 lists the officers on board: "Cap [William D.] Porter, Cap [Robert K.] Riley; Mr. [James] Laning, Mr. [Theo P.] Ferry, and Mr. [George W.] Walker, Masters; Mr. [S.B.] Britton and Mr. [Charles C.] Gray, Master's Mates; Doc [Thomas] Rice, medical department; Mr. [Charles M.] Blazdel, chief engineer; Mr. [Joseph H.] Lewis, Paymaster; Mr. [Matthias] Snyder, Gunner; and Mr. [Thomas] Steel, Carpenter."

26. The shoals near Cape Girardeau again, as on November 29, proved dangerous to the ironclads. On this same trip Commander John Winslow was seriously wounded by a chain that snapped when the grounded gunboat *Benton* was being towed off the sandbar. The delay in getting the gunboats downriver, reported Foote on December 14, set him ten days behind schedule in readying them for active service.

27. As the year was drawing to a close there was great concern about the need for additional personnel to man the ironclads. Foote repeatedly requested that 1,100 men be sent, ideally "seamen from the [Great] Lakes." H. W. Halleck offered, on December 17, some 1,100 or 1,200 unarmed volunteers to help on the gunboats "if you wish them." Foote accepted 1,000, and divided them up among the boats. He also apparently added "two drafts of men from the lakes" by year's end. Park would later recollect that William Porter specifically asked for "forty of the greatest rascals on board" the *Maria Denning* and got, among the forty, some who had "been turned out of irons for our special benefit." Although they were at first impatient with authority, Park recalled, "they were by no means wanting in courage" (see appendix 3). Concern about the general preparedness of such raw and undisciplined recruits evidently prompted Foote's General Orders, No. 3, on December 17: "The officers and men connected with the naval flotilla will consider themselves amenable to the police regulations of the Army while on shore as well as on board, so far as conducting themselves with perfect propriety of conduct, of crossing the lines, abstaining from all approaches to intemperance, a vice which is so destructive to good morals, discipline, and efficiency, that the commander in chief will visit with the utmost rigor of the law all who may be guilty of the slightest degree of intoxication or any violation of laws, rules, regulations, and general orders which are or may be promulgated, either by the military or naval authorities, for the promotion of the highest state of discipline and efficiency in time of war."

1862

January 15th, 1862

I must skip over for the last month as I have been very sick with the Typhod Fever.[1] I was in the Mound City Hospital[2] part of the time. I found the *Essex* laying at Fort Jefferson along with the Iron Clad *St. Louis.*[3] still at work putting the Iron on the *Essex.* General Grant is here with 15000 men.

1. Typhoid fever ("camp fever") was one of the worst killers of the war; Union records show thirty thousand deaths from this disease. It was exacerbated by crowded and squalid conditions, poor sanitation, ill-prepared or tainted food, unclean drinking water, and contamination of rivers and streams by sewage and detritus. Symptoms included severe diarrhea, rash, headache, chills, convulsions, listlessness, and delirium. Mortality was high. Opium, morphine, and quinine were typically used in treatment. Andrew Foote's war diary mentions on January 16 that Commander Roger Perry of USS *Pittsburg* has been severely ill and will "leave this climate as soon as he is able to travel." He, too, had typhoid fever (first mentioned December 28, 1861). "I regret his loss both personally and officially," Foote wrote. He was replaced on *Pittsburg* by Lieutenant Egbert Thompson, under whom Park would later serve. Thompson filled Perry's shoes rather poorly (see appendix 3).

2. Mound City Hospital, like the "city" itself, was a creature of the war. In his personal memoirs, the hospital's first surgeon, John H. Brinton, describes it as having been adapted from "a long row of three- or four-story brick houses, or rather warehouses, built to accommodate the anticipated business of the future city. . . . The buildings stood finished as to their walls, but unfinished as to their interiors. They were just in that state, from which they could readily be converted into a General Hospital, three hundred feet long in front, by one hundred feet deep, capable of accommodating from eight hundred to one thousand patients comfortably." Staffing was very difficult, but eventually a group of nursing sisters from St. Mary's Convent in South Bend arrived and took over responsibilities "very admirably" (*Personal Memoirs of John H. Brinton: Civil War Surgeon, 1861–1865* [New York: Neale, 1914; repr., Carbondale: Southern Illinois University Press, 1996], 40–54).

3. Foote had sent Porter and *Essex* down the river to Fort Jefferson, Kentucky, to protect the advance brigade under General McClernand. A skirmish occurred near Columbus on the

February 2nd

We have had quite a number of running fights with the Rebels Gunboats but they always run under their Batteries at Colombus.[4] one day we had a smart engagement with 3 of their Boats and drove them under their Batteries. we received no damage.[5] Captn. Porter sent a challenge to the Rebls at Columbus to fight all their Boats 5 miles above the Batteries, to which they consented but failed to be their on the appointed day. this morning we left our anchorage and came up to Cairo. Stopped their a short while and then up the Ohio the *St. Louis* & *Taylor* in company.

February 5th

We arrived here at Fort Henry on the Tenessee this morning.[6] we proceded up the River to reconnoiter, the *St. Louis* & *Cincinnati* in company. as soon as we came in sight of the Fort they opened fire on us with a rifle gun they had got. It was the first time I had seen a rifle fired.[7] the shot went over our heads into the woods astern. we was very near 6 miles of the Fort at the time. we returned the fire with our 42 pd rifles but they did not reach the Fort. they put a shot through the Cabin and then we retired down the river in the afternoon. Commodore Foote came up with the *Carrondolet Connestoga Lexington* & *Taylor.* also General Grant and staff with 20,000 men came up on Transports.

11th; Porter reported that one of the rebel gunboats was disabled. He later informed Foote that his men had "behaved like veterans."

4. Columbus, Kentucky, occupied (despite the state's self-proclaimed neutrality) by Confederate General Leonidas Polk.

5. William Porter, in his farewell address to the men of *Essex* (see appendix 1), refers to this engagement at Lucas Bend fighting "craven Rebel gun-boats of vastly superior force" as their first achievement in the war. It was, by the standards of what followed, a very minor skirmish.

6. Heavy rains had swelled the rivers to unusually high levels and created a heavy current, which made getting the boats upstream especially strenuous. But the rushing water also tore Confederate torpedoes and booby traps from their moorings and caused them to drift harmlessly past the fleet. And the high water also mitigated the advantage of the elevated Confederate cliff batteries: Fort Henry was "now upon a level almost with the river; in fact the water had surrounded it, and so high was the stream that our gunboats fought at a great advantage" (Brinton, *Personal Memoirs,* 113–14).

7. Rifled guns, with spiral grooves in the barrels and pointed projectiles, had much greater range, velocity, and accuracy than smoothbores; the technology was new and expensive, and some rifled artillery (e.g., Parrotts) were notoriously prone to malfunction (see Park's entry for August 28, 1862). The 42-pound "rifles" that Park refers to aboard *Essex* are actually

Feb. 6th

This morning after a consultation between the Commanders on board the *Cincinnati* Cap. Porter came on board. He had all hands mustered on the Spar deck where he gave us a speech. he showed us the Rebel flag (which could be seen in the distance) and told us we were going to take itt down and put the Stars and Stripes in its place. All hands gave him three cheers.[8] We then went below and weighed anchor and steamed up towards the Batteries taking the lead and right. The Flag Ship *Cincinnati* and *Carrondolet* taking the cntre and the *St. Louis* holding the left, three wooden boats bringing up the rear. At 11:30 A.M. we took dinner at quarters and the Grog came round at the same time.[9] When we got about 2000 yards of the Battery the *Cincinnati* commenced firing which was the signal for all the boats to open fire. The Fort Immeadtly replied. when the action became general we kept steaming up toward the fort. All the time until we got within about 600 yard's when an ill fated shot came in through the Port bow Porthole and entered the Boilers scalding nearly every man that was on the forward deck at the time. 10 minutes after this the Fort surrended. our boat now dropped down with the current, out of range. getting our killed and wounded on the quarter deck, 33 of our men was scalded some severly some slightly some dead and some had jumped overboard.[10] My poor Friend Andrew Waterman was amongst the latter. I cannot give the names of

---

smoothbores that have been retrofitted according to a rifling system developed early in the war by Charles T. James, a mechanical engineer from Rhode Island. This expedient did not long outlive its inventor, who was mortally wounded when one of his own shells exploded during a demonstration in October 1862.

8. This event is recorded by Henneberry as well and nicely captures the captain's personality (Henneberry calls it "a speech which was characteristic of a Porter") as well as his skill in rallying his crew. The Henneberry diary adds that following the address "all hands went down and had a good song heaving the anchor, everybody joining in the Chorus."

9. Rations of grog had long been customary in the British and American navies; originally made from diluted rum, American "grog" substituted American-made whiskey. Sailors typically received extra rations before and after battle. Alcohol-related problems aboard ships prompted Congress to eliminate "the spirit ration" and to forbid the presence of any "distilled spirituous liquors" on board vessels as of September 1, 1862. Though sailors were offered financial compensation in lieu of the grog, the change was fiercely resented by many. Officers seem to have thought themselves above these regulations: Park, in his later memoir, is scathing in his criticism of the perpetual drunkenness of Egbert Thompson, *Pittsburg*'s captain (see appendix 3).

10. Men who jumped ship or were forced overboard by the explosion, especially those who had never learned to swim, were easy targets for Confederate marksmen. Nonswimmers

all the crew that was wounded. of the Officers Mr. Briton was killed, Messers. McBride & Ford Pilots were scalded to death. Mr. Ferry & Cap Porter severly scalded.[11] The Fort was taken in 1 hour and 15 minutes. The Steamer *Alps* came alongside and took us in tow down the river. we was struck 29 times. The scene on the Quarter deck was sickening to look at. I shall not attempt to describe itt.[12]

---

were ubiquitous in the American navy; two decades after the war a *New York Times* opinion piece ("Sailors Who Cannot Swim," May 3, 1883) recommended "a law requiring all sailors to know how to swim before they shipped." In mid-June 1862, the steam drum of *Essex*'s sister gunboat *Mound City* exploded during a battle, killing many of the officers and crew outright: "This scene of horror was rendered more frightful by the enemy's shooting our wounded and scalded men in the water and by firing into the boats of other vessels . . . which came to the assistance of the . . . victims" (see *ORN*, 1.23.196).

11. While Porter was in "dreadful agony" for weeks following the incident, he eventually recovered and returned to service aboard *Essex* that summer. His face and eyes still bore the physical scars of scalding, according to General Halbert Paine, who interacted with him frequently during the occupation of Baton Rouge (Paine, *A Wisconsin Yankee in the Confederate Bayou Country: The Civil War Reminiscences of a Union General*, ed. Samuel C. Hyde Jr. [Baton Rouge: Louisiana State University Press, 2009], 115). Porter's third master, Theodore Ferry, died in hospital.

12. *Essex*'s first major engagement in the war was also the single-most devastating event in her wartime service. Henneberry notes that at the time of the fateful shot "we were so close to the batteries that we could hear the orders given to load and fire on shore." In addition to members of the ship's crew, eight Indiana soldiers who had been brought on board as sharpshooters were also killed, wounded, or drowned in the chaos. Henneberry says that once the fires were put out and the carnage on the deck attended to, he stayed with his severely wounded captain through much of the night. From the rousing speech and optimistic bravado of the morning through to the horrors of the boiler explosion, it was, in Henneberry's understated words, "a day of conflicting emotions." For another published firsthand account, see the letter from second master of the *Essex* James Laning to Admiral Henry Walke, reprinted in *Century Magazine* 29 (1885): 428–29. Laning records that Porter himself was nearly thrown into the river by the explosion, but a seaman named John Walker rushed through the steam after him and caught him by the waist just in time. He adds that Marshall Ford, who was steering at the time the shot pierced the boiler, "was found at his post at the wheel, standing erect, his left hand holding the spoke and his right hand grasping the signal-bell rope"; sailor James Coffey "was on his knees, in the act of taking a shell from the box to be passed to the loader. . . . He met death in that position." A seaman named Jasper Breas, badly scalded, hearing that the rebels had surrendered, insisted "I must see that with my own eyes before I die." Clambering up to the spar-deck and seeing the Stars and Stripes waving over the fort, "he shouted 'Glory to God!' and sank exhausted on the deck." A "Report of casualties on the U.S.S. Essex" at Fort Henry (29 seamen, as well as 9 soldiers, "4 of whom have since died") was sent to Flag Officer Foote by Executive Officer Robert K. Riley on behalf of the injured captain; it is included in the *Official Records*.

Feb. 7th

This morning we arrived at Mound City where we took off our wounded and then Proceded down to Cairo. shortly after the *St. Louis* arrived with the Commodore and ordered all the spare hands to go on board the *Pittsburgh* to go up and take Fort Donaldson. I was amongst the number.[13] The *Pittsburgh* is Commanded by Leaut., Commd., Egbert Thompson.[14]

Feb. 12th

We left Cairo yesterday the *St. Louis* and *Louisville* in Company. arrived at Paducah at 11 A.M. took in coal and started for the Cumberland River. their were 10,000 Soldiers accompanied us in transports.

Feb. 13th

This evening we met the dispatch Boat *Alps*. She came down to tow us up. she had several men on board belonging to the *Carrondolet* that had been wounded that day. A 120 Pounde shot had penetrated her bow and wounded 9 men. She took the *Louisville* and our Boat in tow. we anchored about 3 miles below the Fort[15] at 11 P.M.

13. Henneberry acknowledges feeling "fortunate" to be among those left on board *Essex:* it remained at Cairo for a time and was then sent to St. Louis for repairs (and indeed a complete, and unauthorized, rebuild under Porter's direction). Henneberry enjoyed what amounted to a lengthy shore leave (and promotion to ship's yeoman) while most of his shipmates—including his friend Hank Ruger and our author, William Park—went back into battle on *Pittsburg.* Foote observed to Gideon Welles on February 11, as he left to support the army in the attack on Fort Donelson, "transferring men from vessel to vessel, as we have to do, is having a demoralizing effect upon them; 28 ran off to-day, hearing that they were again to be sent out of their own vessels."

14. For Park's unflattering portrait of Egbert Thompson, as recorded in his later memoir, see appendix 3.

15. That is, Fort Donelson, described by Admiral David Dixon Porter as "the strongest military work in the entire theatre of war. It was situated on a high bluff on the west bank of the Cumberland River . . . on a peculiarly rugged and inaccessible series of hills which rose abruptly to the height of one hundred feet. . . . The country was densely wooded, but the timber had been felled far out in advance of the breastworks, and the limbs, cleaned and sharpened, were formed into an almost impenetrable abbatis" (Porter, *The Naval History of the Civil War* [1886; Mineola, NY: Dover, 1998], 150). Foote did not consider his naval force sufficiently prepared for the assault on Fort Donelson, especially so soon after Fort Henry, but was compelled into action by the intrepid and impatient Grant.

Feb. 14th

We had a fall of Snow last night and a very hard frost. This forenoon the Commanders and Generals assembeled on board the Flag Ship to consult at 1 P.M. all the Boats got under Weigh and steamed up towards the Fort. the *St. Louis* Flag Ship taking the right. the *Carrondelet* taking the left. the *Louisville* and *Pittsburgh* the Centre and the *Connestoga* & *Lexington* forming a reserve. as soon as we got in sight of the Fort the Rebels opened fire, the first two or three shots falling short. but after that every shot told. We did not fire until we got within a mile when the action became general we gradually neared the Fort loading and firing as rapidly as we could run the guns out. we drove them out of the Lower or Water Battery. when we got about 400 yds from the Upper Battery we commenced firing Grape. The rebels replied with only three guns. Another 10 minutes and I thought they would be obliged to surrender. At this time one of the *Louisvilles* rifle guns burst and disabled another so she had obliged to drop down the stream. at the same time a shot penetrated the Pilot House of *St. Louis*, killing her Pilot,[16] and wounding the Crew and she droped down. our Captain at this time gave the order to the Pilot to back down, which I was very sorrow to here, as I think they must have surrended in a short time. As soon as we was out of range we found that our Boat was rapidly sinking. Two of the Water tight apartments was full of water. We got an awning under her Bow, and then run her on the Bank. We was all night bailing her out.[17] We was 1 hour and a half under fire. We was struck 52 times, all our Flag staff was shot away and our Flag was trailing in the water. One shot came

16. It was actually *Carondelet*'s gun that burst, killing several men. *Louisville* was disabled when her tiller ropes were shot through, making her unmanageable and causing her to drift away from the action. The flagship *St. Louis* (which would be renamed *Baron De Kalb* later in the year) was hit fifty-nine times and severely damaged under the ferocious fire. Flag Officer Andrew Foote was wounded, though not fatally. Altogether, fifty-four men on the six ships (four ironclads, plus two wooden gunboats) were killed or wounded in the battle. Park's observation that it was "the hardest fight for the time it lasted that ever I saw" was shared by many. For his part, Confederate Colonel Nathan Bedford Forrest is said to have asked one of his officers, Rev. Major D. C. Kelly, to appeal for providential assistance during the naval assault: "Parson, for God's sake, pray! Nothing but God Almighty can save that fort!"

17. Park would later reflect on this night—in which the exhausted and shell-shocked crew, waist-deep in frigid water, bailed for long hours—as the occasion that entirely broke his health. He was still only weeks away from his near-fatal bout with typhoid fever, and in greatly weakened condition.

in through the Middle Port and lodged in a barricade we had made with our Bags and Hamocks in front of the Boilers, hurting no one. Itt passed so close to the first Spongers head, that itt burnt the skin and made his nose bleed. Another one came in through the Starboard bow Port, where the crew was working the gun, went through the smoke stack through two escape Pipes, through the wheel & Cabin, and then through the Stern Casemate without hurting any one. 120 pound shot penetrated the Pilot house without doing any damage. Two shots entered our Starboard Bow under water and one the Port. we had only two men wounded. Itt was the hardest fight for the time itt lasted that ever I saw. As soon as the shot holes was covered we went down to Cairo to get repaired.[18] On the 16th the Fort surrended with 15000 Prisoners.[19]

March 4th

This morning we went down the river the *Benton,* Flag Ship,[20] *Cairo, Cincinnati, Carondelet, St. Louis,* and *Taylor* in Company. When we was about 3 miles above Columbus we stopped Steaming and drifted down with the Current. When we got of the Batteries we found that the Rebels had Skeddaled and the Town in Possesion of 2 companies of the 5th Illinois Cavalry.[21] The Boats returned to Cairo with the exception of the *St. Louis* and *Pittsburgh.*

18. While in Cairo, Park and his mates saw the rest of the *Essex* crew, who were still waiting to accompany their damaged vessel to St. Louis. According to Park's later memoir, "all hands on board the *Pittsburgh* were downhearted, as none of us like her, and we all expected to be sent back on board of the *Essex.*"

19. Grant's "no terms except an unconditional and immediate surrender" following his defeat of Confederate forces at Fort Donelson earned him his nickname "Unconditional Surrender" Grant, and a promotion from President Lincoln. The Union victories at Fort Henry and Fort Donelson represented the first significant Union advance into the Confederacy.

20. Eads had built USS *Benton* on much the same plan as the other riverine ironclads, but it was much larger and better fortified, regarded (until the rebuild of *Essex*) as the best gunboat in the Union and the most formidable ironclad ever constructed.

21. The February campaign of Grant and Foote, which subdued Fort Henry, Fort Donelson, Bowling Green, Nashville, and Columbus, effectively brought Kentucky and the greater part of Tennessee back under Federal control, provoking optimism in the North that "another year of vigorous work would bring back all the seceded states" (Alfred Guernsey and Henry Alden, *Harper's Pictorial History of the Civil War* [New York: Gramercy, 1866], 241). Here in Columbus, the navy was too late to be involved, a fact satirically advertised in a broadsheet prepared by some of the cavalry men who took over the local printing office: three men on horseback were pictured above the large title "The Gunboats That Took Columbus."

March 14th

This morning the Fleet came down from Cairo with the Mortar boats in Company. at 1 P.M. we all got under weigh and proceded down the river towards Island no. 10. At 6 P.M. we arrived of Hickman where we all anchored. The troops landed and fired into a Train of Cars filled with Rebels but they escaped. P.S. We have got a Brigade of Soldiers accompanying the Fleet under the Command of Colonel Buford. Next morning got under weigh and started down. 10 A.M. A rebel gunboat was seen ahead. the *Benton* fired a few shots at her but did not do any damage. We all gave chase but she showed us a clean pair of heels and escaped under the Batteries of Island No. 10.

March 16th

We opened fire this morning on the Batteries with 7 Gunboats and 8 Mortars. the Rebels returned the fire with great spirit. Our Mortar shells drove them out of 3 of their encampments. one of their shots stuck the *Benton* killing 2 men and wounding 8.

April 1st

Nothing of importance has occurred up to this date. the mortars still keep up the bombardment assisted by one or two Gunboats each day. A Boats crew of 12 men Volunteered from each of the Boats to spike the guns in the Upper Battery. they started the night being favourable for the expedition. Itt was accomplished without the loss of a single Man.[22]

22. Park's later memoir describes the operation in detail—the sailors approaching the shore with muffled oars, "in such silence that we were less than twenty yards distant when the sentinels at the guns discovered us. They were so surprised at seeing us so close that they cried out, fired their muskets, and ran away. As soon as we were discovered, every man bent to his oar and made the boats fly through the water. . . . There were six guns in the battery and they were all spiked [with rat tail files] in less time than I can write it." The first-person "we" in the memoir should likely not be taken as evidence that Park was among the volunteers (since he makes no such claim here) but as a general assertion of collective credit for the sailors' actions. Within five minutes, he says, the men were back in their boats, making fast for their ships. The soldiers (who kept watch for returning rebels) claimed all the glory, Park observes, though they did none of the work; he appends to his diary a specific commendation of the sailors' actions that night by Gideon Welles (see appendix 2, memo to Flag Officer Andrew Foote, dated April 12, 1862).

April 4th

Yesterday all the Gunboats got into position along the Bank and opened fire on the Floating Battery which we could see across the Point. We kept firing at her nearly all day when she was obliged to shift her position. At Night the *Carondelet* ran the gauntlet past the Batteries when they opened on her from the Batteries. We was in an awful state of suspense expecting she would be sunk but at last we hard her signal guns to let us know that she was all safe, which put our minds at rest.[23]

April 6th

We was very busily engaged yesterday all day coaling ship and getting all ready for running the Blockade and joining the *Carondelet.* At 10 P.M. a barge loaded with pressed hay came alongside to put between our boat and the batteries. At 1 A.M. we put out all lights closed the Ports took in our lines and swung out into the River the night being very favourable with Thunder and Lightning. when we got of the first battery the sentry gave the alarm by firing their muskets. when they opened fire from all their batteries at the same time it poured down one of the most tremendous deluges of rain that I ever saw. When we got about the middle of the Batteries our boat grounded but she backed off all right and we went on our way rejoiceing. Their was not a single shot struck us. At daylight we arrived at New Madrid. after breakfast we went down the river with the *Carondelet* to Riddles Point, where we engaged 3 small batteries and captured them in half an hour. At the same time General Pope was crossing his troops over the Tenessee shore. We went down the river to Merryweather's Landing where we lay all night.

23. Commander Henry Walke volunteered his boat, *Carondelet,* and First Master William R. Hoel of the *Cincinnati,* considered one of the best pilots on the Mississippi, agreed to pilot it on this perilous mission. It took *Carondelet* half an hour, under heavy assault from shore guns and in treacherous and stormy conditions, to outrun the reach of Confederate fire. This was the first attempt of the Union fleet to run the batteries, a tactic repeated two days later by Park's boat, *Pittsburg,* during another thunderstorm; it was attempted more frequently as the war progressed. The ability of the Federal fleet to safely pass the shore batteries effectively neutralized Confederate control of the rivers and allowed the land forces greater freedom of movement. For a firsthand account of *Carondelet*'s passage, see "The War Diary of John G. Morrison, 1861–1865": http://dmna.ny.gov/historic/reghist/civil/infantry/30thInf/30thInf_Diary_Morrison.pdf.

April 7th

This morning the enemy surrended the Island.[24] We captured 5000 Prisoners 9 Transports 1 Gunboats & Floating Battery. We sent all the Prisoners up to Cairo.

April 13th

Yesterday all the Fleet came down the river we hove up our anchor and proceeded down the river in company. We anchored at dark. This morning we saw the smoke of 7 Rebel Gunboats coming up the River. we got up anchor and gave chase firing our Bow guns as we could get them to bear. We chased them under the Guns of Fort Pillow.

April 14th

We got the Mortars in Position this morning. When they commenced their work of death and destruction the Rebels returned the fire with great briskness which made our Gunboats change their Position two or three times.

May 9th

Their has been nothing of any importance going on. The Bombardment is kept up by one Mortar each day and a Gunboat protects her. they lay about 2 miles below the rest of the Fleet. A flag of truce came up today bringing up one of our doctors that was captured at the Battle of Pittsburgh Landing.[25]

24. The successful arrival of *Carondelet* and *Pittsburg* below the batteries of Island No. 10, followed by their silencing of Confederate field batteries, allowed General Pope to cross the river with his troops; this was "the turning point of the siege," according to David Dixon Porter; "the precipitancy with which the enemy retreated when the gunboats appeared below Island No. 10 was astonishing." He adds: "the victory at Island No. 10, although a bloodless one, was as important as the battle of Shiloh. It opened a long stretch of the Mississippi River, down which our forces were continually working their way toward the sea. . . . Neither of these victories would have been won without the aid of the Navy" (Porter, *Naval History,* 163). Andrew Foote, in a missive to Gideon Welles on November 13, 1862, observed, "It is a singular fact that in the captures of Fort Henry and Island No. 10, not a gun was fired by the army" (*ORN,* 1.22.316). See also an eyewitness account of the battery-running by journalist Junius Henri Browne, *Four Years in Secessia* (Detroit: W. H. Davis, 1866), 123–27.

25. The Battle of Pittsburg Landing, better known as the Battle of Shiloh, was to that point the bloodiest armed conflict in American history. Union casualties exceeded thirteen thousand; Confederate losses approached eleven thousand, including General Albert Sidney Johnston, who bled to death after a bullet pierced an artery in his leg.

Commodore Foote left the fleet this evening for his home on the account of sickness. each Boat gave him three cheers as he passed.[26] Capt. C. Daviss succeded him.

May 10th

This morning at 4 A.M. the Mortar was towed into position. The *Cincinnati* guarding her. At 7 A.M. the Rebel Gunboats came round the Point, 8 in number.[27] One of the rams the *Sumpter* made for the *Cincinnati.* she sliped her anchor and stood boldly down towards the ram firing her guns as she could get them to bear. the ram made at her and struck her in the Starboard side. At the same time the *Cincinnati* poured in her broadside dealing death and destruction around. In the mean time all our fleet got under weigh as quiet as possible and arrived at the scene of action; about this time, all the rebel fleet came up likewise, when the action became general. The Secesh ram *Little Rebel* ran into the *Mound City* and stove a hole in her bow. The Rebel Comm. Boat was set on fire. When she hauled down her colors we ceased firing on her when she dropped down the river a little ways she hoisted her colors and commenced firing again. We showed her little mercy this time but

26. In his own diary, John G. Morrison (see note 23, above) recounts Foote's departure: "He looked very pale and feeble as he was passing us. He said if he was able, he would come on board and shake hands with all of us and then he wished that God might bless and protect us." A more detailed account of Foote's emotional departure from the fleet is recorded in Browne's *Four Years in Secessia,* chap. 26. Foote had written to Gideon Welles on April 14 that "the effects of my wound [at Fort Donelson] have quite a dispiriting effect upon me from the increased inflammation and swelling of my foot and leg . . . , depriving me of a good deal of sleep and energy." He went to Washington and was soon elevated to the rank of rear admiral. Just a year later, however, as he was preparing to take over duties as commander of the South Atlantic Squadron, he was taken ill; he died on June 26, 1863.

27. This encounter at Plum Point Bend, near Fort Pillow, Tennessee, was the first engagement of the Western Gunboat Flotilla with the Confederate River Defense Fleet. With the advantage of surprise, the Southern vessels scored a victory (though Park's muted account accords them no glory); they were confident (as it turned out, overconfident) of success if the Union fleet met them at Memphis, which it did a month later. In Park's later memoir he recounts with disgust Captain Egbert Thompson's drunkenness and incompetence during this battle, and the crew's "doing their duty" despite orders or lack thereof: "the guns opened fire on their own responsibility and continued for the remainder of the action." For more on Thompson and the naval Battle of Fort Pillow, see appendix 3.

they getting disgusted with our conduct towards them after hours fighting Skeddadled when we chased them under the Guns of the Fort. The *Mound City* and *Cincinnati* fought duering the whole action. when they was got into shallow water and sunk. their was only four men wounded on our side the Captain of the *Cincinnati* being amongst the number. The rebels tried to board but was repulsed with hot Water.[28]

May 14th

Yesterday the *Mound City* was towed up to Cairo. today the *Cincinnati* was raised and towed up to Cairo to be repaired. Their was a flag of truce came up from the Fort with a prisoner.

June 3rd

Their has been nothing of importance since I wrote last. the Bombardment is still kept up. The *Mound City* has joined the Fleet again. Tow deserters report that they are evacuating the Fort. Three of their Boats showed themselves round the Point to day but a shot from our guns sent them back.

June 4th

I forgot to mention that 6 rams has arrived from Pittsburgh to assist us.[29] This evening one of them was sent round the Point to reconoitre. They opened a heavey fire on her from the Fort for a short time and then a bright flame was seen to issue from the Fort. She proceeded down very cautious and found itt evacuated. They had set fire to everything that would burn: Provisions, Gun Carriages, &c., &c.

28. Steam hoses were used by both Union and Confederate vessels to repel attempted boarding by enemy combatants—to devastating effect. See also, for example, July 16, below.

29. A ram flotilla, consisting of hastily converted river steamers, was added to the Western Flotilla under the direction of Charles Ellet, a brilliant civil engineer without military experience but with a passionate interest in ironclad "ram-boats"; he was commissioned as colonel by Secretary of War Edwin Stanton after the clash of the ironclads off Hampton Roads to design and prepare serviceable rams for use on western waters. Ellet's vessels included *Monarch, Queen of the West, Switzerland,* and *Lancaster,* all of which were captained by a family member—brother, son, or nephew to the colonel. To keep them light and maneuverable, Ellet did not initially fit them with guns.

June 5th

This morning all the Fleet got under weigh and proceeded down the river.[30] Sent some of the troops on shore to take possession of the Fort and hoist the Stars and Stripes and then proceeded on our way.[31] On the way down a large transport was seen ahead. One of the small tugs gave chase and after run of about 3 hours captured her. We anchored at dark about 1½ miles above Memphis.[32]

June 6th

This morning all hands was on the alert expecting a fight. and we was not disappointed for shortly after daylight the Rebel Gunboats made their appearance round the point. 7 in number the rebels opened fire and stood boldly up to meet us. we got under weigh and commenced firing as soon as we could get our guns to bear. Tow of our rams, the *Queen of the West* and *Monarch,* shot out from between our boats and made for the rebels. the *Queen of the West* made at the *Jeff Tompson* and struck her amidship.[33] She made for the

30. By river, the distance from Fort Pillow to Memphis was about seventy miles.

31. Fort Pillow was to remain in Union hands until April 12, 1864, when Confederate Major General Nathan Bedford Forrest attacked the garrison. When Forrest's demand for surrender was refused, a furious assault ensued, in which the Union troops were quickly overwhelmed. According to many contemporary accounts, Federal troops—including a disproportionate number of black soldiers—were murdered in cold blood after they had thrown down their guns. Though accounts of the battle were hotly disputed, the death toll was shocking, and the "Fort Pillow massacre," as it came to be called, became a rallying cry for Union soldiers through the rest of the war. William Park, who was still in service on the river in April 1864, does not record any news about the Battle of Fort Pillow in his journal; in his later memoir, however, he adds a note to the effect that news reached the crew on April 16 that "the rebels had captured Fort Pillow and massacred the garrison."

32. Though Park writes as if on the scene—including such ambiguous, if not misleading, lines as "We anchored at dark," etc. and then speaking of his vessel "returning to take charge of Fort Pillow" after the Battle of Memphis—*Pittsburg* was not in fact with the Union flotilla at Memphis but ordered to stay upriver to "support the army" at the captured fort. In his later memoir, Park is more straightforward, simply declaring that he "had not the pleasure" to participate in the naval contest at Memphis; one reads between the lines both that he was disappointed to have missed that action and that he believed that *Pittsburg* was held back because of Davis's mistrust of Captain Egbert Thompson (see appendix 3).

33. Park mistakes the *Jeff Thompson* for the *Lovell,* which was the first of the Confederate fleet to be disabled and sunk. The *Jeff Thompson* was struck by a shell and run aground, burning, as her crew tried to escape.

Bank where the crew set her on fire and left her. The *Beauregard* made for the *Queen of the West* and struck her in the Paddle Wheel disableing her for the remainder of the action. at this time the *Monarch* came down when the *Beauregard* and *Price* both made at her. She stopped steaming and reversed her engines when the *Beauregard* run into the *Price* and sunk her. Then the *Monarch* made at the *Beauregard* and sunk her. In the mean time the Gunboats disabled the *Bragg, Sumpter* and *Little Rebel.* we sent all our boats to try and save the Crews of the *Price* and *Beauregard.* The *Van Dorin* made her escape down the river. so endend one of the first fights that was fought by rams in any Country. we was 7 miles past the City when the fight was done. Itt was a fine sight for the inhabitans of Memphis. There was thousands of them viewing the fight from the Bluffs in front of the City. the greatest number of them wer Ladies.[34] we then went ashore and hoisted the Stars & Stripes over the Coustom house and Post Office and took charge of the City. Their was only one man wounded on our side.[35] We then started up the river with our boat to take charge of Fort Pillow.

July 1st

We have been engaged getting down to the Levee all the Guns, Shot, Shell, grape and Cannister &c. from the Batteries. When we came here we found that the Rebels had bursted most of their guns. Likewise one 13 inch Mortar before they left here. We went up the Hatchee river in two of our boats and

34. The Battle of Memphis, which lasted "but little over an hour," was the largest inland naval battle in history, involving at least fifteen vessels. It may also have been the most lopsided. The river contest following the Battle of Baton Rouge two months later would be similarly treated as a spectacle by local citizens, including young ladies like Sarah Morgan, who describes it at length in her diary. There, as here, early optimism about the supremacy of the Confederate vessels and their capacity to defend the city would be dashed.

35. The one casualty was Colonel Charles Ellet himself, shot in the leg aboard *Queen of the West.* The wound became infected; confronted with the necessity of amputation, Ellet refused, saying that "like his country, he preferred death to dismemberment." He died fifteen days later. It was his teenage son and namesake, Charlie Rivers Ellet, who, in company with three other Union men from the ram fleet, went ashore to raise the Stars and Stripes over the post office in Memphis and remove Confederate banners from all buildings. For details of the capture of Memphis, see Chester G. Hearn, *Ellet's Brigade: The Strangest Outfit of All* (Baton Rouge: Louisiana State University Press, 2006), 37–40.

captured a small Steamer.[36] The Gun Boat *Cairo* came up to relieve us so that we could go up to Cairo to get repaired. Whilst we lay at Fort Pillow the Rebel Gunboats, *Sumpter, Bragg,* and *Little Rebel* went up to Cairo to get repaired and transferred into Union Boats. This morning we got under Weigh and Started for Cairo. We passed the Gunboat *Sumpter* on her weigh to the Fleet.

July 4th

We arrived at Cairo this evening where we found the *Bragg* had drest ship and fired a salute in honor of the Decelaration of Independence.

July 7th

I was ashore on leave to day when my old Boat the *Essex* came down from St. Louis. I got a boat and went on board to see my old Shipmates. I found them all well. Captain Porter was very glad to see me. He told me he was going to have all his old hands back again, which I was very glad to here.[37] The *Essex* had been completely built over and lenthened. She is 221 feet long 60 ft. wide. She is a two decker, the lower deck for the Guns and the tween deck for the Officers. She mounts 3 nine inch Dalghren guns and two 50 pr Rifles on the forward Battery, one 10 inch Pivot Gun and one 32 pounder in the after Battery. Likewise two brass pieces on the upper deck one 24 pr & one 12 pr rifles. her forward Casement is 28 in thick of solid wood 1 in of India Rubber and 1 in. or Iron. Her side casemates is 18 inches of wood and

36. The seizure took place on June 9, after two deserters from the Confederate army relayed the information concerning its whereabouts to Egbert Thompson. The unnamed steamer accompanied *Pittsburg* to Cairo when she went to be repaired; she was fitted out for use in the Union fleet as USS *General Pillow.*

37. William Porter exercised his seniority in claiming his old crew back from *Pittsburg,* leaving Egbert Thompson to scramble to find replacements for his ship. Shortage of available men was greatly exacerbated by the pall of sickness hanging over the entire Union fleet and the army ranks in the summer of 1862. General Thomas Williams observed on July 24 that "of the 3,200 men brought [to Vicksburg] by him, only 800 were fit for duty; the other three-fourths of his command had died, or were in the hospital with fever. Sometimes as many as ten died in a day." Many of Williams's men (along with hundreds of local slaves) had been engaged in building a navigation channel for gunboats and transports—a grueling and quixotic effort that exposed them to heat stroke, contaminated water, and mosquito-borne disease. Lack of healthy manpower is a persistent subject of official correspondence. See also note 49, below.

¾ of Iron. Her hold is divided into 40 different apartments and every one water tight her Bow is built solid 16 feet from the Stern cased with Iron ¾ thick and has got an Iron stern 3 in. thick. Her Boilers is in the hold and is perfectly secured from shots.[38]

July 9th

Yesterday we was transferred on board the *Essex* where I was told to take my old station (and that is in charge of the Powder Magazine). We was very busily employed all day taking in shot shell Powder &c. We started from Cairo this evening bound for New Orleans.

July 13th

We arrived this morning above Vicksburgh where we found Commodore Farragutt with 9 of his fleet. They had run past the Batteries and joined the upper fleet.[39] Commodore Davis had 5 of his boats and 4 Mortar boats in position.[40] On the passage down we lost a man overboard just above Fort Pillow. His name was Wm. Taylor. He belong's to Plymouth, England. we passed the *Cairo* laying at the Fort. The *St. Louis* and *Mound City* was laying at Memphis. Unfortunately one of our Boilers got burnt out on the passage down and we will be to lay here untill it can be repaired which will take 4 or 5 day's at the least.

38. The makeover of *Essex* was not officially authorized, but undertaken under Porter's direction. It made her the largest and most formidable vessel in the Union ironclad fleet.

39. Against significant odds, Farragut's oceangoing fleet had passed under the Vicksburg batteries in two parallel columns with minimal loss of life (fifteen killed and thirty wounded) in the early-morning hours of June 28. This was the first time in the war that the brown water navy (Western Gunboat Flotilla) and the blue water fleet (West Gulf Blockading Squadron) combined forces.

40. The somewhat testy collaboration of David Farragut, who had overseen the Blockading Squadron along the Gulf and successfully captured New Orleans in late April, and Charles Davis, who had been in charge of operations on the Upper Mississippi since Foote was forced to seek medical leave (see entry for May 9 above, and note 26) marked a new stage in the war on western waters and presaged the transfer of the Western Gunboat Flotilla from the army to the navy, at which time it became known as the Mississippi River Squadron. Vicksburg, the apparently impregnable Confederate stronghold, was now the mutual concern of Farragut and Davis, but their joint efforts failed to defeat the city, which would endure an intermittent yearlong campaign until falling under siege to Ulysses S. Grant on July 4, 1863.

July 16th

We are still laying here getting our Boilers fixed. their was some rumours yesterday that a Rebel Gunboat was going to run past the Fleet. Every one set itt down as absurd. But Davis to make sure sent the *Carondelet, Taylor* and one of the rams to watch the Yazoo river. We was just going to breakfast when we heard heavey firing up the river shortly after the ram made her appearance round the Point follied by the *Taylor* firing her stern Gun. shortly after the Rebel Ram *Arkansas*[41] made her appearance firing at the *Taylor.* Every thing was in confusion. Our transports laying all over the river. the *Arkansas* kept on firing her Broadside, Bow and stern guns as she could get them to bear our boats replying as she came abreast of them, most of the shot skipping of her Iron sides like haill. When she came opposite us we gave her all the guns we could get to bear. a shell from our 10 inch gun penetrated on of her Ports exploding inside. two of our boats got under weigh but was too late to stop her. She got round the Point and under the guns of Vicksburgh. It seems the boats sent to watch her met her coming down the Yazoo. The *Carrondelet* grappled on to her and tried to board but the rebels used the Hot water hose. They drifted down the current together peppering away at each other all the time. At the mouth of the river the *Carrondelet* grounded when her adversary gave chase to the *Taylor.* The *Taylor* got the worst of itt. She got 10 men killed and between 30 and 40 wounded, the *Carrondelet* about the same number. She blew up one of the rams, killing and wounding several when passing the fleet.[42] The Commodores held a consultation together. Farragutt was going

41. This is the first appearance of the "far-famed *Arkansas* ram and terror of the Mississippi River," as Park will call it—the most formidable threat to the Union fleet.

42. The audacity of Captain Isaac Brown in running the gauntlet of the Federal fleet caught everyone off guard and embarrassed both Farragut and Davis. As *Arkansas* rounded the river bend above Vicksburg and "a forest of masts and smokestacks" of Union vessels came into view, Brown determined to steam as close to them as possible, to create confusion and to avoid being rammed by the immobile ships. Despite the close-range firing of *Essex* and other gunboats as it passed, *Arkansas* reached the safety of Vicksburg, where cheering crowds were lined up along the bluffs to greet her. When some of these citizens crowded eagerly aboard the ram, the grim toll of her passage was immediately evident and stifled the exuberance. According to Acting Master's Mate J. A. Wilson, "The scene around the gun deck . . . was ghastly in the extreme. Blood and brains bespattered everything, whilst arms, legs, and several headless trunks were strewn about." Casualties aboard *Arkansas* were 16 killed, and as many wounded (some critically). But she had inflicted terrible loss on the Union fleet—over 120 killed and wounded.

to run past the Batteries and sink the *Arkansas* or cut her out.[43] The upper fleet was to draw the fire of the upper batteries. At dark they all got under weigh. As soon as they rounded the Point the rebels opened fire from the Batteries when the Mortars from both fleets opened fire the Boats opened fire about the same time when the firing became general. It was the heaviest cannonading that I ever heard. It lasted about 1 ½ hours. And now we are all suspence to know whither they have taken the boat or not.

July 17th

Farragutt's fleet passed the batteries with the loss of 5 men. They did not succeed in taking the boat. They said they could not see her.[44] Our boilers are now repaired and we are ready for any emergency.

July 22nd

During the past days we have run down to the point and tried our guns on Vicksburgh. To day Com. Faragutt. Davis and our Captain made arrangements to send the *Essex* down past the Batteries and tackle the Ram while Davis engaged the upper Batteries and Farragutt the Lower ones. At 4 A.M. all hands was called and the ship cleared for action. At 5 A.M. we got under weigh accompanied by the upper Fleet. At 6 A.M. we rounded the Point. When the Ball commenced[45] the upper Fleet opened on the Batteries. We got under a full head of steam and made right for the ram, not firing a gun. as soon as the rebels saw our move they opened from every gun they could get to bear on

43. Farragut felt his reputation was at stake and urged an immediate pursuit of *Arkansas,* but Davis was hesitant. At 7:00 p.m. that night, the fleet descended the river with the sole objective of destroying the ram, but in the darkness the gunners of Farragut's ships were unable to locate her.

44. *Arkansas* was painted a dull chocolate-brown, which helped camouflage her as she lay under the bluff in the darkness. In the unflattering description of Sarah Morgan, who was eager to catch a glimpse of the ram once it reached Baton Rouge in early August, *Arkansas* was "a heavy, clumsy, rusty, ugly flatboat with a great square box in the centre, while great cannon put their noses out at the sides, and in front" (Morgan, *Civil War Diary,* 191).

45. Several variants on this phrase, military slang for commencement of a battle, are used in the *Essex* diaries, which depend on different associations. Sometimes "the ball got rolling" or "the ball commenced a rolling" (Henneberry); elsewhere, "the ball opened," or "the Ball commenced," as here, an ironic allusion to war as a formal dance.

us. When we was about 40 yards from her she fired into us but her shots did not penetrate. We intended to run into her amidships but she was prepared for us. She started her engines and we mearly glanced along her side and ran into the bank. as we struck her we gave her our 3 bow guns which went crashing through her sides. We now found ourselves unsupported by either of the Fleets (the Lower fleet was laying at anchor yet) and in the middle of their Batteries. Cap. Porter gave the order to turn round and go down the river which we did in good style. We came to anchor amidst the deafning Cheers of the Soldiers ashore and Faragutts Fleet at 8:15 A.M. Making two hours that we was under fire of the guns of Vicksburgh. There was only two Shots penetrated. One shell exploded in the casement killing 1 man and wounding 3.[46]

July 24th

Fore the last few day's the Commanders have been preparing to abandoned the Seige of Vicksburgh.[47] Yesterday the Mortar Boats left their Position and was towed down the river, and to day all the Fleet left our boat bringing up the rear. Before we left we tried the range of our rifle guns on the Ram.

July 26th

We arrived of Baton Rouge at 7 P.M. and anchored in the Stream. The rest of the fleet proceeded down the River to New Orleans. Nothing of any importance occurred on the passage down except some guerrillas fired into the leading boats without doing any damage.

46. Henneberry and Galligan identify the fatality as Peter White, who had been scalded in the Fort Henry disaster in February. The wounded included Joseph Stanley and Frank Wilson, the former of whom would not survive the war (see Park's entry for January 2, 1864).

47. Farragut, who had not been enthusiastic about bringing his seagoing ships up the Mississippi in the first place, was now, following the humiliation with *Arkansas,* more than ready to return down the river. *Essex* went with him as far as Baton Rouge. At the same time, Vicksburg was abandoned by General Williams, whose land forces were so decimated by sickness as to be useless; he limped back with his remaining men to Baton Rouge. Flag Officer Davis, rankling under this desertion by both army and navy support, took his own remaining boats north to Helena without formal authorization, writing in his diary on August 1: "There is no knowing what crazy project the Department may have in view or how this move of mine may be taken. But . . . the only course now to be pursued is to yield to the climate and postpone any further action at Vicksburg till the fever season is over" (*ORN,* 1.23.271–72).

August 5th

Yesterday an accident happened on board. One of the men got shot as he was stepping into a boat to go on a foraging expedition.[48] He died this morning. Very near all the Ships Company is on board the Hospital Boat with the Swamp Fever.[49] This morning the Rebels under General Breckenridge[50] attacked the City to drive our troops out.[51] The ram *Arkansas* was to Co-operate with them by destroying the Fleet or driving us down the river. We can see the smoke of the ram round a bend in the river but She has not come down yet. The rebels made the attack at 4 A.M. Gradualy driving our troops in until we opened fire on them from the Gunboats our shells doing tremendous execution.[52] they fought until 9 O clock when they had obliged to retreat after a heavy loss. Our side suffered severly. But the rebels lost 2 men

48. Unnamed here, he is identified in the Henneberry and Galligan journals as George Myers, from Michigan, "an old hand on the boat" whose loss was deeply regretted. He was buried in Baton Rouge along with J. Brenner, another "old hand" who had succumbed to typhoid fever the same day.

49. A dispatch from the assistant surgeon aboard *Benton,* H. Beauchamp, to Flag Officer Davis on July 25, had put "40 per cent of our crews upon the sick lists of their respective vessels." "The effects of this climate, with its combined influence of temperature and miasmatic poison, which at this season of the year exerts a most pernicious influence upon those coming from a more northern latitude," presents the risk of "disabling our entire squadron." The hospital boat that Park mentions here may have been *Red Rover,* a well-supplied vessel with "bathrooms, laundry, elevator for the sick from the lower to the upper deck, amputating room, nine different water-closets, gauze blinds to the windows to keep the cinders and smoke from annoying the sick, two separate kitchens for sick and well, and a regular corps of nurses" (*ORN,* 1.23.153–54). But *Red Rover* was likely soon overwhelmed with the sheer numbers of ailing men; Park says in his later memoir that "Doctor Rice, our surgeon . . . took possession of an old wharf boat and converted it into a hospital and there our men were conveyed one after the other as they fell sick, until the *Essex* was left with about a third of her crew on board." (The wharfmaster at Baton Rouge, with whom Rice would have made these arrangements, was Pierre ["Pete"] Millet, Celeste Repp's uncle.)

50. John Cabal Breckinridge had been President James Buchanan's vice president and ran unsuccessfully against Lincoln in 1860. He joined the Confederate army as brigadier general in November 1861 and enjoyed great acclaim in the South.

51. Baton Rouge had been under military occupation by Federal troops since shortly after the fall of New Orleans in late April. For discussion of the Federal presence and how it affected the city's inhabitants, including Matilda Victor, headmistress of St. Mary's Academy, see the afterword.

52. It was strategic firing from the gunboats—*Essex, Sumter, Kineo,* and *Katahdin*—as depleted as they were in manpower (*Essex* had "not enough to man three guns, says Park), that

to our one. The 21st Indina Regt. won great praise for their bravery. General Williams was shot through the heart when he was leading the 21st to charge.[53] The 7th Vermont got disgraced and their colors taken away for Cowardice.[54] The *Tennesee* came up from New Orleans. We got 14 vollinteers from her to fight the ram. And 6 from the Gunboat *Kineo.* We could not get enough to man three guns and obliged to make the remainder up with niggers that had never seen a gun before.[55] We had about 50 men on board, Officers and all.

---

decisively turned the tide of the Battle of Baton Rouge. An officer from the fleet went ashore and signaled the vessels from the roof of the State Capitol, which allowed for deadly accuracy in targeting Breckinridge's men. The Confederate ram *Arkansas* had been expected to neutralize the effectiveness of the Union ships but failed to arrive in time because of engine trouble.

53. General Thomas Williams was respected and liked by the "secesh" inhabitants of Baton Rouge, who valued his gentlemanly demeanor and concern for their protection and welfare. He was sincerely mourned by many in the city—less so by his own men, according to many accounts; there were, in fact, whispers that his death resulted from a well-aimed Union rather than Confederate minie ball. For more on Williams, see the afterword.

54. The Seventh Vermont was censured by Benjamin Butler for a friendly-fire incident with the Twenty-First Indiana, as well as for later failure to support that unit in the chaos of battle. The circumstances and the impartiality of the judgment are still much disputed. For a detailed account of the controversy, see Jeffrey D. Marshall, "'Butler's Rotten Breath of Calumny': Major General Benjamin F. Butler and the Censure of the Seventh Vermont Infantry Regiment," *Vermont History* 72 (2004): 23–54. See also Philip E. Faller, *The Indiana Jackass Regiment in the Civil War: A History of the 21st Infantry/1st Heavy Artillery Regiment, with a Roster* (Jefferson, NC: McFarland, 2013), 50–74.

55. This is Park's first reference to former slaves, or "contrabands," serving aboard *Essex.* As Union ships penetrated the heartland of the Confederacy, black men and boys (sometimes whole families) flocked to the vessels. Crew shortages were such that they were often set to work performing routine chores on the boats; the most promising might then be given a position at the bottom end of the sailors' ranks and assigned to dangerous or unpleasant tasks such as coal heaving and firing the furnaces. In this instance, necessity prompted manning of the guns by contrabands; crew shortages increasingly allowed for black sailors to attain new levels of responsibility and status. By late November 1862, Henneberry says that "every night we receive 6 or 8 negroes on board." In crowded quarters, it was a challenging social experiment for the white sailors, among whom racism of an often extreme kind was rife. Few Northern or foreign-born tars, Park among them, had had prior social interaction with African Americans. Regulations in the Mississippi Squadron enforced strict segregation aboard ships: blacks were messmates and shift-mates with one another. Henneberry complains later in the fall (November 17) that all the black hands were "allowed to go on shore to meeting [i.e., church services], while white men asking the same privilege were refused." On the whole, a wary cooperation prevailed under conditions of necessity for all concerned. See also Park's entry for September 6, below.

August 6th

Last night was a night of suspense to every man on board the *Essex.* very few closed their ey's. I stood Quarter Masters watch and had the first watch.[56] I strained my eyes to try and see if she was coming down but their was no move. The smoke could be seen in the same position as itt was all day. After breakfast we got under weigh and stood up towards the Point accompanied by the *Gunboat No. 9*[57] and the Ram *Sumpter.* As soon as we came in sight of the *Arkansas* she opened fire with her stern guns. (She was laying made fast to the bank.) we replied with our bow guns. At this time *No. 9* and the *Sumpter* turned round and ran back towards Baton Rouge. They said the rebels was driving our troops out. But the truth of it was they thought they would get far enough of; so in case that the *Arkansas* sank the *Essex* they would have a chance to escape.[58] In this trying emergency Capt. Porter Steamed up determined to riske another battle with the Iron Monster. We kept a rapid fire up for nearly ½ an hour. The ram did not return it. All her Crew abandoned her and set her on fire. All hands was nearly mad with joy to think that they had got such an easy Victory. for they had made up their minds for a death struggle. we steamed up to her to see if we could not put the fire out. But it was too late. The Flames was issueing out of the Ports. We steamed up past her and kept a good distance of her for fear of her Magazine exploding.

56. Park's later memoir confirms that "As all our Quartermasters were sick. I took one of their places," adding that "Captain Porter never closed his eyes the whole night; he was on deck during the whole of my watch keeping a sharp lookout for the ram."

57. That is, *Cayuga.* Farragut's gunboats in the Gulf Blockading Squadron were known by numbers as well as names: *Sciota* was *Gunboat No. 1; Winona, No. 2; Kineo, No. 3; Wissahickon, No. 4; Kennebec, No. 5; Pinola, No. 6; Itasca, No. 7; Katahdin, No. 8; Cayuga, No. 9.* A *New York Times* article published August 11, 1862, observed that "these are as much alike in appearance as nine blackbirds, and are distinguishable only by the figure on the smoke-pipe of each one." *Cayuga* was the vessel on which *Essex*'s gunner's mate, William Young, had served with great valor during the taking of New Orleans.

58. Park's interpretation of the sudden departure of the two other Union vessels, *Cayuga* and *Sumter,* mirrors that of his captain, William Porter. The claims and counterclaims of the respective officers, acrimonious at times, continued at length in official correspondence until a court of inquiry was held in New Orleans in November. By then, Porter had been "kicked upstairs" and owned the title of commodore, so could afford to condescend to those he had earlier accused of cowardice: to Captain Donald Fairfax of *Cayuga* he wrote, "Whatever prejudicial feeling there was certainly forced on my mind from your apparent absence of assistance to the *Essex* in the attack is now entirely removed."

She burnt her fastenings ashore and drifted into the stream. she burnt for 3 hours when her Powder Magazine ignited and blew up with a tremendous explosion. I counted 14 shots that had penetrated her Iron sides.[59] two of her Men came on board. they said her engines got out of order and they set her on fire.[60] She mounted 10 guns and had a crew of 180 men. Leut. Stevens Commanded her. I heard Capt. Porter say that if he had Command of such a boat as her he would sweep every thing out of the river. Such was the Fate of the Far famed *Arkansas* Ram and the terror of the Mississippi River.[61] On the road down to Baton Rouge tow of the men quarled and drew their nives

59. Most Confederate accounts deny that *Essex* inflicted any damage at all: "We were not struck by the *Essex,* nor do I think we struck her" (George W. Gift, "The Story of the Arkansas," *Southern Historical Society Papers,* vol. 12; quoted in H. Allen Gosnell, *Guns on the Western Waters: The Story of River Gunboats in the Civil War* [Baton Rouge: Louisiana State University Press, 1949], 135). Park clearly believed otherwise, as did Porter.

60. Park's description of the demise of the dreaded Confederate ram, including the witness of two of her crew members (natives of New Orleans who deserted, according to a Confederate report), is unexceptionally factual—unlike William Porter's first boastful and misleading report to Farragut: "This morning at 8 a.m. I steamed up the river and at 10 a.m. attacked the rebel ram *Arkansas* and blew her up. There is not now a fragment of her left." Farragut, for whom, since Vicksburg, *Arkansas* had become something of a white whale, was likely the happiest man in the Union when he received news of the Confederate ram's demise—a fact that Porter was pleased to exploit. Porter continued to insist, in official correspondence, that *Essex* was responsible for the fire and explosion aboard *Arkansas,* repeatedly denying that she had been scuttled by her captain, Henry Kennedy Stevens, once she proved helpless to respond to *Essex*'s attack. Sarah Morgan's diary reports the escaping *Arkansas* crew members as saying that the Union ironclad's first shot "had set ours afire"—which lends credence to Porter's early claim (Morgan, *Civil War Diary,* 194). Given the difficulties that had plagued her starboard engine for days, it is clear that *Arkansas* would have been destroyed by the guns of *Essex* had Stevens not beat them to it; in sacrificing the ram, the captain kept her from falling into enemy hands and allowed his men to escape. Indeed, Farragut, in private correspondence long after the event, gives his adoptive brother his due: "Although Bill Porter did not destroy her, he was the cause, and thought his shells did the work; for they [the men of *Arkansas*] would hardly have destroyed her unless he had made the attack. I insist that Porter is entitled to the credit of it" (Loyall Farragut, *The Life of David Glasgow Farragut* [New York: D. Appleton, 1882], 289). The Confederate crewmen, now shipless, went first to Jackson, Mississippi, and were then ordered to Port Hudson, where they would once again take up arms against *Essex* (see Charles W. Read, "Reminiscences of the Confederate States Navy," *Southern Historical Society Papers* 1 [1876]: 362).

61. *Arkansas* had been in active service for only twenty-three days; her loss was devastating to Southern aspirations to retake control of the Mississippi waterways.

and stabbed each other several times before any one could interfear. One of them was stabbed in the abdomen and died next day.[62]

August 10th

This morning we started up the river on a forageing expedition about 9 miles above the City. we went ashore to a Plantation and got a good supply of Sheep Turkey's, chickens, &c &c from their. we proceeded up the river to a place called Bayou Sara where we captured 50,000 dollars worth of Sugar.[63] We lay their until the *Sumpter* and two transports came up. We loaded the transports and convoyed them down to Baton Rouge leaving the *Sumpter* to guard the remainder. The same night one of the *Sumpter* boats came down and told us she was aground. Capt. Porter dispatched a transport up to her assistance with an Officer and 4 of our men on board. On the passage up our men went ashore to destroy a boat at Port Hudson when they was surrounded and captured by Guerrillas.[64] The transport could not get the *Sumpter* off, so the Crew abandoned and came down to Baton Rouge.[65] We immeadtly got under

62. Henneberry adds that the man whose wound was fatal was named Morgan, a troublesome and unpopular shipmate who had come aboard at St. Louis (after the rebuild of *Essex*): "Some of the boys says he is from the Joliet State Prison [in Joliet, Illinois]. The soldiers crowded down to the boat to learn the result of the fight, and received it with joy." In his later memoir, Park says that the culprit in Morgan's death (who entered the fray after the initial altercation) was never identified or punished, though the stabbing was witnessed by many in the crew.

63. Bayou Sara was a thriving and prosperous river port in the 1860s, the terminus of the West Feliciana Railroad. According to contemporary records, it housed some of the most extensive and heavily stocked stores in Louisiana outside of New Orleans.

64. Captain Porter, in a letter to General Butler in early September, claimed that the seamen, unnamed, and the officer, Spencer Kellogg, were murdered by the guerillas the next day. He demanded that "retribution be carried out." Butler, without evidence, doubted Porter's assertion that the men were killed. Park's later memoir confirms that three of the four men were freed in a prisoner exchange. Spencer Kellogg (his full name was Spencer Kellogg Brown), fourth master of *Essex*, was taken to Richmond, Virginia, and hanged as a spy on September 25, 1863. He was twenty-one years old, a favorite of his captain and popular with his mates. Porter was incensed with the execution and with the charge of spying, which he vehemently denied ("The Execution of Spencer Kellogg," *New York Times*, October 4, 1863), though the facts were well substantiated (see *Spencer Kellogg Brown: His Life in Kansas and His Death as a Spy, 1842–1863, as Disclosed in His Diary*, ed. George Gardner Smith (New York: Appleton, 1903).

65. Henneberry expresses outrage at the cowardice of the captain in abandoning his vessel: "The Capt. Of the *Sumpter* basely deserted his boat and got on board the transport with his crew

weigh and proceeded up to Bayou Sara where we found the *Sumptcr* burnt to the water's edge. The Capt then gave the inhabitants warning to leave as he was going to burn the Town down. we left the same night for Baton Rouge.

August 20th

Our troops have been preparing to evacuate this place. this morning they all left for New Orleans, the Gunboats and vessels belonging to Farragutts fleet going with them. We kept one boat. her name is the *Angelo American* for to tow and assist us up the river. we put one of our 50 pound Rifles and a 13 pounder on board of her.

August 23rd

We left Baton Rouge this morning and proceeded up the River. on the passage up we sent the *Angelo American* on a forageing expedition. She succeeded very well. we came to anchor of Bayou Sara where we found the Coal heap afire. it made Captain Porter very angry as itt was the only place we could get Coal. He immeaditly opened fire on the Town. not doing any damage. Itt was only meant to frighten the People out.[66]

---

and proceeded down to Baton Rouge. Capt. Porter was justly Indignant when he heard the news and he ordered Capt. [Henry Erben] to report to Washington and we now steamed up and found the boat in flames. The rebels burned her. This is one of the most disgraceful acts of cowardice that ever has been heard of a man professing to be a fighting man. . . . If Capt. Porter had his way about It he would string him up." In his haste in abandoning the boat, Erben apparently left the ship's signal book and log on board, which fell into Confederate hands. A formal investigation of the loss of *Sumter* in early October 1862 resulted in charges against Erben being dismissed. He was given command of USS *Pinola* later in the Civil War and promoted to commodore in 1892 and rear admiral in 1894. Porter's high-handedness in sending Erben home without authorization drew exasperated comment from Gideon Welles. Indeed, Welles took the opportunity to inform Porter that there would be, in addition to an investigation of Erben's conduct on *Sumter*, a similar investigation of Porter's exaggerated and fiercely contested claims regarding the destruction of *Arkansas*.

66. Porter's firing on Bayou Sara echoes Farragut's bombardment of Baton Rouge on May 28 after his men were attacked by guerillas. In all such cases, civilians paid the price for the provocation and harassment from on shore (here, the destruction of precious coal) and the forceful reactions from the Federal fleet. Bayou Sara was shortly to be completely destroyed; Baton Rouge suffered significant destruction as well. For more on life in Baton Rouge during this period, see the "Matilda Victor" section of the afterword.

August 24th

Opened fire in ernest on the town this morning. Kept up the fire for about ½ an hour when we moored two boats and went ashore and commenced setting fire to the Town.[67] There was a party of Guerrillas came down and fired at us but we very soon made them retreat with a shell from the Ship. There was a great many valuable things got in the Houses. I got a good number of valuable Books.[68] Most of the furniture was removed out off the Houses before we went ashore. We burnt all the Houses excepting two and they belong to Union Families. Capt. Porter dispatched the *Angelo American* to New Orleans for Coal.

67. Henneberry adds that Porter gave the women and children two hours to leave the city before commencing the attack on Bayou Sara.

68. Though most "foraging" expeditions did not turn into wholesale pillaging and vandalism, those that did were a source of long and bitter memory in Louisiana and across the South. In a September 11 dispatch to his commanding officer, the captain of *Katahdin,* Francis Asbury Roe, complained about being forced into complicity in an episode involving soldiers from one of the Union transports at Donaldsonville, forty miles south of Baton Rouge: "A company of troops had entered a large mansion situated near to the landing of the steamer *St. Maurice,* had pillaged it in a brutal manner, and carried off wines, liquors, silver plate, and clothing belonging to ladies. I am informed that several of the soldiers were drunk from the use of the liquors and wines thus appropriated. During this time the *Katahdin* was at anchor with her guns trained upon shore over the *St. Maurice* for her protection. I respectfully request instructions if the guns of the *Katahdin* are to be used for the protection of soldiers upon a marauding expedition, and if I am to use them in the protection of drunken, undisciplined, and licentious troops in the wanton pillage of a private mansion. . . . I confess, sir, that I blush to report that while the troops of the *St. Maurice* were thus engaged in this unsoldierly and ungallant, not to say disgraceful, operation, I opened my fire upon guerrillas hovering in the rear, apparently occupied in preventing such acts of the United States troops. I feel quite ready to place the *Katahdin* and her guns under the fire of an enemy; I am desirous of encountering enemies, and of injuring them in every manly manner; but I cannot further prostitute the dignity of my profession, as I conceive I have done today, without an earnest and respectful appeal to your authority. It is disgraceful and humiliating to me to be ordered upon guard duty of soldiers employed in pillaging ladies' dresses and petticoats, and I respectfully request that I may be relieved from such service." The equivocal and mocking response of General Benjamin Butler, to whom the note was forwarded, may indicate why such behavior continued despite its formal prohibition: "The acts of the troops in pillaging (if true) are without palliation or excuse. Certainly no more to be justified than this improper, bombastic, and ridiculous rhodomontade of a sublieutenant of the Navy" (*ORN,* 1.19.191–92).

August 28th

The last two or three days Boats were sent to the Plantations for Provisions which they generealy obtained.[69] To day we got under weigh and started down the river towards Port Hudson where we heard the Rebels were building Batteries.[70] We opened fire with our Stern guns. After firing a few round's unfourtanately our 10 inch gun burst without doing any damage. We could see earthworks but no guns. We then returned to Bayou Sara, where we threw the remainder of the gun overboard.

August 30th

The *Angelo American* arrived yesterday with Coal. as she was passing Port Hudson the Rebels opened fire on her with field pieces and musketry. there

69. A somewhat euphemistic reference to Union personnel demanding supplies from those left to defend Southern plantations—typically women and black servants—who had no choice but to permit the Federal troops to "help themselves." In some cases, plantation owners were sympathetic to the Union cause, which is likely the case with "Ackland's Plantation," mentioned in the next entry. In that case, the owner seems to be at home, familiar to the men, and willing to offer provisions. As Park indicates with respect to the burning of Bayou Sara, "Union families" were well known to the troops and generally protected. Similarly in Baton Rouge, a few Union homes were spared from the kind of looting and vandalism that Sarah Morgan's and others suffered.

70. The fortification of Port Hudson was crucial to the Confederacy holding open a supply route along the Lower Mississippi. A small village about twenty miles northwest of Baton Rouge and fifty miles below the mouth of the Red River, it was a railway depot as well as steamboat port. The high bluffs on the eastern bank commanded an excellent view in both directions along the river and were well suited to long-range guns; a plateau at the base likewise allowed for the presence of shore batteries. The narrowness of the channel and the sharp elbow turn on the north end of the battery placements made passing the fort extremely dangerous from either direction. Behind the fort was a maze of creeks, bayous, and swamps that defied approach by Northern soldiers. A member of the 174th New York Regiment under Banks's command (identified only as "J.M.M.") wrote in a letter home: "Have you any idea of a Louisiana swamp? I think not. There was no use talking about marching, it was get through the best way you can; mud and water, old logs and underbrush every step, taking us in up as far as one leg could go at a time, and in some places there were long vines under the mud to catch our feet and trip us up. O, it was beautiful" (online at www.dmna.state.ny.us/historic/reghist/civil/infantry/174thInf/174thInfCWN.htm). *Essex* was to run past the batteries on September 7, sustaining considerable damage in the process, and then to spend much of her service in the spring and early summer of 1863 in the vicinity of Port Hudson until the fort's eventual surrender in July.

was about 20 shots struck her without doing much damage. there was two men wounded.[71] This morning we got under weigh and proceeded up the river the *Angelo* taking us in tow. we anchored of the Mouth of Red River. we went ashore on Ackland's Plantation. He supplied us with all we required as we was short of Provisions. We then Proceeded up the River to Natchez.

September 2nd

We arrived at Natchez. We found some coal laying on the Levee on the West side of the River. Commenced taking itt in. I went with a party on a forageing expedition and to get a few bales of Cotton to protect the Boiler and Machinery of the *Angelo American* and was very successful. Capt. Porter sent a boats crew on shore to the City to get some ice for the sick. Just as the Boat was shoveing of from the shore after getting the ice about 300 of the inhabitans came down with shotguns muskets &c and fired into the Boat killing 1 man and wounding 7.[72] We immediately opened our Batteries and commenced Shelling the City. We kept the fire up for 2 ½ hours. The inhabitans kept up a fire of Musketry all the time. Our shells set fire to several houses Under the Hill and did a great deal of damage to the City. We then got under weigh and proceeded up the River. P.S. we burst one of our 9 inch guns.

September 4th

We arrived in sight of Vicksburgh this morning. Proceeded up slowly to reconnitre when a battery opened on us out of the bush about 3 miles below where the Fleet laid before they evacuated. We exchanged a few shots with them, then turned and went down the river.[73]

71. Two men were killed, not wounded, according to the *Official Records*.

72. Henneberry and Galligan identify the officer accompanying the shore party as Matt B. Snyder, who was among the wounded; he was to survive the war and to become a well-known stage and screen actor in the age of silent film. Of the sailors who accompanied Snyder, one was killed and five wounded—only two returning to the boat unscathed. This incident, closely following the capture of officer Spencer Kellogg with his shore party, signals the increasingly deadly stakes of interaction between the boats' crews and the population along the shores.

73. Porter's intent had been to rejoin the upper fleet, but new batteries on both side of the river caused him to rethink his options.

September 5th

Today I met with a slight accident as we was coming down the river. I was going with a foreageing Party to get some Provisions. I had a Cutlass and revolver on at the time. Leaving the Ship instead of stepping into the Boat I stepped over board and made a hole in the water. The *Essex* was ½ mile down the river before they could stop her weigh. I was about 15 minutes in the water before they Picked me up. I kept the Cutlass and Pistol all the time. I got on board and put on some dry clothes and went with the expedition.[74]

September 6th

We arrived at Natchez to day and Capt. Porter demanded the surrender of the Town. The Mayor and the City authorities came on board and delivered itt up and agreed to all the Propositions that Capt. Porter made to them.[75] We then proceeded down the river to Sandersons Plantation where we went on shore and got all we required. We had a slave on board belonging to Sanderson and he wanted his son a boy about 12 years old.[76] One man volunteered to go

74. This "slight accident," as he calls it, could easily have been the death of William Park. Not only were Confederate snipers along the riverbanks ready always to finish off unfortunates in such a situation, but many sailors simply drowned once in the water, having never learned to swim. Park must not have been one of those since he was fifteen minutes in the river before being picked up, and weighed down by weapons. His self-deprecation about "making a hole in the water" and his nonchalance about changing into dry clothes and then proceeding with the foraging expedition accord nicely with his friend Ruger's later assessment that he was a steady, unflappable, and dutiful shipmate.

75. The destructive bombardment of Natchez following the attack on Porter's men (September 2) had apparently prompted the mayor and inhabitants to seek rapprochement rather than endure further firing. Natchez had actually surrendered previously to Captain J. S. Palmer of the *Iroquois* in May; it now did so again to Porter. Henneberry's version of the encounter has little of "demand" from the captain of *Essex*. The mayor, he says, offered to hoist the Stars and Stripes over the town, and Porter continued downriver. Union troops under General Ulysses Grant occupied the city in 1863. Many of the plantation owners around Natchez had opposed secession and lacked a strong attachment to the Confederacy.

76. Edward Galligan's journal identifies the slave as George Black (possibly a sobriquet); he served as a blacksmith and armorer aboard *Essex*. Galligan was apparently the unnamed sailor who accompanied Park. In his own journal he describes bringing back not only the boy but also "sheep, veals, and fowls." He also says he "broke a set of stalks [stocks] with an ax," freeing three women and one young man, an act of dubious merit to the slaves, since they were apparently not taken back to *Essex*.

with me to get him. we had to go 3 miles back in the bush for him where all the slaves was at work. We pressed a wagon and 4 Horses that was their into our service and I went out for him. He came with us very willingly, without even seeing his Mother who was working another part of the field. In fact we could brought the whole of them very easy. they all wanted to go with us but we had more of them on board than we had provisions for. We then proceeded down the River.

September 7th

This morning we passed Bayou Sara at 3 A.M. when all hands was called to Quarters and everything prepared for running past the Batteries at Port Hudson. As soon as they saw us they opened fire from their Batteries. We replied aiming for where we could see the flash of their guns. We was about one hour under the fire of the guns and was struck a great number of times. two of their rifled shells penetrated and exploded inside wounding one man slightly. one of them burst in the Doctors shop destroying more Medicine in one second than the whole ships company would use in a year. Passed Baton Rouge at 8 A.M. and arrived at New Orleans at 11 P.M.

September 13th

Capt. Porter left us this morning for Washington. When we arrived here Capt. Porter received dispatch from the Secretary of the Navey, also his Promotion and a letter of thanks for the Ship's Company for destroying the *Arkansas* Ram. He was promoted to Commodore. he made a very stirring speech to the ships Company before he left.[77] Most of the Officers left with

77. A copy of the speech, which was recorded by both William Park and James Henneberry, may be found in appendix 1. An always colorful and controversial figure, known to many as "Dirty Bill," William David Porter was in Park's later words "the idol" of his men. Henneberry, in his own notation for September 14, says "Cap Porter by his courage and bravery has endeared himself to every man on board. There is not a man on board but feels very lonesome at [his] leaving." In the assessment of Secretary of the Navy Gideon Welles: "Like all the Porters, he is a courageous, daring, troublesome, reckless officer." Welles's fuller description of William's younger brother, David Dixon Porter, further delineates the family character: "He has great energy, excessive and sometimes not over-scrupulous ambition, is impressed with and boastful of his own powers, given to exaggeration in relation to himself—a Porter infirmity,—is not generous to older and superior living officers . . . but is kind and patronizing to favorites

him.[78] The Officers and Crew of the *Angelo American* came on board. they was formerly the Crew of the *Sumpter.*

September 15th

Captain Caldwell our new Captain took Command of the *Essex* this morning.[79]

November 12th

Nothing of any importance has occurred since the last date. We have been laying at New Orleans since we arrived first getting repaired and the Ship calked.[80] This morning we started up the River. Passed the Rebel Transport *Louis D'Orr* and one of our Gunboats exchanging Prisoners.

November 19th

We arrived at Donelsonville[81] on the 14th where we found two of our Gunboats laying. There is about 5000 of our Soldiers laying here. On the 18th get under weigh and started up the River for Baton Rouge where we arrived this morning.

November 25th

This morning discovered the Ship to be on fire in one of the Coal Bunker's. it was soon extinguished without any damage to the Boat. Got under weigh

---

who are juniors and generally to official inferiors." (For Park's later assessment of Captain William Porter, see appendix 3.) Porter's promotion to commodore, ostensibly a reward for the destruction of *Arkansas,* served also to remove him from the fleet in which his relations with many fellow officers had been sorely strained. It coincided closely with the elevation of his brother David Dixon Porter to commander of the Mississippi Squadron, replacing Charles Davis. (Davis was made chief of the Bureau of Navigation in Washington, D.C. and promoted to rear admiral early in 1863.)

78. Henneberry mentions by name [Robert K.] Riley, [Thomas] Steel, Mr. Foster, [D. P.] Rosenmiller, [M. Harry] Wyatt, and "little Willie" (Willie Coates, a ship's boy).

79. Charles Henry Bromedge Caldwell was former commander of the gunboat *Itasca.*

80. Henneberry recounts the curiosity and disdain *Essex* attracts at her anchorage in New Orleans: "The People here crowd down every night to look at the *Essex.* She is held in very little esteem by the officers of Farragut's fleet; they cast slurs and use all kinds of names to express their contempt for her, but I think she will out live them."

81. That is, Donaldsonville, about forty miles south of Baton Rouge.

and anchored abreast of the R.R. Depot. Sent a Boat on shore to search the Depot. Found about 300 barrels of Molasses.

November 26th

This morning got under weigh and made fast to the Bank opposite the Depot and commenced taking on board the Molasses. Got itt all on board and dropped down to the City and Anchored at 3 P.M. Two of the Gunboats arrived from New Orleans. They brought up a mail for us. They left the same night for Donelsonville.

December 1st

This morning got under weigh and started down the River. Yesterday a Conscript and his Wife & family came on board from the City to go to New Orleans.[82]

December 2nd

We arrived here at New Orleans to day and went alongside the store Ship *Fearnot*[83] and commenced taking out the Molasses and taking in Provisions, Shot, Shell, &c.

December 11th

Yesterday we started from New Orleans up the river. Passed by Donelsonville this morning and proceeded up the river to Placqumine where we anchored. we found 4 of our Gunboats laying here.

December 12th

Got under weigh this morning and proceeded up the River, accompanied by the Gunboats *Sciota, Kenio* and *Winnona.* Came to Anchor about 3 miles below the Batteries of Port Hudson.

82. "The rebels have been trying to force the husband into the army and for that reason he has left his home and goes into a strange place with a large and helpless family on his hands to support" (Henneberry journal, November 30, 1862).

83. USS *Fearnot* was commissioned in August 1861 as a supply ship to the Union blockade. She sailed out of Key West, Florida, and then, after the fall of New Orleans, relocated there.

December 13th

This morning the Rebels came down in strong force opposite the Boats on the West side of the River. They put up a Nigger on the Levee to decoy a boat ashore. The *Kenio* sent a boat ashore to bring him off. As the Boat neared the shore the Nigger jumped down behind the Levee and the Rebels opened a heavee fire of Musketry on the Boat.[84] All the Boats immediately opened a fire of Shells and Sharpnel on the Rebels which soon dispesed them. Shorty after the *Kenio* and *Scitoa* went down the river. Their was no one hurt in the Boat.

December 14th

This morning we was roused out of our slumbers by the report of 3 guns close to us. during the night the Rebels had brought a battery of artillery down opposite the ships and at daybreak they opened on the *Winnona.* All hands was called to Quarters and a heavy fire was opened on them. The fire was too hot for the *Winnona.* she sliped her cable and came under our lee. as soon as the Rebels saw that they ceased firing. only two shots struck us. the most of their fire was directed to the *Winnona.* she was struck 24 times. one of her Masters Mates was killed. we got under weigh and convoyed the *Winnona* down the River. The Rebels kept up a fire of musketry on us for about 16 miles down the River. we replied by shelling every piece of Bush, House and Plantation to within 7 miles of Baton Rouge.[85] We came to anchor of Baton Rouge and the *Winnona* proceeded down the River.

84. This cruel tactic became fairly common as the war progressed and more and more blacks sought shelter on the passing Union gunboats. Whether the "decoy" was forced to perform this function by threats of violence or offered incentives for cooperating with the "secesh" ambush, his role was perilous in the extreme.

85. Here again the harassment of small arms from shore, answered by the big guns of the Federal fleet, proved ruinous to landowners along the river. As one witness recounts: "'Bombs bursting in air' every few days gave assurance that the 'guerrillas,' as a hastily organized band of rowdies and bullies . . . chose to style themselves, had 'run in and fired off and run out again,' making just enough demonstration to call a return fire from the gunboats . . . [causing us] shudders of unutterable agony for the safety of aged and defenseless friends. The townspeople actually made excavations in their yards and covered them with planks for refuge in a bombardment. Some of the plank coverings were struck and shattered by fiery missiles, so the wretched inhabitants had to dig tunnels by which they could obtain shelter beyond the covered entrance. Plans and diagrams for these were passed around, and neighbor helped neighbor in the life-saving work. It was a terrible state of things, no military organizations at

December 17th

This morning at daylight a large fleet was seen coming up the River. it proved to be a part of General Banks expedition accompanied by the Sloop of War *Richmond* and several Gunboats.[86] we got under weigh and stood in for the town. we fired a few shells to clear the town of the Confed's and made fast alongside of the Bank. The transports came alongside and the troops landed across our decks.[87]

December 24th

For the last few days troops has been coming up at the rate of about 1 Regiment per day. we got under weigh and proceeded up to Port Hudson to recconitre. found it about the same as we left itt. turned and came back.

December 29th

We got under weigh this morning and proceeded up to reconnitre the Batteries. found them the same as we left them. Came back down the river to Baton Rouge. Last night the State house was burned down. it is supposed that itt was set on fire by some of the Secesh prisoners that was confined their.[88]

---

hand to control the rowdy element on the Confederate side, and the Federals claiming to have no other way of putting a stop to these senseless raids except by firing from their gunboats" (Eliza McHatton Ripley, *From Flag to Flag: A Woman's Adventures and Experience in the South during the War, in Mexico, and in Cuba* [New York: D. Appleton and Co., 1889], 24–25).

86. Nathaniel Prentiss Banks, who had suffered repeated defeat by Stonewall Jackson in the Shenandoah campaign, was reassigned to New Orleans in December to replace General Benjamin Butler as commander of the Department of the Gulf. He was responsible not only for conducting military operations but also for overseeing the civil administration of Union-held territory in Louisiana. Many, including Gideon Welles, secretary of the navy, doubted his ability to keep a tight rein on Southern partisans. His approach was clearly more conciliatory than Butler's; he immediately opened churches that Butler had closed (for authorizing days of prayer and fasting for the Confederacy, and refusing to pray for President Lincoln), freed some political prisoners, and returned property that Federal forces had sequestered. His wife, Mary Theodosia Palmer Banks, who joined him in New Orleans, had her own formula for occupying a rebel city: she was famous for hosting lavish parties for Unionists; Matilda Victor almost certainly enjoyed the Banks's hospitality during her stay in New Orleans (see the afterword).

87. For an image of the events described here, see figure 12.

88. The fire turned out to have been accidentally set by Union soldiers inhabiting the building.

Figures 1 (*above*) and 2 (*left*). Celeste's father, John Diedrich Repp, a butcher and meat dealer in the Baton Rouge Market, is likely the stocky, mustached gentleman pictured in these 1859 photographs. Celeste's younger brothers, Henry (9) and William (6), bereft of their mother since 1855, would have been apprenticing and performing simple chores rather than attending school, as their sisters were. They may well be two of the boys pictured in the second photo. John Repp died in early 1860, shortly after these pictures were taken. Both images courtesy of the State Library of Louisiana.

Figure 3. This daguerreotype of William Little Park was donated by his granddaughter, Virginia A. Park, to the Newberry Library in Chicago, along with a retrospective memoir of his wartime service. Though undated, the image was likely taken in Chicago in September 1861, just prior to the commencement of Park's three-year term with the Union brown water navy. He was twenty-five and already a veteran sailor, having fought with British forces in the Crimean War. Image courtesy of the Newberry Library, MS 10035.

Figure 4. William David Porter, 1863. Unlike the dashing portrait sketched by Bill Travis in the early months of the war (published in *Harper's Weekly,* March 1, 1862), this Library of Congress image captures a war-weary, though still dauntless Porter just after his tenure on *Essex* ended. "Though his character as a private citizen was far from spotless," Park observes, "his reckless daring and utter contempt of danger made him the idol of the crew."

Figure 5. Gunners of the USS *Essex*. William L. Park is at bottom left; seated next to him is gunner's mate William ("Bill") Young, who had won a Medal of Honor for his previous service on USS *Cayuga* during the capture of New Orleans (April 24–25, 1862). Standing behind are Gordon F. Tracy (*left*) and Charles James Drew (*right*), both quarter gunners like Park himself. William Young transferred to the *Essex* in July 1862, and Tracy joined the crew in October 1862, so this photo was taken sometime after that—probably in occupied New Orleans or Baton Rouge, where there were numerous studios doing a brisk business in photography of military personnel. This image appears in Francis Trevelyan Miller's *Photographic History of the Civil War*, vol. 6, *The Navies* (where Drew's first name is mistakenly given as "Thomas," and Tracy is misidentified as "Terry"). Courtesy of the Missouri History Museum.

Figures 6 and 7. *Above:* members of the crew of USS *Essex* on the waterfront of Baton Rouge take a break from coaling ship—an arduous, tedious, and dirty job. *Below: Essex* moored off Baton Rouge. Photo above courtesy of G. H. Suydam Collection, Mss. 1394; below, Andrew D. Lytle Album Photograph Collection, Mss. 3708; both in the Louisiana and Lower Mississippi Valley Collections, LSU Libraries, Baton Rouge. Both photos were taken by local photographer Andrew D. Lytle, evidently on the same day in the summer of 1862.

Figure 8. A group of unidentified Union naval officers poses for a formal portrait by local photographer Andrew D. Lytle in occupied Baton Rouge, ca. 1862. In Sarah Morgan's words, "The naval officers all appear like gentlemen, and certainly produced that impression on all who saw them." Courtesy of Andrew D. Lytle Collection, Mss. 893, 1254, Louisiana and Lower Mississippi Valley Collections, LSU Libraries, Baton Rouge.

Figures 9 and 10. *Above:* Union General Thomas Williams. Few, if any, other Federal officers enjoyed comparable trust and respect in the South. His concern for protection of the welfare and personal property of local families prompted cooperative, even congenial relations with the citizens of occupied Baton Rouge, many of whom mourned his death at the Battle of Baton Rouge (August 5, 1862). Courtesy of the Library of Congress. *Below:* granite baptismal font donated by the Williams family to the parishioners of St. James Episcopal Church in Baton Rouge, in thanks for their kindness to him during his tenure in that city. Williams attended St. James while in Baton Rouge, as did Sarah Morgan, who called him "a good man" whom "we all liked." Photo courtesy of Fred Frey.

Figure 11. Baton Rouge endured bombardment from Farragut's gunboats on May 27, 1862. Then, less than three months later, following the Battle of Baton Rouge, a third of the city was burned by Federal troops under the command of Halbert Paine. Matilda Victor's school was damaged in the first incident, and her outbuildings and fences, as well as a cottage, were fired in the second. Here, a resident whose property was designated for destruction—possibly Colonel Andrew Matta, who lived just two blocks west of St. Mary's Academy—surveys the burned-out ruins of his home. Courtesy of Andrew D. Lytle Collection, Mss. 893, 1254, Louisiana and Lower Mississippi Valley Collections, LSU Libraries, Baton Rouge.

Figure 12. *Recapture of Baton Rouge, La., December 17th, 1862: Federal troops under General Grover driving off the Confederates and occupying the city.* This line drawing, based on a sketch by Frank H. Schell, was published in Frank Leslie's *The Soldier in Our Civil War* (New York: Stanley Bradley, 1893). USS *Essex* is prominently featured just offshore. Park's journal entry for the day notes that "we fired a few shells to clear the town of Confed's and made fast alongside of the bank. The transports came alongside and the troops landed across our decks."

Figure 13. This photo of the Federal encampment (Augur's Division) in Baton Rouge, early 1863, was taken by Andrew Lytle from the upper story of the Heroman Building on the corner of Florida and Church (Third) Streets, looking east along Florida. Baton Rouge would be the staging area for the Port Hudson campaign and siege, in which USS *Essex* played a prominent role. Courtesy of Andrew D. Lytle Collection, Mss. 893, 1254, Louisiana and Lower Mississippi Valley Collections, LSU Libraries, Baton Rouge.

Figure 14. USS *Hartford,* the flagship of Admiral David Farragut, off Baton Rouge. This was the ship on which Matilda Victor and two female companions escaped Baton Rouge on May 27, 1862. Farragut later wrote two letters on Matilda's behalf in support of her claims, as a "loyal Northern woman," for financial reparation for the loss of her school and livelihood under Federal bombardment and occupation. Courtesy of Andrew D. Lytle Collection, Mss. 893, 1254, Louisiana and Lower Mississippi Valley Collections, LSU Libraries, Baton Rouge.

Figures 15 and 16. The location of these 1863 photos (sometimes wrongly assumed to be one of the Davis plantations near Vicksburg) is a "contraband camp" in Baton Rouge "formerly used as a female seminary." Until now, the school in question has never been identified. The property is Matilda Victor's St. Mary's Academy, in which Celeste Repp and her sister Alice (as well as many daughters of prominent residents) had studied. These are the only known photographs of St. Mary's buildings and show only a small portion of the campus. Photo above courtesy of Marshall Dunham Photograph Album, Mss. 3241; below, G. H. Suydam Collection, Mss. 1394; both in the Louisiana and Lower Mississippi Valley Collections, LSU Libraries, Baton Rouge.

Figure 17. *Fr. Darius Hubert, S.J.*, by Alexandre Alaux, a well-known painter of portraits, historical tableaux, and religious subjects, active in New Orleans between 1869 and 1932. Fr. Hubert is wearing his Confederate service medal from the Army of Northern Virginia as well as a unique gold medal struck for him by the City of Savannah, Georgia, as a token of thanks for his valiant ministry there during the yellow fever epidemic in 1876. This oil-on-canvas portrait, dating to the mid-1880s, was donated to the Museum of the Confederacy (MOC), Richmond, Virginia, by a Confederate Ladies Memorial Association; it is reproduced here courtesy of the MOC. A similar portrait is held by Confederate Memorial Hall in New Orleans; for several decades after the hall was built in 1891 for and by Confederate veterans, the Hubert portrait hung next to those of Stonewall Jackson and Robert E. Lee.

Figure 18. New Orleans Jesuits, 1888. Fr. Darius Hubert is in the bottom row, second from right; next to him on the far right is Fr. Francis Gautrelet, his friend of fifty years and superior for much of that time. Fr. Gautrelet said of Darius Hubert that "the passion of his life was self-sacrifice." Three years after this photo was taken, Fr. Hubert suffered a stroke and was moved to Macon, Georgia, where he died on June 14, 1893. From the folded page of a Jesuit scrapbook, this photo is reproduced courtesy of Archives of the New Orleans Province, Society of Jesus, Loyola New Orleans University Monroe Library.

Figure 19. *Consolation* (1908), by John Hauser, a well-known Cincinnati artist, from a photo-image of a wartime painting. The original (1863) version of this iconic image of a Sister of Mercy reading to an injured soldier in a Union tent hospital is said to have been commissioned by President Lincoln and hung in a White House gallery, but the sentimental backstory—that General Ulysses S. Grant had witnessed the scene firsthand and mentioned it to the president—is likely fanciful. The name of the wartime artist, sometimes given as Florence Meyer, is unknown, and the original painting is lost. The setting is clearly Vicksburg, Mississippi, though the Mercy Sisters of the Vicksburg House were unlikely to be found in the role depicted here; they spent most of the war on the run with Confederate troops. Image courtesy of Sisters of Mercy of the Americas, Mercy Heritage Center, Belmont, North Carolina.

Figure 20. Sisters of Mercy Convent in Vicksburg, Mississippi, built in 1868, the year that Celeste Repp (Sister Mary Euphrasia) was received into the order. She spent her early years as a nun here, teaching at St. Francis Xavier Academy, before moving to Pass Christian to teach African American children. This rather bucolic image of the convent and adjoining property was taken in 1876 by Henry J. Herrick, a Canadian-born Vicksburg photographer. Courtesy of the Old Court House Museum in Vicksburg.

Figure 21. Confederate Veterans Memorial Monument in Baton Rouge, with local veterans, 1886. The statue at the top of the monument, representing "the beau ideal of a patriotic citizen," was modeled on the eminent local Confederate soldier Andrew Stewart Herron, Celeste Repp's adoptive cousin and her godparent. The base of the monument eventually cracked, and the statue was moved from its original location (North Blvd. at Third Street) to the grounds of the Old State Capitol. This image, from the *Elks Souvenir of Baton Rouge,* is reproduced courtesy of Special Collections, LSU Libraries, Baton Rouge.

1863

January 1st 1863

Yesterday the Mail arrived. itt brought the news of the Battle of Fredicksburgh.[1] Yesterday morning their was a large number of Negros came down to the Bank of the river. we sent Boats and brought them on board. Likewise this morning their was about 60 men women and Children when a Band of Guerallis came down and shot one of them tied another one both hands and feet then threw him into the River. That is what they call making an example to prevent the Niggers from running away. Boats was sent from the vessels to bring the remainder accross. This evening we shifted our position closer to the shore to prevent such scenes in future.[2]

January 2nd

This morning sent a boat on shore and took 30 Contraband's (alias nigger's) accross to the City.[3] In the forenoon the Transport *Landis* and *St. Mary's*

1. This battle, fought December 11–15, 1862, in and around Fredericksburg, Virginia, was a major defeat for the Federal army under Major General Ambrose Burnside. Union casualties more than doubled those suffered by Robert E. Lee's Army of Northern Virginia. Park, who has no family in the United States, generally gets his news about the eastern and western theaters of the war from his shipmates, including James Henneberry, for whom every "mail" contains newspapers from his home in Chicago.

2. Another incident of extraordinarily callous cruelty toward slaves by guerillas (perpetrated, ironically, on the day the Emancipation Proclamation was issued), which raised the stakes of interaction between the gunboat crews and fleeing blacks. It seems not to have deterred *Essex* from offering safe passage along the river to contraband camps, despite the ambivalence of many of the sailors toward abolition.

3. That is, Baton Rouge. Matilda Victor's school property, which had served as a Union hospital facility through the summer of 1862, had been transformed by early 1863 into a contra-

landed one Rgt. of Infantry and A Company of Cavalry on the West side of the River. in the afternoon the *Landis* came alongside and supplied us with Coal.

January 5th

The last two day's some of the Contraband's brought word that the Rebels had got some more guns mounted and was laying Torpedo's below Port Hudson on purpose to destroy the *Essex.* This morning we got under weigh and proceeded up to reconnitre. We found itt was a false rumour. We turned back and anchored of the Depot on the West Side of the River at Baton Rouge. One of our Gunboats came up and brought the News of the Capture of the Gunboat *Harriet Lane* at Galveston in Texas and the Captain of the Gunboat *Westfield* had blowen that boat up with all hands on board to prevent her falling into the hands of the Rebels.[4]

January 9th

Nothing of any importance has occurred the last few days. It has been raining heavey and the river is rapidly riseing. Our Cavalry went to day up the West side of the river to reconniter. They Captured 3 of the Rebel signal men. The Prisoners say that the Rebels is preparing their Gunboats and 15 Transports to Capture the *Richmond* Sloop of War and the *Essex,* now laying here. The same as they Captured the *Harriet Lane.* We are making preparations to give them a warm reception.

January 12th

Yesterday we went up the river as far as Port Hudson to reconnitre. We went within the range of their guns but they did not fire. As we was coming down the river a party of Rebels was cheering for Jeff Davis. We fired a gun at

---

band hostel, the subject of several well-known McPherson & Oliver photographs (figures 15 and 16) (see the afterword).

4. USS *Westfield's* destruction was instigated by the captain after she ran aground on a sandbar near Pelican Island on January 1, during the successful recapture of Galveston by Confederate forces. Commander William Renshaw poured turpentine over the deck and laid a fuse trail of powder from the magazine. When he lit the fuse, the boat exploded before he and the thirteen crew members still aboard could escape; all died in the conflagration. The sunken remains of *Westfield,* including its five-ton Dahlgren cannon, were recovered in 2009.

them. The Shell exploded right in the middle of the group. We arrived here at 7 P.M. when we heard that our Pickets had been driven in on boath Sides of the river. This morning our troops evacuated the West side of the river and crossed over to B. Rouge.

January 19th

Nothing of importance since the last date. Yesterday we went up to Port Hudson. Found that the enemy had been strengthing his Batteries also adding another Water Battery. On our passage down the River we picked up a Torpedo.[5] Sent two of the boats to get it. one of the Boats landed on the shore and cut the wires attached to itt. The torpedo was a small iron Barrel containing about 100 pounds of Powder made fast and buoyed up by a large Cask so that it would be about 6 feet under Water. Had wires attached leading to the Shore. The boats made a line fast to the Cask and towed it on board. We all thought itt was meant to explode by a Galvanic Battery on shore. The rebels fully expected that they would blow us up for they had soldiers stationed all down the river ready to pick us up. They fired at the boat several times on the passage down. This morning took the Torpedo on shore to try and see how itt worked. Got a long line fastned to the wire that led inside of the Torpedo and a boat get hold of the other and pulled out into the river. as soon as they tightned the line the Torpedo went of with a tremendous explosion, scattering all round the Boats Crew splintering the oar in one of the men's hands. A piece of it struck one of the men on board the ship nearly cutting his foot in two. The Torpedo is made to go off by Friction so we must be carefull the next time we go up the river.

5. The use of floating explosive devices increased along with the presence of the Federal fleet on Southern waterways, and the crew of the *Essex* became not only more vigilant in watching for them but also curious about their construction. Park, as an ordnance man, is particularly interested in the variety and creativity of the torpedoes' construction, and describes many of them in detail. The use of torpedoes, like other tactics of the guerillas, was hated and feared by the sailors—hated because it was inconsistent with conventional warfare ("not in the regular line of fair stand-up, give-and-take naval fighting") and feared because it was effective. An iron vessel like *Essex* could be quickly sunk by such a mine if it detonated under the ship's waterline. The large and unusual torpedo found by *Essex* in late February and described by Park below (Feb. 27 entry) was the subject of a brief article in *Harper's Weekly* (April 18, 1863, 250), which includes a picture and a sectional view of the device.

January 22nd

Yesterday General Banks arrived from New Orleans. In the afternoon he came on board accompanied by Major General Auger[6] and their respective Staffs to inspect the *Essex*. He appeared to be well pleased with all the interior arrangements and thought she was a very strong Boat. To day we went alongside of a Coal Brig and filled up with Coal. The river rapidly rising.

January 27th

The River is still rising. One day last week A Regement of Nigger's arrived from New Orleans. The White soldiers and the Niggers don't seem to agree so well as the Newspapers would have us to imagine.[7] Yesterday one of our Transports went to A Plantation and got a load of Corn from a Union Man. At night A party of guerrillas came and burnt the remainder of his Corn Crib's.[8] This morning two deserters came board from Port Hudson. They brought a double Barrel shot gun apiece. Their news was not of much importance.

Feburary 1st

Nothing worthy of note since last date. The River is still rising.[9] Yesterday we sent up to Port Hudson. On the passage up we was fired into by a band of Guerillas doing us no damage. We fired a few shells into the bush which soon scattered them. On the passage down we were fired into again by the same parties. We opened a brisk fire of shrapnel and Cannister on them for a few minutes. When they Skedaddled we proceeded down the river and came to anchor here at 4 P.M.

6. Christopher Columbus Augur had led a division under Nathaniel Banks at the Battle of Cedar Mountain (Culpeper County, Virginia) in August 1862, where he was severely wounded. Rejoining his corps in November, he was appointed major general by Lincoln and transferred to the Army of the Gulf. There, in partnership again with Banks, he would command the left wing of the army in the siege of Port Hudson.

7. Park's ironic tone reflects the widespread ambivalence of those whose purported objective in emancipating slaves is at odds with their own entrenched racial prejudices. See also appendix 3.

8. Retribution against any who cooperated with "the enemy" (in all parts of the country) could be harsh, at times much harsher and more violent than that described here.

9. Henneberry reports in early February that "the river has risen 26 feet and is still rising," sometimes as much as two feet in twenty-four hours, and that the surrounding countryside is flooded. In his later memoir, Park observes in April 1863 that "the war has already turned

February 7th

Several Regements of Soldiers arrived here from New York last week. Yesterday one Brigade of Infantry and a Battery of Artillery went down the river to Placquemine. Last night we got information that the Rebels was going to float a Torpedo down under our bows and blow us up; after dark we got under weigh and shifted our position to the other side of the River. This morning we got under weigh and proceeded up the River about 7 miles to a house where the Rebels were making Torpedo's. we fired a few rounds of Grape and Cannister at itt and then sent one of the boats ashore to set fire to the place. They found a good deal of rope and wire also two baynotes a Cartouche Box and a knapsack.[10] We came down and anchored in our old position off the depot.[11]

February 15th

The River is still rising. Two transports loaded with troops and one Mortar Boat arrived here last week. On the 12th the General sent out 65 waggons, and 14 men to guard them, on a foraging expedition for Corn. The Rebels Gobbled them all up. This morning we got under weigh to go on our weekly trip to Port Hudson. We got about halfway there when we had obliged to turn back on account of the strong current, likewise being short of Coal. Some parts of the River the Current was so strong that itt took us 5 hours to go 3 Miles. We Anchored of the depot at 4:30 P.M.

February 16th

This morning a Nigger brought word that the Rebels had been planting Torpedo's during the night, about 3 miles above here. We got under weigh and

---

this fertile and rich part of the country into an uninhabitable swamp" and that the floodwaters merely made the scene more pitiful: "the gardens and orchards are all under water and a current of muddy water is running through the cotton and cane fields at the rate of six miles an hour. . . . The water stood as high as the second story windows of the buildings situated in the low ground, and I suppose that the catfish are feeding in the parlours of many of the planters dwelling houses."

10. Park obviously intends "bayonets" here. Henneberry adds that the occupants had been startled from their meal by the grape and canister shot, leaving uneaten food on the table. The shore party, led by John C. Parker, acting master of *Essex,* gained not only trophies but useful intelligence about how the torpedoes were made.

11. That is, at Baton Rouge.

proceeded up to the place when two boats crews landed and commenced getting the torpedo's out of the River. We picked up four and all the apparatus belonging to them. We came back and anchored in our old position. The torpedo's are different from the other one we picked up. These are large demijohns covered with basket work placed inside of a barrel containing about 70 pounds of Powder. We broke two of them to see how they were fixed inside. A piece of wood extended from the neck of the demijohn to the bottom. In the middle of the wood the friction tube was made fast and a wire to the tube leading through the cork of the demijohn to set it off. We saved the Powder to return itt to the Rebels the first time we attack Port Hudson. I think it is better Powder than ours. I think the *Essex* is getting rather obnoxious to the Rebels, by what the deserters report. They say that the Confederate Government has offered 100,000 dollars to any one that will capture or destroy the *Essex.* I suppose that is the reason so many torpedo's is in the river. we hear there is 12 more between this place and Port Hudson. Captain Caldwell handsomely rewarded the Nigger that brought us the information by giving him a piece of pork and some biscut.[12]

February 18th

Last night two Contrbands brought intelligence that the Rebels were going to float torpedo's down to the vessel to blow her up. We got under weigh and made fast to the bank, out of the current. This morning commenced tearing down the depot to make a raft for catching the torpedo's that might be floated down whilst we lay at anchor. In the Forenoon we tried to explode the remaining torpedo's but they would not go off. In the afternoon the *Landies* tow boat brought up two Mortar Schooners, and a Coal brig alongside. We commenced taking on coal. The *Laurel Hill* went up the river this morning with a Company of Cavalry to a plantation to get some Cotton and Sugar. The Rebels planted a battery below here about 7 miles from the City. Two of the Cavalry came down and gave us the information. We sent a boat across the river to tell the General to send some troops up to capture the Battery as our vessel

12. Park's sense of irony is again evident here—the huge financial reward offered by "secesh" authorities for capture or destruction of *Essex* set alongside the "handsome reward" of pork and biscuit given by the ship's captain to a black informant for information that helped protect *Essex.* Contrabands are increasingly mentioned by Park as bringing intelligence about torpedoes and other threats to the Union fleet.

was taking in coal. The General replied that he was afraid that the enemy had more troops than he had to send (although he has got 30,000 men here). So we had to leave the Coal Brig and go up the river. as soon as the enemy saw us coming they left and the *Laurel Hill* came down the river with us.

February 20th

Yesterday filled up with Coal. In the afternoon the *Mississippi* Sloop of War came up from New Orleans. She brought up a Mortar Schooner with her. This morning the *Richmond* Sloop of War went down the river to New Orleans.[13]

February 23rd

On the 21st the Confederate Steamer *Frolic* came down with a flag of truce to exchange Prisoners. She lay here until this morning when the *New Brunswick* brought the Prisoners up from New Orleans when she proceeded up the river. This afternoon the Captain of the *Mississippi* and General Grover[14] came on board to inspect the ship. When they left we gave them a salute of 13 Guns.

February 24th

This morning got under weigh and proceeded up to Port Hudson. On the passage up we met the confedrate Steamer *General Quitman* with a flag of truce. Coming down with a load of exchanged Prisoners. They were our men that were captured at Galveston, also the Crew of the U.S. Ram *Queen of the West* which had run by the Batteries of Vicksburgh. She was captured in the Red River, by the treachery of her Pilot taking her under a masked Battery where she had her Steam pipe cut by a shot, when her crew jumped overboard to escape the steam and hot water.[15] There were three Boats laying under the

13. Henneberry, in mentioning *Richmond*'s departure, and her replacement on the river by *Mississippi*, expresses impatience for similar relief for his own boat: "When will the *Essex* be relieved? Ans. When she is no more." It is doubtless a credit to her perceived importance that she is in service almost continuously, except when in need of repairs.

14. General Cuvier Grover had recently been transferred to the Department of the Gulf, having won renown (and promotion) for bravery in the eastern theater at the Battles of Williamsburg and Seven Pines, as well as the Second Battle of Bull Run (Manassas). The 13-gun salute by the ship's crew here evidently owes to respect for his exploits on the battlefield.

15. *Queen of the West* was part of the Ellet ram fleet that saw first action at Fort Pillow and Memphis in June 1862 and then tried in vain to sink *Arkansas* at Vicksburg, in company

Batteries. On our passage down the Rebel pickets fired into the Ports but we did not return the fire. They did not hurt any one. We anchored in our old position at 3 P.M. The *Quitman* went up the river at 6 P.M.

February 27th

Last night the River rose 5 inches. This morning we received information that the Rebels were going to attack this place. Longstreet was marching on itt with 40,000 men.[16] Their rams were to attack the Fleet at the same time. The soldiers on shore has been busey building batteries and throwing up entrenchments. They have got 16 siege guns in position. part of that number commands the river. All the Mortar boats has droped down the river below the Town out of the way. We are prepared to give them a warm reception. In the afternoon a cask was seen floating past with a lot of cotton on top of it. we sent a boat to see what it was. The boat hauled it into the shore. It was a large Torpedo containing upwards of 200 pounds of Powder. They opened one end of it. when they saw a lot of machinery something like a clock in motion they got water and damped the Powder and then took the Machinery out. It was meant to go off at a set time. It has two percussion caps with hammers to strike them by springs attached to the machinery. I don't know their reason for sending it down without they expected us to take it on board the same

---

with *Essex,* on July 22. Here, Park is reflecting the allegation that a replacement pilot who was steering *Queen* when she grounded on February 14, 1863, directly under the guns of Fort DeRussy, was a Confederate sympathizer, and had deliberately put her in harm's way. David Dixon Porter, in his memoirs, refers to the grisly scene on board, when those wounded and killed by the relentless firing of the shore batteries into the helpless boat were then engulfed in scalding water and steam from the shattered pipe. For more on this incident, see Steven M. Mayeux, *Earthen Walls, Iron Men: Fort DeRussy, Louisiana, and the Defense of Red River* (Knoxville: University of Tennessee Press, 2007), 18–34.

16. General James Longstreet, who had graduated from West Point in the same class as Union Generals Henry Halleck, William Tecumseh Sherman, and Ulysses S. Grant, became Robert E. Lee's "Old War Horse" in the summer of 1862 and was one of the Confederacy's most prominent and controversial military leaders. The rumor of his moving toward Port Hudson was mistaken; Longstreet was in Virginia in February 1863 and would remain in the eastern theater until September, when he was sent, with parts of his First Corps of the Army of Northern Virginia, to assist Braxton Bragg and the Army of Tennessee. He did not set foot in Louisiana during the war, though he settled in New Orleans after surrender.

as we did the other ones, when it would have gone of and blown the ship to pieces.[17] In the evening the tow boat *Landies* arrived with a store ship and a Mortar Schooner.

March 2nd

Yesterday several Transports arrived with batteries of Artillery. The Gun Boat *Albatross* and a Mortar Schooner came up from Plaquemine. Last night after dark we got under weigh and crossed over to the East side of the River. we took up our position about ¼ of a mile above the City. For the last two day's there has been roumours that the Confedrates has captured another of our Gun boats up the river that had run past the batteries at Vicksburgh. Her name is the *Indinola* an iron clad and built in the Monitor style.[18] Several transports arrived here today with stores &c &c. This evening the *Landies* arrived with a barque in tow loaded with Stores.

March 5th

Yesterday morning as we were crossing to the West side of the river a part of the Port Engine broke down. The Engineers belonging to the *Mississippi* came on board to inspect it. they concluded we should be obliged to go down the river to New Orleans to get repaired. We started from Baton Rouge at 6 P.M. Passed one of our Gunboats at Placquemine. This morning we passed the Sloop of War *Portsmouth* laying at Carrolton. Arrived here at New Orleans 10 A.M. There were 3 first class Sloops of War 1 Second Class and 5 Gunboats laying here, besides Foreign War vessels.

17. See note 5, above.

18. *Indianola,* which had joined the Mississippi Squadron on January 23, had indeed been captured on February 24, when she was attacked by both the Confederate ram *Webb* and *Queen of the West,* now under rebel command, near the mouth of the Red River. While her captors worked on salvaging her for their own use, they were surprised by a ghostly ironclad floating downstream toward them and hastily exploded *Indianola*'s magazines to prevent her possible recapture. The "ironclad" was actually a clever wooden dummy raft fitted out by Admiral David Dixon Porter and floated down the river to draw Confederate fire—possibly the most ingenious hoax of the war. Park and the other tars would doubtless have enjoyed that joke at the "Rebs'" expense. *Harper's Weekly* (April 11, 1863) recounted the incident in "Admiral Porter's Dummy." Steven M. Mayeux revisits the story at length in *Earthen Walls, Iron Men,* 37–79.

March 8th

For the last two days all hands has been employed taking in coal. Provisions, Shell, ammunition &c, &c. Had men from the Shore reparing the engines and Boilers. We also took on board two 12 Pound brass Guns. Yesterday the transport *Mississippi*[19] arrived from New York. She brought a Mail and a Regment of Cavalry. Last night General Bank came on board and stayed a short time, then left for Baton Rouge. This morning the tow boat *Reliance* came alongside to tow us up the River. at 7 A.M. got up steam and proceeded up the river. at 3 P.M. Passed the *Portsmouth* laying at Carrolton.

March 11th

We arrived at Baton Rouge last night. On the passage up six transports passed us loaded with army waggons and Soldiers for this place. This morning the Fleet arrived from New Orleans composed of the following Ships. The first Class Sloop of War *Hartford,* 24 Guns with the Flag of Rear Admiral Farragut on board, the *Richmond,* 24 Guns, the *Monongahlia,* 11 Guns, the *Genesee,* 11 Guns. The Gunboat *Albatross* went up the river toward Port Hudson this morning. This evening we commenced to coal ship. At 8 P.M. The *Albatross* and *Kenio* Gunboat came down the River.

March 12th

This morning the *Albatross* convoyed two transports loaded with troops about 10 miles up the river. the *Genesee* took two Mortar boats up to the same place. The Gunboat *Sachem* arrived from New Orleans. General Banks reviewed all the troops here today. In the evening we finished coaling and got under weigh. We proceeded up the river and anchored where the other vessels were.

March 13th

This morning at daylight we got under weigh and proceeded up the river, followed by the Gun boats *Albatross, Sachem* and *Genesee* and three transports loaded with troops. the transports had two Mortar boats in tow. When we

19. Not to be confused with the steam frigate USS *Mississippi* in Farragut's fleet (see Park's entries for February 20, above, and March 14 through March 17).

got up to Prophets Island[20] the transports landed the troops about four miles below the Batteries of Port Hudson. We went up and reconnitred the Batteries. Their were four transports laying there. We sent a boat down to tell the Gunboats and Mortars to come up. They anchored at the Head of Prophets Island. We anchored about a mile from their lower earth works. We can see their pickets on the Levee about 700 yards ahead. They don't seem too pay any attention to us at all. As it was getting dark we fired a couple of nine inch shell where we saw their pickets standing to keep them awake. At 10 P.M. A transport brought up 4 Mortar Boats.

March 14th

This morning the Admiral arrived with the *Hartford, Richmond, Mississippi, Monongahelia,* and *Kenio.* Farragut gave our Captain the command of the Mortar Boats during the morning they were getting into position. At 3 P.M. the Mortars opened fire on the Batteries. They made some splendid practice. At 4.30 P.M. We opened fire on their lower Batteries with our 9 inch guns, every shell going into the Batteries. At 5.30 made a signal for the mortars to cease firing. The Amiral has made up his mind to run past the Batteries to night with the vessels he brought up; also the *Genesee* and *Albatross.*[21] We have to lay here and protect the Mortar Boats with the *Sachem.* When he is passing the *Essex* and *Sachem* is to attack the lower Battery and draw their fire.

March 15th

Last night set in foggy but toward 11 Oclock it cleared of and the stars shone out quite bright which showed us the Fleet under weigh and up abreast of us. We immediately got under weigh and moved about 300 yards nearer to the batteryies where we were within good shelling distance and called all hands to quarters. The fleet was to pass in the following order, the Flag Ship

20. Prophet's (or Prophet) Island, now normally spelled Profit Island, six miles south of Port Hudson, served as a convenient anchorage for *Essex* during the months leading up to the siege of the Confederate garrison there.

21. When General Banks was delayed in reaching Port Hudson from Baton Rouge, Farragut decided to push past the fort without waiting for army support, confident he could take control of the junction of the Red and Mississippi Rivers with his ships and thus interrupt the Confederate supply corridor to Vicksburg.

Hartford to lead with the *Albatross* on the off side of her, the *Richmond* next with the *Genesee* on her off side, the *Monongehela* next with the *Kenio* on her off side, and the Sloop of War *Mississippi* to fetch up the rear.[22] The fleet moved up until opposite the Lower battery when a rocket was sent up from the opposite shore and Bang goes the guns from the lower battery followed by the broadsides of the Ships. The *Essex* and *Sachem* opened on the lower battery. At the same time the mortars opened fire, followed by the fire of the whole of their batteries, which were not less than 3 miles long. What with the roar of the Mortars the broadsides of the Ships and the Batteries and the bursting of the Shells was terrific.[23] At 1 Oclock we could see that one of the Sloops had passed round the Point and wondered what the Batteries were keeping up such a tremendous fire on, when presently the *Richmond* and *Genesee* droped down disabled followed shortly after by the *Monongehela* and *Kenio.* Still the batteries kept up their fire when a small boat hailed us and told us that the *Mississippi* was hard and fast under the Batteries and they wanted a boat to go up and take the crew off. The boat came alongside full of men and two of them wounded.[24] We dispatch a boat to the *Richmond* to tell them of the disaster when he sent the *Genessee* up to their relief, but before she got half up the *Mississippi* was seen to be on fire. In the meantime another boat load of men came on board, when we got up anchor and crossed over to the opposite shore to pick up any of the men that mite have swam ashore when

22. In Farragut's attempt to run past the batteries of Port Hudson, the three initial pairs of Federal vessels were lashed together, with *Mississippi* following unaccompanied. Only Farragut's own flagship and *Albatross* were successful in maneuvering past the shoals and twists of the river and outrunning enemy guns. Four other vessels were disabled and dropped down the river with the current. *Mississippi,* a venerable oceangoing steam frigate with an illustrious career, enveloped in heavy smoke from all the guns, ran hard aground and endured a prolonged and devastating bombardment as her captain, Melancton Smith, attempted to free her. Eventually abandoned and fired with her dead still aboard, she came off the bank and drifted downriver until she sank in a massive explosion that could be seen for miles up and down the river.

23. In nearby Clinton, Sarah Morgan heard the barrage of the guns and commented in her journal, "What an awful sound! I thought I had heard a bombardment before; but Baton Rouge was child's play compared to this" (Morgan, *The Civil War Diary of a Southern Woman,* ed. Charles East [New York: Simon and Schuster/Touchstone, 1992], 439).

24. Henneberry reports that there had initially been 7 injured in the lifeboat, but "five jumped overboard with the agonies of their wounds."

we got their a good many of her men came on board.[25] It was seen that the *Mississippi* had drifted clear of the Bank and was coming down the river all the after part on fire the flames mounting over her Main and Mizzen mast heads, we shoved out from the shore for fear she got foul of us. When she got opposite the Mortar boats her guns got heated and began to go of which made it a beautiful, but rather dangerous picture. She drifted down the river about 10 miles before her Magazine exploded which shook the *Essex* at that distance the same as if she had run aground. As soon as she had passed, we got some more men of the shore; then crossed the river, and took up our position ahead of the Mortar Boats. By the accounts of the men. I am given to think that all her wounded was left in her to burn, as the only wounded that was saved was the two that came on board of our Boat, by the accounts of the men. The shot was plunging through boath sides of her. They fought the Batteries for one hour after she grounded before they left her; they say that they know of 50 or 60 that was killed or badly wounded before they left, so the wounded in proportion to the killed must be tremendous. They had only 4 boats[26] on board, and the rush to get into them amongst the hury and confusion the wounded men was left to their fate. Out of a crew of 340 men 117 is missing.[27] The *Richmond* had a shot through her steam chest which disabled her and the *Genesee* accompanied her down. the *Richmond* had 3 men killed and 13 wounded. The *Kenio* had her ruder shot away. The *Monongahela* had her

25. By Henneberry's count, *Essex* picked up about sixty sailors and twelve officers: "as they arrived on board they presented a sight truly heart-rending." From the bluffs, Confederate Colonel Isaiah Steedman saw the chaos on the river and the flaming *Mississippi,* "a dying ship manned by dead men," as "the grandest, most sublime and terrible scene of my life." All around him, fellow soldiers raised a piercing rebel yell to signal their victory. *Mississippi*'s executive officer never forgot the sound: in his *Autobiography of George Dewey: Admiral of the Navy* (New York: Scribner's, 1913), he recalls thinking as he heard it for the first and only time in his career, "How they must hate us."

26. That is, lifeboats; those on the starboard side, facing the bluffs, had all been destroyed by enemy fire.

27. Some of the missing that Park counts here were rescued, thirty-nine were captured; upward of sixty aboard the *Mississippi* at the beginning of the action that night were killed. The horror of injured men being "left to their fate" on a flaming and doomed ship obviously haunted Park, though Captain Smith and Lieutenant Dewey later claimed that all survivors were removed before the ship was abandoned. David Farragut, who learned about *Mississippi*'s fate a few days later from a Confederate newspaper, seemed, somewhat pitilessly, to take the casualty count in stride.

wheel ropes shot away and they drifted down together. The men belonging to the *Monongahela* reports that one of the rebel boats tried to ram her when they gave her a shot with her 200 pound rifle which sent her down stern first. It is probably true as two bales of cotton was picked up this morning floating in the river. The *Monongahela* had 5 men killed and 22 wounded. The Flag ship *Hartford* and the *Albatross* were the only two that passed the Batteries. We don't know what their loss were as we have had no communication with them yet. Shortly after they passed the Batteries we could see the reflection of a large fire across the point but dont know whither it was on shore or one of the boats that they had captured as none of the transports was seen under the batteries this morning. This morning at 10 O clock we heard the report of three big guns which we conclude is a sign that the Admiral is all right. General Banks sent an officer to communate with the Admiral. He came on board of our Boat. The General wished to know if the Admiral would cooperate with him for an attack on Port Hudson as he had cut of their railroad communication with Jackson[28] and had his army 4 miles of Port Hudson. As the Admiral was not here I don't know the result. He wished to know what all the Bombardment and firing was about last night.[29]

March 17th

Yesterday a vessel arrived with shells and ammunition for the Mortar Boats. In the afternoon we sent the *Sachem* down the River to communicate with the army. She could not find them. On the passage she found the remains of the *Mississippi,* only her after Magazine had exploded; and her hull had sunk in shoal water. Her fore Mast was still standing and her forward battery out of the water. This morning three transports loaded with troops arrived from

28. That is, Jackson, Louisiana, about twenty miles northeast of Port Hudson.

29. Park's record of the visit of the general's envoy indicates the disconnect between Banks and Farragut, who had been expected to attack Port Hudson together with a joint land and naval force. A letter written by a soldier of the 174th New York Infantry, identified only by the initials "J.M.M.," contains an account of Banks's men, "driving in the enemies pickets" and then halting for the night on the March 14, "snug in our blankets, listening, those that were not too sleepy, to the whistling of the shells over our heads from the gun boats trying to pass the batteries at P. Hudson. . . . The next morning we started back [to Baton Rouge]. Gen. B said we had accomplished all that we came for; well, he was satisfied, so was I" (www.dmna.state.ny.us/historic/reghist/civil/infantry/174thInf/174thInfCWN.htm).

Baton Rouge. They landed on the West side of the River, to try and communicate with the Admiral. In the afternoon the *Monongahela* came up to try the range of her guns on the batteries. She got a little to close, when the lower batter opened fire on her. We went to quarters and threw a few shells into the battery to draw their attention, until the *Monongahela* dropped out of the range. We are anchored within range of their batteries but they have not fired a shot at us yet. I expect they are saving all their ammunition for the wooden Boats, or else they must think that the *Essex* is impregnable.

March 19th

The Soldiers tried to communicate with the Admiral, but could not on account of the Levee being cut above and the Swamp overflowed. Yesterday the *Richmond* picked up a bottle with a letter in it, floating down the River from the Flag ship. They had only one man killed and two wounded. In the evening the transports went down the River. Just as it was getting dark the Soldiers went up the river opposite the Batteries and set fire to a house belonging to Benjamin the Rebel Secretary of War.[30] This morning the three transports returned loading with troops. they landed them on the West side of the River. during the day whenever any of the Soldiers attempted to go in front or past the Batteries the Rebels would open fire on them from the Batteries. The Soldiers kept them pretty close to their guns all day. The Gunboat *Winona* arrived here today from Placquemine. The *Monongahela* and *Genesee* was trying the range of their rifle guns on the Batteries. The *Genesee* made some splendid shooting. Some of her shells exploded right in the batteries. She was laying nearly 5 miles of at the time. This evening just as it was getting dark two Rebel transports came down the river and went under the Batteries. I suppose that the Admiral must have passed Red River and gone up to communicate with the upper fleet.

30. Judah P. Benjamin, born in 1811 in the West Indies to Sephardi Jewish parents, moved in 1828 to New Orleans. He married into a wealthy Creole family and enjoyed prosperity as a planter, and political eminence as a lawyer and statesman. He was appointed by Jefferson Davis as first attorney general of the Confederacy and then in September was made secretary of war. Benjamin never returned to Louisiana; fleeing with Jefferson Davis toward Georgia after Appomattox, he escaped capture and made his way to England under an assumed name. He died in Paris in 1884. For more on Benjamin, and other Southern Jews who served the Confederacy, see Robert N. Rosen, *The Jewish Confederates* (Columbia: University of South Carolina Press, 2000).

March 20th

Last night the Gunboats *Winona* and *Kenio* went down the River during the night. The Rebel transports were very busy going and coming. This morning theire were four of them discharging cargo under the Batteries. In the afternoon the *Monongahela* came alongside and opened fire on the nearest boat with her 200 pound Rifle. She made some very wild shooting. The Rebels hoisted a flag on the stern of their boat in derision. The *Genesee* then opened on them with her 100 pounder, the shots gong so close that three of the boats got up steam and left for a cooler climate.

March 21st

Last night the *Winona* came up the River with two transports loaded with Soldiers and Artillery. They landed on the West side of the River. Our transport has been going and coming all day bringing up troops and supplies. Four of the rebel transports came down under the Batteries this morning, in the afternoon the *Genesee* came alongside and opened fire on them with her rifled gun, at the second shot they all got up stern and skaddaled. We saw a party of Rebs at work in the lower Battery. We gave them a few shells when they left.

March 25th

There has been nothing of importance going on for the last few days. The *Monongahela* has been taking in stores and provisions for the Flag Ship *Hartford*. I suppose she intends to run past the Batteries, the first favourable opportunity. Three deserters came on board from the Batteries. They were conscripts from East Tennessee. They could not give much information as they had only been three weeks there. They head[31] their were between 35 & 40,000 in the Batteries, and the men were on half rations.[32] Yesterday a Company of our Cavlery went out on a reconnicence about 10 miles up the River. They Captured 17 Prisoners and burnt two transports that were taking in wood on the river bank. As they were passing the Batteries on the road down they[33] opened fire on them with shells doing no damage to our men.

31. He intends "heard."

32. The reduction in rations reflects the impact of the Union presence above Port Hudson (i.e., Farragut's two vessels), making supplying the fort more difficult.

33. That is, the Confederates.

During the night some of the Soldiers went up and set fire to a large Suga house that was in front of the Batteries to spite the Rebs, they opened a heavy fire on them without doing any damage to our men. To day the Soldiers burnt another Sugar Mill. In the afternoon some of the Artillery went up on the West side and opened fire on the Batteries. Most of their shot fell short. The Bebs did not reply.

March 27th

Yesterday morning a transport arrived with a mail. Soon after all the Soldiers on the West side of the River embarked on transports and went down towards Baton Rouge. In the Afternoon all the Mortar Boats was towed down the River. After dark we got under weigh and droped down the river about a mile when we anchored about a cable's length ahead of the rest of the Fleet.

March 28th

Last night the *Monongahela* left for New Orleans. Today the remainder of the Fleet left for Baton Rouge and vicinity Leaving the *Essex* here to look at Port Hudson, and I suppose to give them warning when the enemy sends their rams and cotton boats down to attack us, so they will have time to clear out.[34]

March 31st

Nothing of importance has occurred since last date. The *Winona* came up each day to see that we were all right. This afternoon we got up anchor and dropped down the river to the foot of Prophets Island. In the evening three Contrabands came on board. They brought no information.

April 3rd

Nothing has occurred since last date. We picked up a letter that the rebels had stuck in a piece of drift wood and sent down from the Fort. They wished to know why Mr. Banks and his Yankees did not attack the Batteries, also an invitation for the Fleet to attack them promising not to sink more than half of the Fleet and four of the Mortar Boats, and a lot more nonsense.

34. *Essex* will be, up until the siege of the fort begins in earnest on May 8, the chief (and often only) Union vessel assigned to Port Hudson. Park's mordant take on the situation is that *Essex* is essentially the canary in the coal mine for the rest of the fleet.

The *Winona* came up yesterday and anchored alongside. This evening three Contrabands came on board. They brought news that the rams and Cotton boats were getting ready to attack us. We got up anchor and moved up close to the point of the Island.

April 6th

Yesterday morning we got under weigh and proceeded down the river to Baton Rouge. On the passage down we passed the *Genessee* about 10 miles below Prophets Island. The *Winona* anchored in company with her. We arrived at Baton Rouge in the forenoon and anchored alongside a Coal Brig. General Banks has left here and gone down the river with the most of his army leaving here one Brigade to protect the City. They expect the Rebels will attack the City every day.[35] The *Richmond* and Mortar Boats are laying here. We took in Coal today and cleaned the Boilers out.

April 7th

Last night we heard heavy firing in the direction of Port Hudson. We got up steam and proceeded up the river and anchored where the *Genesee* was laying. This morning we all got under weigh and proceeded up the river, the *Genesee* and *Winona* leading. We went up the passage between the Island and the Batteries. When we came in sight of the Batteries we found that the Rebels had cut down all the Trees between the lower Battery and the place where the Mortar Boats lay. We dropped down the river on the West side where the *Genesee* and *Winona* were laying. They had captured three Prisoners and they report that two of the upper Fleet and the *Albitross*[36] were above the Batteries. The *Albitross* had captured one of their transports and burnt her. The Batteries opened fire on her which accounts for the heavey firing we heard. The *Genesee* opened fire on the Batteries with her rifle firing at intervals during the afternoon as signal to let the upper Fleet know that we were laying here. We dropped down below the Island and made fast to the West bank of

35. Such apprehensions proved unwarranted; following the Battle of Baton Rouge in August 1862, Confederates troops never attempted to retake the city.

36. That is, USS *Albatross*, the vessel that had safely passed the batteries with the flagship *Hartford* on March 14.

the river. We sent a party on shore to cut down the trees on a point so that we could get a good view up the River.

April 8th

Last night the *Winona* hailed as she passed. She reported that two Contrabands had come from the Flag ship on board the *Genesee* and they report that an officer from the flag Ship had left her one hour before they did, in a Skiff to communicate with us. The *Winona* was on her road down to Baton Rouge to see if the skiff had passed us in the dark. This afternoon the Tug Boat *Ida* brought us news of his safe arrival at Baton Rouge. Also Admiral Farragut's dispatch to communicate with him tonight (Wednesday). We took in our lines and proceeded up the river and anchored at the head of the Island.

April 10th

Yesterday the *Winona* arrived from Baton Rouge. This morning we got under weigh and proceeded down the River about 10 miles to a large Crevasse where the water was overflowing the whole Country to get some sugar for the Ships use from one of the sugar mills that was surrounded by water. We dispatched a boat in for a load. When the *Winona* came down and reported that the Rebel ram *Webb* had arrived under the Batteries. The *Winona* turned and went back again. As soon as the boat returned with the sugar we got under weigh and went up the river, and anchored at the head of the Island ahead of the other boats.

April 13th

Nothing of importance has occurred since last date. Last night we got up anchor and made fast to the Island. This morning some of the Rebels were showing themselves a little too close to the Ship when we opened on them with our Rifled Guns. They Skdadled. The *Winona* got under weigh and gave them a parting salute. She then crossed the River and made fast to the West Bank.

April 15th

Last night the *Richmond* arrived to communicate with the Admiral. She had a stand rigged at her Main royal Mast head, so that the Signal Man could see the Admiral Ship over the trees across the point. This morning the Admiral fired three guns to let us know that he was above. We answered it by firing two five second shells into the air. They held communication across the point with greatest of ease.[37] We have not heard what it was about yet.

April 16th

This morning the *Genessee* went down to Baton Rouge. In the afternoon heavey firing was heard in the direction of the Admiral's Ship. The *Richmond* tried to signalize to know what the meaning of it was, but could not attract their attention.

April 20th

There has been nothing of importance since last date. Last night the *Genessee* arrived from Baton Rouge. This morning the *Genessee* and *Winona* went down the River. Every day the whole of our ships Company goes ashore on the Island to amuse themselves. Some playing games some Shooting and some Fishing.[38]

April 23rd

Two days ago twenty Contrabands came down on the West side of the river from Point Coupee. They say they were starving. Their Master sent them down for the Yankee's to feed them. Last night the *Genessee* arrived. Wee sent

37. This was greatly assisted, no doubt, by the earlier removal of trees on the point (April 7) between the two arms of the river. Signaling with flags in a secure coded language was a sophisticated and highly specialized skill; navy signal books in the Civil War were weighted with lead so that they would sink when thrown overboard, making it impossible for the enemy to recover them. The accusation that Captain Henry Erben of USS *Sumter* had carelessly let the ship's signal book fall into Confederate hands the previous summer when he abandoned ship at Bayou Sara is part of what prompted a formal investigation of his actions (see August 10, 1862, above, and note 65).

38. This is Park's only reference to recreation or games in his diary; he seems not, by temperament, naturally drawn to such amusements. Henneberry, by contrast, is eager to get off the boat whenever he can, is a serious fisherman, enjoys roughhousing and skylarking and all forms of diversion from the routine of sailoring. During this relatively long lull between engagements, the men of *Essex* formed baseball teams, fifteen to a side, and, according to Henneberry, played frequently and earnestly on Prophet's Island.

the niggers down to Baton Rouge. To day the Admiral came down the River and fired his signal guns. The *Richmond* has been making signals to him all the afternoon.

April 25th

Yesterday evening the Admiral went up the River. This morning two Transports arrived from New York. One of them brought Potatoes, Onions, and fresh Beef packed in ice. The other Transport brought a Mail and took five of our men home whose time had expired.[39] The Transports and *Genessee* went down the River in the Afternoon. The later vessel went to join the Blockading Squadron of Mobile. In the evening we got under weigh with the *Richmond* and proceeded down the river. the *Richmond* went down to Baton Rouge. We came down to the foot of the Island and made fast to the West bank of the River.

April 27th

This morning we got under weigh and proceeded down the River about four miles to Lobdales Plantation[40] where we came to anchor and sent a party on shore to procure some sugar for Ships use. On the road down the *Richmond* passed us going up, in the Afternoon she passed us on the road down to Baton Rouge.

39. Henneberry's notation for the same day is more specific. He lists two officers discharged for "conduct unbecoming gentlemen" (fighting and drunkenness)—2nd Assistant Engineer Mr. [W. H.] Manning, and Acting Gunner Mr. [C. W.] Long; two sent home on sick leave—D. W. Fuglestead and James Waiting (?); two whose term of service had expired—D. Crew and Thomas Gramon (?); and Robert McQuinn, who for unspecified reasons is "ordered to report to New York."

40. The W. S. Lobdell and Co. sugar plantation was on the west side of the Mississippi between Prophet's Island and Baton Rouge. A detailed color map (1858) showing landowner names along the river between Natchez and Baton Rouge may be found at the Louisiana Digital Map Library: http://usgwarchives.org/maps/louisiana. Sarah Morgan's family sheltered briefly with the Lobdells in August 1862 when they fled Baton Rouge; Abraham Lobdell was himself shortly forced to evacuate with his family—his slaves seized and his property stripped and vandalized by Federals (Morgan, *Civil War Diary*, 206–8). By the time Park writes here, the plantation was abandoned, and Union forces simply helped themselves to such goods as they required.

May 1st

Since last date the Tug Boat *Ida* brought up 200 bushels of Coal for us. This afternoon the *Richmond* passed us on the road to Port Hudson. We hove up anchor and followed her. She anchored abreast of Prophet Island. We anchored ahead of her.

May 3rd

The Admiral was expected above the batteries yesterday for to communicate but he has not made his appearance yet. This morning a transport arrived from Baton Rouge. She brought the intelligence that two Regments of Illinois Cavalry had arrived at Baton Rouge from Tennessee in 15 days. They had marched through the whole of the Southern Confederacy. During the Raid they had five skrimeges and only lost 1 man killed and 5 wounded. They captured and paroled 1200 prisoners and brought 60 into Baton Rouge. They destroyed 200 Railway Cars, 10 Engines, 25 Depots, 85 Railway Bridges and immense quantaties of stores, besides destroying the Mobile and Jackson Railroad and all the railroads and Telegraph stations in their route. It was the most daring and successful Raid that has been accomplished this war.[41]

May 5th

This morning the Transport *Iberville* came up the River with a Flag of truce and 250 Prisoners to exchange. Shortly after the Rebel transport *Starlight* came down the River for the same purpose, when both boats made a landing at the Island and exchanged their Prisoners, and then proceeded to their respective destinations. In the forenoon the Admiral came in sight above the point and fired a number of guns. The *Richmond* has been making signal's to

41. Grierson's Raid, as it came to be known, was indeed the most audacious and triumphant Union cavalry expedition of the war. Colonel Benjamin Grierson (a former music teacher, who had overcome a long-standing fear of horses) led a brigade consisting of the Sixth and Seventh Illinois and Second Iowa cavalry regiments (1,700 men, though nearly 200 of the slowest were sent home after three days) through hostile territory untraveled to that point by any Union military personnel. Leaving La Grange, Tennessee, on April 17, he and his men reached Baton Rouge on May 2, having wreaked havoc all along the way and effectively distracted Confederate attention and resources from Grant's army, which was approaching Vicksburg along the west bank of the Mississippi. Some of the numbers Park gives here warrant correction by official records.

him all day. The Tug boat *Ida* has been sent down with dispatches, to bring up the Mortar Boats and all available vessels in the River.

May 7th

Yesterday the Admiral went up the River. In the afternoon the *Ida* brought up a Mortar boat. To day the *Ida* brought up another Mortar Boar and a Mail, also Signal men from the Army to our boat.

May 8th

This morning we got under weigh and proceeded up towards the Batteries and anchored about a mile from the lower one. The remainder of the Mortar Boats came up from Baton Rouge, when the Transport *Sallie Robinson* and *Ida* commenced towing them into position astern of us. At 1.30 P.M. Our Boat and the Mortars opened fire on the Batteries.[42] We gave all our attention to the lower one. We kept up a heavey fire for one hour and a half when we ceased firing. Nearly every shell went into the Battery. The Mortar kept up a fire for two hours. We sent a party to cut down some trees and set fire to a fence about half a mile from the Battery which they accomplished. The Reb's never attempted to disturb them, in fact they have never fired a shot at us yet. The party also captured a bale of cotton which they rolled into the river and one of the men got on top of it and paddled it alongside. It was used by the Rebels for their Pickets to lay behind the last time we were here.

May 9th

Last night the Mortar boats opened fire at 11 O'clock, and kept up a continual bombardment for two hours. We fired a round from our bow guns to help the general uproar. The Rebels commenced firing across the river I suppose thinking that some of the boats were going to run past. This morning we got under weigh and anchored about 300 yard's nearer the Batteries. The Mortar boats moved up to the place we left and opened fire on them. They ceased firing at dinner time. In the afternoon the *Richmond* came up alongside of

42. The bombardment of Port Hudson, commenced now in earnest, will continue for two months. Upriver, the campaign that will ultimately subdue Vicksburg is well under way, with Grant's Army of the Tennessee being supported by the upper fleet of the Mississippi Squadron under the command of David Dixon Porter.

us and opened fire with her 100 pound rifle to try the range. She fired a few rounds and then went back to her old position.

May 10th

Last night the Bummers[43] opened fire on the Batteries from 10 to 11 O'clock. During the night the Rebels threw up a fresh earthwork and placed Cotton bales in front of it. This morning the Mortars opened fire at 4 O'clock which the Rebs replied to from the new battery and the lower one. We beat to Quarters and opened fire on them which we kept up for two hours and a quarter when the batteries ceased firing. Just before the fireing ceased the *Richmond* came up and delivered her broadside and then went down to her old position. The Rebs made very poor shooting. They only struck the *Essex* once and that did not penetrate the Iron. Three of the Mortar boats were struck once each without doing any damage. I don't know what damage our shots did as it was dark when we commenced and not wind enough to carry the smoke away. We were obliged to watch the flash of their guns, so that we could point our guns in the right direction. After we ceased fireing the Rebels rolled all the cotton that was in front of the new work into the bush out of our sight. I expect they will have a strong battery erected before tomorrow morning. This evening we put a coating of tallow on our forward casemate to help the shot to glance off.[44]

May 11th

Last night the Bummers kept up a heavy fire on the batteries from 12 to 1 O'clock. After they ceased firing. We all dropped down to our old position which we left on Saturday. This morning the *Iberville* came up with a flag of truce and 500 prisoners to exchange. She went to within half a mile of the

43. "Bummers" is a Civil War term frequently used pejoratively to denote malingerers, men who hang behind in order to scavenge. For sailors of the inland navy, however, "bummers" was a slang term for the mortar schooners and their crews, presumably a variant on "bombers."

44. This was a tactic used by sailors on both Confederate and Union ironclads: a thick coating of rendered animal fat (tallow was used principally for making soap and candles) would be spread on the casemate as a lubricant so that shot and shell would slide or deflect off the surface. At Hampton Roads, CSS *Virginia*'s sloping sides were covered with tallow; during the fighting the fat actually caught fire so that "it seemed that she was literally frying from the burning grease from one end to the other."

lower battery, when the Rebel boat *Starlight* came down and took the Prisoners on board. The Rebel Officers that came with the *Starlight* were kind enough to exchange papers with us. Their papers contained the account of a battle in Virginia between Hooker's and Lee's forces, one account states that the Union army was victorious, the other account that the Rebels were. I don't know which is correct but am given to think by their allowing a partial defeat that the Union army is victorius.[45]

May 13th

On the night of the 11th The Mortars kept up a rapid fire for an hour. We fired several rounds from our guns. Last night the Mortars fired for one hour and a half. This morning the Rebels were seen at work reparing damages, when we opened fire on them with our guns. The first shell made them "Skeddadle." Two Contrabands came on board the *Richmond* to day from the Batteries. They report that they are evacuating Port Hudson, and that the most of the troops had left their this morning to intercept General Grant, who was marching on Jackson. There is very few men to be seen walking around inside the Batteries to day. We also miss a number of their guns which were in sight yesterday.

May 14th

Last night the Bummers opened fire for one hour. This Afternoon the *Genessee* came up from New Orleans. She came up astern of us and commenced firing at the upper Batteries with her 100 pound Rifle. She made some excellent shots. In the evening she dropped down and anchored alongside of the *Richmond.*

May 17th

Nothing of importance has occurred since last date. The Mortars fires one hour each night. This morning the Transport *Antona* came up with stores for the Fleet. In the evening the Mortars and *Essex* opened fire on the lower

45. Newspapers were prized by the combatants but notoriously undependable, as local "Rebel" and "Yankee" papers tended to stress their own side's strength and the enemy's weakness. The battle referenced here is Chancellorsville, a major Confederate victory by the Army of Northern Virginia, as the sailors were later to learn (see May 23).

batteries to obtain the range. We ceased firing after half an hours practice. The *Genessee* came up and opened fire. She got a little closer than the Rebels liked when they opened fire on her from the Middle battery (or Citadel) without doing any damage. The *Genessee* anchored astern of us.

May 18th

This morning the *Antona* came alongside and supplied us with Powder and Shell. In the Afternoon the *Monongahela* came up from New Orleans with Admiral Farragutt on board. He left the *Hartford* in Red River and came down the Atchafalaya River in a transport to Breashear City and from their to New Orleans. The *Richmond* saluted him with 17 guns.[46] A party of our Soldiers went up the West side of the River this afternoon and captured 12 prisoners and about 50 head of cattle in front of the batteries with loosing a man.[47] In the evening the *Monongahela* got under weigh and went down the river.

May 20th

The Mortars still fire at night. This morning the Gunboat *Kineo* came up from New Orleans. She brought up 100 rifle shells for the *Essex*. she anchored astern of the Mortar Boats. The *Genesee* went down the river as the *Kineo* came up. A part of our army has left Baton Rouge and are now in the rear of Port Hudson. We heard heavy firing in that direction this afternoon. The river is falling rapidly. It has fell three feet this last week.

May 22nd

Yesterday we heard heavy fireing in the direction of our troops. This morning a white Officer and a company of niggers came from the army. They brought a few prisoners which they captured on the road. The Officer reports that the fireing was caused by some of the Nigger regiements skirmishing with Rebel

46. This is the first time the men have seen their flag officer since March 14, when he managed to get past the Port Hudson batteries with *Hartford* and *Albatross*. Though he had come downriver a number of times to communicate with the fleet by signaling across the point (see, e.g., April 15), prudence dictated that he rejoin his men below the fort by a roundabout route. Military tradition assigns the number of guns used to honor an officer or head of state according to rank; an "Under Secretary of the Navy" merits a 17-gun salute.

47. That is, "without losing a man."

Pickets. He gives them great praise but thinks they are too rash and all wishing for a fight.[48] This afternoon several transports loaded with troops came up and landed them opposite the island on the Port Hudson side of the river out of sight of the Batteries. The *Genessee* came up and took her position on the West side of the river to prevent any of the rebel pickets or spies seeing what was doing. The *Richmond* has been signalizing all the afternoon across the Point to some of the upper Fleet. I expect this place will be attacked soon.[49] The Mortars still keep the Secesh awake each night.

May 23rd

We have heard some good news from the Upper Fleet to day. They report that Bank's and his army crossed the river at Bayou Sara and are now three miles from Port Hudson. Also that General Grant and Sherman had attacked the Rebels (in Mississippi) under Johnstone and defeated them capturing 61 Guns. In the afternoon we got under weigh and crossed to see what effect the Mortar shells took. They fired three shells apiece when we were over and made some excellent shots. After they ceased firing we took up our old position. In the evening the *Monongahela* came up with the Admiral on board. She brought some percussion shells for our rifels. Also a Mail with New York papers confirming the repulse of Hookers army in Virginia.

May 24th

This morning we picked up a piece of paper floating down on a piece of wood from Port Hudson. Wrote on it were these words. Farragutt you renegade what is the good of throwing away so many shells. That does no harm. If you want Port Hudson come and take it. you will find plenty of Cotton. "Signed." Stonewall.[50] This afternoon at 1.30 P.M. we got under weigh and proceeded up toward the Batteries on a reconnicence. (The Mortars opened fire when

48. The officers who led colored units spoke frequently of this combination of admirable valor and occasionally dangerous impetuousness and lack of discipline.

49. The arrival of large numbers of ground forces, the return of Farragut, and the busy "signalizing" of *Richmond* all suggest to Park, quite accurately, the beginning of a major joint offensive to subdue Port Hudson.

50. Stonewall Jackson had actually died two weeks earlier, on May 10, from pneumonia and complications from amputation surgery after he was wounded by friendly fire at Chancellors-

we started.) We found the lower Batteries deserted. When we opened fire on the Citadel, which the Rebs returned, we still kept going ahead. One of their shells struck our forward port, exploding and wounding slightly three of No. three guns crew. As soon as their wounds were dressed they returned to their stations. In the meantime the *Monongahela, Richmond, Genessee* and *Kineo* came up within a good shelling distance astern of us and opened with their rifled guns. We kept up a heavy fire on the Citadel when the rebs were obliged to "Skeddale" although we could see their Officers trying to bring them up to the scratch two different times. At last we dismounted two of their guns. When three more of their bluff batteries opened on us we very soon paid our respects to them. When two of them ceased fireing at this time the admiral made our recall when we dropped down to our old station and anchored at 5 P.M. I think if the troops had been ready we might have carried the place by storm in a very short time. We have heard fireing in the direction of the Army all the evening. The *Essex* was struck four times without doing any damage. Their were no one hurt on any of the other Boats. The Admiral gave the *Essex* great praise. He said he never saw quicker or better fireing in all his life.[51]

May 25th

To day a party of the Illinois Cavalry came through the lower batteries and came down alongside. Their Officers came on board.[52] They report that General Sherman had arrived from New Orleans with his forces and that Port Hudson was surrounded. They were going to occupy the lower batteries to night ready to storm the Citadel tomorrow. In the evening the Fleet moved up and anchored abreast of us. We moved up and anchored abreast of the lower batteries. The Mortars are moveing up and takeing their position between the Admiral and our boat.

---

ville. That the Confederates attribute such a taunt to him and that Park does not comment may suggest that news of Jackson's demise, despite the newspapers, had not yet reached troops along the Mississippi.

51. This is a nice inclusion in a diary that lacks any hint of self-conscious bravado; the commendation for good work from the fleet commander obviously meant a great deal to Park.

52. These are some of the men from Grierson's Raid, mentioned with such awe by Park above (May 3). Having recovered in Baton Rouge from their dramatic overland expedition, they are now part of Banks's large force.

May 26th

Last night the vessels above the Batteries commenced firing at 12 O'clock and kept up a heavy fire until 5 O'clock this morning. When the Mortars opened and fired for two hours. Their has been fireing at intervals all last night and to day between the Rebs and our troops. this evening they kept up a very heavy connonade for about one and a half hours when we saw a back smoke rise above the trees and the fireing ceased. This afternoon we saw a party at work on their breastworks. We opened fire and dispersed them. There is a rumour flying round that we are going to storm the place tomorrow. The Mortars is to keep up a continual bombardment to night and the Fleet is to get under weigh at 4 O'clock. The Troops is to make the advance at the same time. W.L.P.[53]

May 27th

Last night the bummers kept up a continual fire all night. The army opened at daybreak and has kept up a continual roar of Artillery all day excepting a short intervil at noon. At 7 O'clock in the morning all the Fleet got under weigh and opened fire on the batteries. We went in the *Essex* to within three hundred years of their lower Redout and silenced two of their batteries. The wooden boats were half a mile astern of us. We were engaged about 1 hour and half when the Admiral made our recall and we dropped down to our Anchorage. The Rebs made very poor shooting. They did not strike us once. The army has met with some successes and some disasters. The right wing is commanded by Banks in person, the Left by Sherman and the Centre by Arguer and Witzel.[54] In the morning Bank's troops made a rush on the upper battery and captured itt, turning the guns of it on the rebels. They have been trying to drive him out of it all day but has not succeeded. Witzel in the Centre

53. Here, William Park signs his initials—apparently in anticipation of mortal combat the next day. It is the only point in the diary that he does so and would seem to suggest some portent of his death.

54. In addition to Banks, the generals mentioned here are Thomas W. Sherman, Christopher Columbus Augur (see January 22, above), and Godfrey Weitzel. Though Banks had the overwhelming advantage in numbers, he did not give a specific time for each unit to act; Weitzel, with Cuvier Grover, attacked the north and northeast at dawn. Augur and Sherman attacked the east and southeast at noon. The piecemeal and ill-considered attack across treacherous terrain resulted in a huge number of Union casualties, despite significant odds in their favor. Park's account paints a generous view of apparent Union successes on the field.

captured 700 prisoners and a battery of Artillery. In the evening Sherman received a flag of truce stating that they would surrender if allowed to march out with the honour of War, which our Generals refused. The rebels then stated that they would fight as long as they had a man left And made a dash at Sherman's position and drove him back with loss. Sherman then received reinforcements and drove the rebels back inside their entrenchments. As it was getting dark the rebels opened fire from two batteries on Banks position. The Fleet got under weigh and proceeded up to draw some of the fire from him. as soon as the rebels saw us, they ceased fireing and we dropped back to our old position as it was getting dark. Both Sides ceased fireing at 8 O'clock.

May 28th

During the night we could hear a tremendous fire of Musketry in the direction of our right wing. We heard to day it was caused by the rebels recapturing the battery that our troops captured in the morning. The Rebels during the night mounted two rifle guns on the lower redout for the benefit of the *Essex.* at half past 6 they opened fire from them, also one gun from the Citadel which we replied to. Also the Bummers. The remainder of the Fleet dropped out of range. We fired for about 1 hour and half when our ammunition ran short and then went to breakfast. As soon as we ceased fireing the rebels got an accurate aim, maeking every shot tell. The shots that missed the *Essex* struck the Mortars astern of us. They kept up a heavy fire for three hours. When one of the Mortar shells fell upon and disabled one of their guns they took the other one out of range and ceased fireing. They struck the *Essex* 12 times.[55] Two fifty pound rifle shells penetrated our forward casemate without doing any damage. One of the Mortar boats was struck 16 times. Their were no one hurt on our side. In the afternoon we got a supply of ammunition from the *Richmond.* The troops on both sides has been burying the dead all day under a flag of truce. The loss on our side was severe. General Sherman was wounded.[56] This evening just at 7 O'clock the time allowed for the flag of truce to expire. We heard heavey

55. In Henneberry's colorful description, they "plowed up our decks as good as an Illinois farmer could do."

56. The severity of Sherman's wounds, requiring amputation of his right leg, prompted a premature obituary in his hometown paper in Newport, Rhode Island. Though his active war service ended, Sherman returned to an administrative post in New Orleans until the end of the war and stayed with the army until 1870.

artillery fired three or four times in rapid succession and then a continual roar of Musketry which lasted for one hour and a half and then ceased. We are now in great suspence to know what it means.

May 29th

An Officer came on board to day from the Army. He reports that the fireing was caused by the Rebels making a Sortie trying to cut their way out through our lines. They were repulsed with tremendous slaughter. Last night the Mortars opened on the batteries throwing a shell every five minutes. The rebels replied with one of their rifled guns from the lower redout fireing at the flash of the Mortars. Some of their shots came rather to close to be comfortable. At 3 O'clock we ceased fireing and dropped down out of range taking up our old positions what we occupied when we first came here.

May 31st

Last night and night before the Mortars fired from 11 to 4 O'clock. The rebels opened from their lower redout in reply. Only one of their shots grazed us. This evening the Mortars opened on the batteries. The *Essex, Monongahela, Gennesee* and *Richmond* opened with their rifled guns. The enemy replied, the first shot penetrating our forward casemate, doing no damage. None of the other vessels were struck. We fired for one hour and then ceased.

June 2nd

The mortars keep bombarding each night. The *Antona* came up and supplied us with ammunition. The troops are building Batteries to plant siege guns in. They are to be manned by Sailors from the Fleet. Some Soldier Officers came on board this evening. They report that Weitzel's division has captured the whole of the upper breastworks but cannot advance on account of the Redouts on the inside the enemy's breastworks. Weitzel has made our front batteries. They also report that our forces captured 799 Cavalry without fireing a shot. They were coming to reinforce the Garrison.

June 4th

The bombardment still continues. Last night the Rebels opened fire on our troops from their heavy guns shelling the woods where our men were building batteries. The Mortars and *Gennessee* commenced shelling the batteries to draw their attention. The fire was kept up on boath till two O'clock this morning. In the forenoon about six hundered niggers came down on the West side of the river opposite the vessels. The *Landies* came up and took them down the river. In the Afternoon the Naval Brigade went on shore under the command of the First Leaut. of the *Richmond.* Their were four Guns Crews, three of them belonging to the *Richmond* and one to the *Essex.* They are to work four nine inch Dalghren guns that the soldiers has got in position.[57]

June 5th

The Bummers still keep the enemy awake. They shelled the batteries for two hours this Forenoon. At dinner time General Dwight[58] and Staff came on board. The General says they are only waiting for the Naval Battery to get ready when they will open the Ball with 80 guns. He expects Port Hudson to fall before a week expires. This evening the *Ida* came alongside with Coal. The Mortars gave them another stirring up this evening.

June 7th

The bombardment is still kept up. Yesterday the batteries commenced shelling the troops. We opened fire which soon silenced them. we kept up the fire for half an hour and then ceased. Some of our men came down from the battery this morning. the[59] say that they can only work by night at the battery as the Rebels keeps shelling them by day. they will not have the guns in position before tomorrow night.

57. Park will later volunteer to replace one of the sailors manning the guns on shore after the latter comes down sick (see July 5, below, and appendix 3).

58. General William Dwight's service at Port Hudson was something of a second coming. He had begun the war in the eastern theater and been severely wounded and left for dead on the field at Williamsburg on May 5, 1862. Found by Confederates, he was taken to a prisoner of war camp, where he recovered and was then released in a prisoner exchange on November 15. Despite his near-death experience, he survived the war. Two younger brothers died in the conflict: Wilder Dwight was mortally wounded at Antietam; Captain Howard Dwight was killed by guerillas during the Port Hudson campaign.

59. "They."

June 10th

The Mortars fire each night from 10 O'clock to 4 in the morning. Yesterday the *Antona* came up. she brought the *Essex* a 100 pound Parrott Rifle. We took on board the Carriage and Ammunition. this morning we went alongside the *Richmond* and took the gun on board. The Army has got several 8 and 10 inch Mortars in position. Last night and to day they have keept up a heavy fire on the Rebel works.

June 12th

The bombardment is still kept up. The army keeps shelling night and day. Yesterday we tried our 100 pound rifle on the Batteries. She answers first rate, every shot taking effect. To day some of the Army Officers came on board. They report that they had received news through Rebel sources that Grant had captured Vicksburgh. Mr. Sheppard the Officer that has charge of the guns crew on shore from our boat came on board this morning. he say's they have kept up a steady fire for three day's and nights on the Rebel works. they have made a breach in the intrenchments in two places by the Naval Battery and dismounted two of the Rebel guns. the enemy don't return the fire from their big guns. they reply with Musketry. The deserters that come in report that it is rather hot inside.[60] We can see several tents underneath the bluffs close to the river. The *Gennessee* and *Richmond* had a little amusement to day shelling them out with their Rifle guns.

June 13th

This Forenoon we got under weigh and proceeded up toward the batteries. At 11 O'clock we opened fire on the lower redout and made a signal for the Mortars to commence fireing. the *Monongahela, Richmond* and *Gennessee* remained at anchor fireing their Rifled guns. at 12 O'clock we ceased fireing and dropped down to our old anchorage. The Rebels did not return the fire. After dinner we got under weigh and came to anchor opposite the old lower battery. The *Gennessee* came up and anchored on the opposite side of

60. The increasing flow of deserters may reflect the bad news for the Confederacy coming down the river from Vicksburg, now under prolonged and devastating siege; Confederate officers at Port Hudson commented on the tide of defections and the way it impacted both strategy and morale.

the river. As soon as she had anchored the Rebels opened fire on her which she returned. We assisted her with our guns and soon silenced the battery. The Rebels opened from two other batteries and kept up a steady fire until 4 O'clock when we went to supper and the *Gennessee* dropped down about 400 yards when they ceased fireing. After super the Mortars were towed up and took position astern of us. As soon as they anchored they opened fire and obtained their range then ceased fireing.

June 14th

Yesterday General Banks sent in a flag of truce demanding the surrender of Port Hudson. General Gardiner (the Rebel General) replied that he would not surrender as long "as he had a Man left or a horse to eat."[61] Last night the Mortars opened at 11 O'clock firing at five minutes intervals. at 12 a dispatch came from General Banks to fire for two hours as rapidly as they could. as soon as they commenced the Rebels opened fire on us with two Rifled guns. all their shots went over doing no damage. at two O'clock we ceased fireing. Between three and four O'clock Our shore batteries opened fire keeping up a continues and heavy fire untill 9 O'clock. Sometimes their would be a lull for a minute and then it would commence with redoubled fury and volleys of Musketry with occasional Cheering. We were all in great suspense to know the news. In the forenoon some of the soldiers Officers came on board. they report that Generals Weitzel and Grover had captured the upper works. as soon as our men captured the works the Rebels tried to cut their way out through the lower end but the Indinia battery and Michgan troops that were stationed their repulsed them with tremendous slaughter. Their dead can be plainly seen stretched out on their earthworks and along the side of the bluff. the Rebels dare not remove them for our sharpshooters. Skirmishing and fireing has Been continued the whole day.

June 18th

Their has been nothing going on of any importance the last few days. Generals Witezel and Grover were obliged to evacuate the works through not being

61. While this is one of the more colorful responses to a demand for surrender, it is characteristic of Confederate tenacity and bravado throughout the war, even when odds were dramatically against them.

supported. Several of our regiments Skeddaled. they would not face the music.[62] Yesterday and today our Pickets and the Rebels on the lower end of the works made an agreement not to fire on each other. Our troops is advancing and throwing up new batteries right under their nose. they can see our men at work not more than 400 yards from them. we are getting a thirteen gun battery in position that will sweep the whole of their works. The reason they don't fire they say they will not be the first to break the agreement and our Sharpshooters wont fire until the battery is completed. Their is good feeling between both parties.[63] Yesterday our Captain and doctor went up and spoke to some of the Rebel Officers and gave them some papers. The Rebel Officers think they can hold it against all the force that Banks can bring against itt. The Privates told our Pickets that it was only madness to attemp to storm it. if we would only lay still for two weeks they would be obliged to surrender for the want of Provision. The *Monongahela* went down the River this evening to Placquemine where the guerrellies is at work. they burnt the government stores there and three Transports.

June 21st

Nothing of importance since last date. The Mortars has ceased bombarding. the Generals are afraid that they will hurt our own men. The *Tennessee* arrived with Stores and ammunition for the Fleet last night. She went down the river. this evening the Tug came alongside with coal.

62. Though Park reports this obvious lack of discipline very matter-of-factly, his disdain for such shirking is clear. The failure of Union command to effect an orderly and decisive victory at Port Hudson, despite outnumbering the Confederate defenders four to one, is generally laid at the feet of General Nathaniel Banks, a political general with few military skills and little effective authority on the field (see, e.g., the biography by James G. Hollandsworth Jr., *Pretense of Glory: The Life of General Nathaniel P. Banks* [Baton Rouge: Louisiana State University Press, 1998]). Union casualties in the failed assault of June 14 were 1,792; Confederate, 47.

63. This entry affords a remarkable insight into the etiquette of war still fought on intimate face-to-face footing, where hostile parties not only agree to a temporary cease-fire but talk candidly about potential outcomes: Union officers sharing newspapers (likely detailing the deteriorating situation for the defenders of Vicksburg); Confederate officers responding that they believe their dug-in troops can hold out perpetually against the ineffectual Banks; ordinary rebel soldiers confessing that attack is hardly necessary, since supplies are dwindling so rapidly. It was indeed, in the end, siege rather than storm that quelled Port Hudson. There is something hauntingly poignant about Park's comment that "there is a good feeling between both parties," in a fierce and bloody campaign that took more than five thousand lives.

June 27th

Yesterday our batteries were completed. in the afternoon they opened on the lower redout. The Mortar boats opened fire at the same time. the *Essex* and *Gennessee* assisted with their rifled guns. The rebels replied from four batteries directing their shots at our boat. In the middle of the fireing the *Richmond* came up the river a little way and fired two broadsides. most of the shells exploded over our boat. None of them reached the battery.[64] She then dropped down and anchored out of range. We fired untill supper time and as soon as supper was over we commenced fireing again until dark. The rebels kept up a heavy fire all the time. We silenced one of their batteries. they struck us three times. two of them glanced of our casemates. the other one a 10 inch shot passed through one of our Smoke Stacks, nocked the trail of one of our 12 pound Howitzers through the upper deck taking one of the beams in the passage into the coal bunker on top of the boilers, glancing through the end of the bunker through the Cook's galley into the Wheel, narrowly escapeing one of the steam pipes. no one was hurt on our side. This morning we fired a few rounds but had to cease on account of our Sharpshooters who were digging rifle pits close under the rebel batteries.

June 28th

The shore batteries still keep up the fire on the redout. This morning the *Gennessee* was sent down to Donldsonville. the rebels were marching on that place. We can see the Rebel Sharpshooters and our men fireing at each other all day long. no sooner is a head or hand seen above the rifle pitts than twenty shots is fired at it. Our men are making zig-zag approaches up the rebel works. They are nearly up out the top of the bluff.

July 1st

The bombardment is still kept up. Last night a party of our men made a dash into the rebel rifle pitt on a reconnicence. The rebels repulsed them with a loss of nine men. Our men captured a Secesh Officer and brought him out with them. Last night a dispatch came on board requesting our vessel to assist a new battery that was building on the West side of the river in front

64. Henneberry quotes Captain Caldwell as saying caustically that "two more broadsides from the *Richmond* would silence the *Essex*."

of the rebel works when they opened fire. This forenoon the rebels opened fire on them. We got under weigh and proceeded across the river where we opened fire with our 100 pound rifle. The rebels ceased fireing at the battery and commenced paying their respects to our boat with six of their guns. The *Richmond* opened fire on the upper guns with her rifle. We fired until 12 O'clock when the rebs ceased and then came back and anchored in our old position. None of their shots struck us.

July 2nd

This morning a dispatch came on board Stating that the rebels had attacked Springfield Landing (A place where all our Army stores are landed at. It is about four miles below here.) We got under weigh as quick as possible, and proceeded down to the Landing. We arrived their to late for the fun. The guard stationed their had repulsed them, with considerable loss on boath sides. They[65] had not time to do much damage. In the Forenoon the *Gennesee* and *Tennessee* arrived. The Admiral had his Flag on the later vessel. In the evening the *Reliance* came up alongside. She brought up Commander Townsend, a new Captain for the *Essex*. Our old Captain has been promoted and is to report at Washington.[66]

July 3rd

This morning we got underweigh and went up the River to our old station ahead of the Mortar boats. The batteries are pretty quite today. their has been no fireing with big guns, only a few shots between the Sharpshooters on either side. In the afternoon the *Reliance* came alongside and took Captain Caldwell down to New Orleans. as he left the Ships Company gave him three Cheers.

July 5th

Yesterday the batteries on the West side of the River kept up a heavey fire nearly all day. The Rebels did not fire much in return. At 12 O'clock all the

65. That is, the enemy

66. Another changing of the guard on *Essex,* far less emotional than the departure of William Porter, though Caldwell gets "three cheers" as he leaves (next date). The new captain, Robert Townsend, had previously been in command of USS *Miami,* part of the mortar flotilla below New Orleans.

vessels fired a National Salute of 21 Guns in honor of the 4th. Today the batteries are exchanging a few shots at intervals. The *Monongahela* came up to day and reported that the Guerrillas are swarming along the bank's of the River. They had fired into and disabled several of our Transports. She went down the River again. Tomorrow I am going to the batteries on shore if all goes well. So I must take my leave of the Journal for a short time until I get back.[67]

July 12th

Below Donaldsonville. Last night I arrived on board. The *Winona* brought our men down from Port Hudson. On the 7th We got the news of the Capture of Vicksburgh. when the dispatch was read to each Regiment it was greeted with tremendeous cheers. at 12 O'Clock the Army and Navy fired each a salute of one hundred guns.[68] On the 8th a flag of truce was sent into Port Hudson communicateing the intelligence. The same day the Rebel General Gardiner surrendered Port Hudson unconditionally with a garrison of 5000 men and 50 Guns. Since I left the *Essex* she has had several skrimmages down here with Artillery and Sharpshooters. the rebels had 14 pieces planted behind the Levee. They disabled one of the wooden boats and killed several men belonging to the other vessels. The *Monongahela* lashed alongside and towed us up to Donaldsonville[69] this afternoon where the Gunboat *Princess Royal* was laying.

67. Park will be on shore with the naval battery for only a few days before Port Hudson surrenders. When given a short period of liberty before returning to his boat, according to his later memoir, he chose to spend it among the Confederate prisoners, conversing with them about their prior service (many had earlier fought at Fort Donelson; some had manned the old nemesis CSS *Arkansas*), their battle fatigue, and their astonishment at the fall of Vicksburg. Here again, he evidences regard for, and curiosity about, those with whom he has been engaged in bloody conflict for several months.

68. The news from Gettysburg did not reach the men until July 15, but the fall of Vicksburg and of Gettysburg within a twenty-four-hour period in the first week of July signaled the turning point of the war. The immediate effect of these two major Union victories was to cripple morale on the Confederate side and to boost it among the Federals.

69. *Essex* was to be based at Donaldsonville, forty miles downriver from Baton Rouge, until early March 1864, providing naval protection to Fort Butler. The town had been bombarded by Farragut's fleet in the summer of 1862, and most of its properties looted and destroyed by Federal soldiers (see Park's journal entry for August 24, 1862, and the accompanying note). Union forces occupied the area, set local black families to work on the deserted plantations, and with help from contraband men built a star-shaped garrison, naming it for General Benjamin

July 14th

Yesterday our troops here were fighting nearly all day. The Rebels were found to be in force. they were in position about two miles from the river. they captured two pieces of Artillery and drove our men back. In the evening our men were reinforced by four batteries of Artillery and regained their old position. This morning every thing is quite. There are some rumours flying round that the Rebels left during the night. This afternoon the *Monongahela* left for Baton Rouge. The *Princess Royal* left and went down the River. The *Arazona* passed down bound for New Orleans.

July 15th

This morning our troops went on a reconnicence and found the enemy in force. they exchanged a few shots and came back to their old position where they are drawn up in line of battle waiting for reinforcements. All the transports are busily employed bringing troops and stores from Port Hudson. two boats loaded with troops arrived to day. One boat loaded with prisoners passed down for New Orleans. We received good news by Telegraph from New Orleans to day stating that the Potomac Army under General Meade had defeated Lee's Army at Gettysburgh, Pa. capturing 28,000 Prisoners.

July 16th

This morning the Steamboat *Imperial* passed down bound from St. Louis to New Orleans. she is the first boat that has got through since the war commenced.[70] The *Winona* brought up the Mail and proceeded on up the river.

Butler; on February 9, 1863, the First Louisiana (Union) Volunteers, under the command of Colonel Richard Holcomb, raised the Stars and Stripes. In the last few days of June 1863, the fort lightly occupied—principally by members of the Twenty-Sixth Maine Infantry Regiment—Confederate troops attempted to seize it but were repulsed with heavy losses; fugitive slaves and free blacks who had helped build the fort joined in its defense. Confederate forces continued to harass the fort for several weeks, and Park refers periodically to rumors that another assault is expected, but none was ever attempted. For an account of the building of the fort and an eyewitness report of the attack on Fort Butler, see George Gilbert Smith, *Leaves from a Soldier's Diary: The Personal Record of Lieutenant George G. Smith* (Putnam, CT: Smith, 1906), 35–40; 80–83.

70. Park notes the milestone made famous by President Lincoln's words in a letter to James Conkling (August 27, 1863): "The Father of Waters again goes unvexed to the sea."

the *Monongahela* came down this evening. The *Princess Royal* came up and anchored. She went down the river to see if all was clear.

July 19th

Nothing of importance since last date. General Grover's Division of troops are still arriving from Port Hudson. The Rebels has made good their retreat towards Texas. Several transports came down from Vicksburgh loaded with cattle and Oats for the Army. They report that General Ransom has occupied Natchez and is going to fortify the City. Yesterday the *Winona* passed towing store Ship. all the Mortar boats were towed down to New Orleans this morning.

July 23rd

The last few day's the Transports has been employed carring Troops down the river. likewise Prisoners that were captured at Vicksburgh and Port Hudson. Yesterday the *Monongahela* and *Princess Royal* went up the River. This evening the *Richmond* passed down on her road to New Orleans.

July 29th

Nothing of importance since last date. Yesterday Morning the *Monongahela* and *Princess Royal* passed down to New Orleans, the last of Farragutt's Fleet up the River excepting the *Essex*. In the afternoon the Gunboat *Kenwood* belonging to Porters Fleet brought down a coal barge alongside of us to supply us with coal. The *Kenwood* is what they term a tin clad. she is a Stern wheel Steamer carring 6 guns, two twenty four pound Howitzers in each broadside and two 42 pounders in the bow. She is covered with Boiler iron round the outside and ¾ iron on the forward casemate backed with six inches of wood. She went up the river again. To day General Grover and most of the troops that were here went down the river.

July 31st

This evening Admiral Porter came down the river, on board his Flag Ship, *Black Hawk*, accompanied by the wooden Gunboat *Conestoga*. He stoped here about one hour and then proceeded down the river.[71] The *Black Hawk*

71. The visit allowed for a reunion of sorts for some of the original *Essex* sailors since many of their old officers (including D. P. Rosenmiller, fourth master under William Porter and pro-

used to be a river Packet. she has got heavy wooden casemates around her and mounts some six or eight guns.[72]

August 6th

Nothing of importance since last date. All the Soldiers has left here with the exception of the Regement to garrison the Fort. Some of the Soldiers went up the river to Baton Rouge and some down to New Orleans. Last night the Admiral passed up the river on board the *Black Hawk,* also the *Conestoga,* convoying six Transports up the river.

August 10

Yesterday morning twenty five of our crew left for home, their time having expired.[73] In the evening a dispatch came on board stating that the rebels were going to attack some of our troops twelve miles up the river. we got under weigh and proceeded up to the place where we arrived at 8 P.M. We found the Gunboat *Kenwood* laying there. It was a false alarm. This morning we got under weigh and came down to our old station of Donaldsonville.

---

moted several times thereafter) were now attached to *Black Hawk.* Park mentions Rosenmiller again on February 22, 1864, by which time he has taken command of the gunboat *Alexandria* (formerly *St. Mary*).

72. Although Park's description is neutral and accurate as far as it goes, Henneberry alludes to the tars' "disappointment on seeing the *Black Hawk,* for . . . we find her to be only a common transport boat having scarcely no protection for her Battery of 7 Broadside guns. She was formerly the old *Uncle Sam.*" The presence of two different naval vessels named *Black Hawk* in the Union fleet—one a sidewheel river steamer that became Admiral Porter's tinclad flagship, the other a transport steamer that David Dixon Porter, in his own memoirs unhelpfully (and with considerable disdain) calls "General Banks' flagship"—has caused a good deal of subsequent confusion. Compare, for example, Porter's *Naval History of the Civil War,* 500; Thomas O. Selfridge in *Battles and Leaders of the Civil War,* vol. 4: *Retreat with Honor* (New York: Castle, 1956), 363 and note; Gary D. Joiner, *Mr. Lincoln's Brown Water Navy* (London: Rowman and Littlefield, 2007), 148; and Myron J. Smith Jr., *The Timberclads in the Civil War* (Jefferson, NC: McFarland, 2008), 370, 449. Henneberry's description muddies the water by combining elements attributed to both vessels.

73. Most of these are "one year men," who signed up for a shorter term of service than Park. But one of the last and best of the original officers, John Mammon, also left the ship at this point, after two years with *Essex.* Henneberry adds that all the soldiers currently assigned to the gunboat received their discharge as well.

August 15th

Since last date a large number of Transports loaded with Troops passed down to New Orleans. I think they are part of Grant's army going to reinforce Banks. Yesterday five of General Ellets fleet passed down the river.[74] They are meant for large river Transports fitted up to carry about one thousand Soldiers and covered with Boiler Iron to protect them from Musketry. They are for keeping the river clear of Guerrillas. This evening we fired of our rifled guns to clear them out. we set out two barrels as Targets to fire at and sunk both of them.

August 20th

A great many Transports has passed down loaded with troops since last date. Ellets Fleet has gone up the river again. Yesterday a small steam boat came down the river from Port Hudson to act as a tender to our boat. She was captured up the Yazoo River. The Rebs had used her as an armed patrol boat. Her name is the *St. Mary's.* Our Engineers are working on her getting her ready for service. This evening the Soldiers in the fort were practising fireing at target with big guns. They did not strike itt.[75]

74. "General Ellet" is Alfred W. Ellet. Following the death of his brother Charles Ellet Jr. from a wound suffered at the Battle of Memphis, Alfred took over command of the ram fleet; he was promoted by Secretary of War Edwin Stanton to brigadier general of the newly formed Mississippi Marine Brigade in late 1862, which added large steam transports to the Ellet rams. Recruiting handbills for the Ellet fleet promised easy soldiering, free of marching and the normal hardships of war: "no trenches to dig; no rebel houses to guard; no picket duty to perform; no danger of camps in the mud; always a chance to sleep under cover; no chance of short rations." Convalescent soldiers were especially invited to enlist. Without any normative chain of command in either the army or navy and with an open-ended assignment ("keeping the river free of guerillas," as Park says here), the Brigade became a controversial rogue unit, known for intrepid skirmishing but also for dubious, sometimes lawless behavior—notoriously, the burning of Austin, Mississippi, in May 1863. For a graphic account by an unwilling—or at least subsequently penitent—participant, see *Warfare along the Mississippi: The Letters of Lieutenant Colonel George E. Currie,* ed. Norman E. Clarke Sr. (Ann Arbor: Edwards, 1961), chap. 9. The Brigade was decommissioned in the summer of 1864.

75. Park's back-to-back references to target practice by the ship's crew on his own gunboat (August 15) and by soldiers in the fort, with very different results, are offered without comment, but he is obviously keeping score.

August 25th

Nothing of importance since last date. Several Transports has passed down with Cavalry on board. This morning the dispatch boat *De Soto* came down the river. She brought us a mail, also Provisions and Ammunition. In the afternoon she went up the river again. The *De Soto* is one of the boats that was Captured at Island No. 10. She carries five guns and Casemated to protect her from Musketry. This evening four transports passed down loaded with troops. I hear their destination is Mobile. Some say Galveston. This evening our tender (the *St. Mary's*) went down to New Orleans on duty.[76]

August 30th

Every thing quite as usual. Several transports passed by loaded with troops since last date. This morning the Gunboat *Estrilla* came up from New Orleans. She is to assist us in keeping the river clear between Donaldsonville and New Orleans.[77] She started down the river again on her patrol. In the afternoon our tender arrived from below. The men on board of her report that a large expedition is getting ready at New Orleans. Between thirty and forty large Ocean transports is anchored in the stream loaded with troops ready for a start. Their destination is kept Secret.[78]

76. Among those sent to New Orleans aboard *St. Mary's* were James Henneberry and Hank Ruger, who, in addition to gathering ship's stores, enjoyed several days of well-lubricated "ease and luxury" in the Crescent City before returning on August 30. The men reported that although the official destination of the large Federal fleet gathering there was given as Mobile, word on the street suggested Galveston.

77. *Estrella* had been captured as a blockade-runner in late 1862 and commissioned for Federal gunboat service shortly thereafter. For her shared role in "keeping the river clear between Donaldsonville and New Orleans," see note 85, below.

78. As Park later confirms, the "secret" destination was in fact Texas. On September 8, four Union gunboats and troop transports carrying nearly five thousand soldiers, under the command of General William Franklin and Navy Captain Frederick Crocker, attempted to seize Fort Griffin at Sabine Pass below Port Arthur and establish a foothold in Texas. The attack was a spectacular and mortifying disaster: the Davis Guards, a company of forty-four Confederate defenders of the fort, destroyed two gunboats, scattered the rest of the fleet, and captured more than two hundred sailors without a single casualty on their side, thus forcing a skedaddle back to New Orleans. Word of the outcome had evidently not reached the men by September 13; Park never reports it.

September 3rd

For the last two day's a number of Ocean transports passed here bound up the river. also several river boats. Last night and to day they all passed down loaded with troops.

September 10th

Yesterday our tender went down to New Orleans for stores. In the evening the Gunboat *Kenwood* came down the river and anchored astern. The Admiral sent her down to tow up the *St. Mary's.* This morning she went up the river and left a Pilot and Engineer to take the boat up.

September 13th

The *St. Mary's* came up the river to day. The Officers belonging to the *Kenwood* took charge of her and proceeded on up the river. Our men that went down in her report that the expedition that was fitting out at New Orleans had left their for Texas.

September 18th

For the last two day's several transports loaded with Army wagons came down the river and landed them here (at Donaldsonville). This morning the passenger Packet *Hanniable*[79] run on to a snag and sunk about four miles above here. We sent the transport *Starlight* to her assistance. She was on her passage between New Orleans and St. Louis. No one hurt on board. This afternoon the *Kenwood* brought dispatches down the river for our Captain. She went up the river to Baton Rouge again. In the evening two transports loaded with Cavalry came down and landed them here.

September 21st

Yesterday the dispatch boat *New National* came down the river. she brought us a Mail and provisions. she is the same class vessel as the *De Soto.* In the evening she left for Cairo. This morning the transport *Polar Star* came down towing a barge loaded with ice. She brought a new gun for us a one hundered

79. That is, *Hannibal.*

pounder Parrote rifle and a supply of ice. We got the gun on board in the Forenoon. in the afternoon she left.

September 25th

Night before last a party of guerrillas came in and "gobbled" up 25 of our Cavelry and a Telegraph opperator that were on the East side of the river guarding the Telegraph without fireing a shot.[80] Last night about 11 Oclock some person on the East side of the river hailed the *Essex* saying the guerrillas were coming again and told us which direction to fire. All hands were called to quarters. When we opened fire the voice from the shore telling us where to direct our shots. They also opened fire from the guns in the Fort. we kept up a spirited bombardment for about one hour firing in different directions as the voice told us. At last the Captain begin to think that it was one of the rebs that was directing opperations so we sent a few shells flying in the direction of the voice when everything was quite. This morning some of the inhabitans came on board. They said their were no guerillas near their last night. It was some drunken soldiers that hailed the boat. By good luck none of the people got hurt although several shots passed through their houses.[81] To day some steamboats took up an expedition of Cavelry and landed them on the East side of the river about 5 miles above here. They are going to try and clear out the guerillas on that side of the river. This evening a rumour came on board that the rebels were marching in force to attack the Fort. we got every thing in readiness to give them a warm reception. But the rumour proved to be a false alarm.

October 1st

Nothing of importance since last date. The expedition returned from the East side of the river without success. they did not find a single 'reb.' to day two

80. These were all personnel attached to *Essex*, captured in a daring raid. The increase in guerilla harassment on the east side of the river near Donaldsonville leads to reinforcement of the gunboat with additional personnel and artillery, and shore parties sent to clear them out, with limited success.

81. As if local householders don't have enough to worry about, Federal soldiers here invite needless destruction of property and enormous risk to innocent lives in a drunken game.

tin Clads came down the river this morning to assist us in keeping the river open between New Orleans and Baton Rouge. They are the same class boats as the *Kenwood.* I have not learnt their names yet. One is numbered *19* and the other *27.*[82] Number *19* left this evening for New Orleans.

October 4th

This morning *No. 19* came up from New Orleans. she brought us a Mail and proceeded on up the river. *No. 27* got under weigh and went up the river about four miles to protect the wreck of the *Hanniable.*

October 9th

This morning the dispatch boat *General Lyon* came down the river. she brought down a mail. In the evening she left for Cairo. Six Caulkers came down on her to Caulk our decks.

October 12th

Since last date several transports passed down loaded with Cavelry. This morning the tin Clad *St. Clair* (alais *No. 19*) came down from above and anchored.

October 16th

Yesterday the Tin Clad *Agossa* (alais *27*) came down. the *St. Clair* took her place. This evening the *Agossa* went down to New Orleans for Stores.

October 21st

Yesterday the Steamer *Hannibal* went up the river. The Bell boat *Champion* has been at work raising her for the last two or three days. The *Saint Clair* came down and gave us a supply of wood and Coal. This morning the *Agossa* arrived from New Orleans with a supply of Provisions, and some stores for the

82. The Federal tinclads had numbers painted on their pilothouses to help with identification: *Kenwood* was *No. 14*. As Park will later indicate, *No. 19 = St. Clair; No. 27 = Argosy* (though Park misnames her *Agossa* or *Argossa*). For a history of the Union tinclad fleet, see Myron J. Smith Jr., *Tinclads in the Civil War: Union Light-Draught Gunboat Operations on Western Waters, 1862–1865* (Jefferson, NC: McFarland, 2009).

Caulkers, also a Mail. In the afternoon she went up the river to get a supply of wood and returned in the evening.

October 23rd

This morning the tin Clad *Springfield* arrived from Cairo. She brought down the Fleet Surgeon and Paymaster and one Million and a half of dollars to pay the Soldiers at New Orleans. They transferred the money on board the *Agossa* when she started for Orleans. In the afternoon the *Springfield* returned to Cairo.

October 25th

Yesterday the *Saint Clair* went up the river. This morning the *Agossa* arrived from New Orleans. Yesterday a shell exploded in the Fort killing one man and wounding several others one severely. It was done through carlessness. It seems that some of the soldiers got hold of a loaded shell and was taking the Powder out of it when one of them that was smokeing knocked the ashes out of his pipe on the shell, when it exploded.

October 27th

Yesterday morning the *St. Clair* came down the river. also the dispatch boat *New National* came down from Cairo. She brought down a draft of 24 men to help fill up our compliment.[83] This morning she started for Cairo.

November 5th

Nothing of importance since last date. Last night the *St. Clair* went down to New Orleans. To day the *Steamer B.* brought down a barge of Coal for us. also a Mail. In the evening she left for Cairo.

November 9th

Yesterday the dispatch boat *General Lyons* came down with the Mail, some stores and lumber to sheath over the upper deck. This morning she left for Cairo. In the evening the *St. Clair* arrived from New Orleans.

83. These are replacements for those who mustered out on August 9.

November 24th

Nothing of importance since last date. The garrison on shore here has been expecting an attack from a party of rebs that has been lurking round here for the last week. a Battery of artillery came up from New Orleans and landed. Yesterday the *New National* came down from Cairo, she brought us two nine inch guns and a supply of ammunition in exchange for our two fifty pound riffles and thirty two pounder smooth bore, which she takes up to Cairo. She left this evening.

December 1st

Every thing quite since last date, not the least excitement. To day the Captain gave all the old hands twenty dollars each and forty eight hours liberty to go to New Orleans six men at a time.[84] The first six went down this morning, on the Baton Rouge Packet *New Orleans.*

December 8th

Yesterday the *General Lyons* brought down the Mail. In the evening she left for Cairo. This morning the ram *General Price* came down from Cairo. She brought down a Coal barge. The *Price* carries two nine inch guns and two Howitzers on the upper deck. She was one of the boats that was captured at Memphis. She belongs to the first division of Gunboats under the command of Captain Townsend.[85]

84. Periods of inactivity had a tendency to create problems aboard ship, as restlessness led to various forms of misconduct. Townsend here is not only allowing for some of the men to let off steam but also rewarding particularly the "old hands," who are by now well into their third year of service. Such gestures no doubt strengthened loyalty between sailors and their captain. Townsend may have been feeling especially generous after a party of army officers inspected the boat and watched an ammunition drill a few days earlier. Henneberry comments that "they expressed entire satisfaction with the manner we handled our guns, and well they might for [there is] not a better drilled ships company in the fleet. She has always had the name of it and always carries off the 'palm'" (Henneberry journal, November 26, 1863). One assumes Park himself enjoyed two days' leave from the ship (and his journal) prior to his next entry on December 8.

85. Admiral Porter had organized a divisional structure for monitoring the entire length of the Mississippi: *Essex*, captained by Townsend, was the lead vessel, responsible for guarding the "first district" between New Orleans and Donaldsonville (see also Park's entry for August 20,

December 15th

Yesterday the Caulkers finished their job.[86] They went up to Port Hudson on the *St. Clair.* Last night the *Argossa* captured the Steam Boat *Ben Franklin* landing Powder and stores for the Rebels about twelve miles above here. she put a prize crew on board and sent her down here. Our Captain has confiscated her and is going to send her to Cairo. The *Franklin* is one of the New Orleans and Baton Rouge Packets.

December 23rd

Yesterday the dispatch boat *New National* arrived from Cairo. She brought us a Mail and Provisions. Last night she left for Cairo. Mr. Ruger our Surgeon's Steward and Wm. Young Gunners Mate went up on her.[87] They are both going home.

December 28th

This morning one of the men belonging to the First Louisiana Regiment shot himself. He was a German. It seems he had promised to marry one of his fair Country women as soon as he had money enough to pay for the Ceremony.

1863). "Second district" was Donaldsonville to Morganzia; "Third district," Morganzia to Fort Adams; "Fourth district," Fort Adams to Natchez; "Fifth district," Natchez to Vicksburg; "Sixth district," Vicksburg to the Arkansas River; "Seventh district," Arkansas River to Memphis; "Eighth district," Memphis to Columbus; "Ninth district," Cairo to the head of the Tennessee River; "Tenth district," Cumberland River and Upper Ohio (see Joiner, *Mr. Lincoln's Brown Water Navy,* 172).

86. Commenced on October 9; see Park's entry of that date. *Essex* had also been entirely repainted during the same period, the breastwork on her gun deck now colored green.

87. Both men were close to Park. Hank Ruger was James Henneberry's "chum" who talked him into enlisting; though Park and Henneberry seem not to have forged any kind of relationship, Park and Ruger remained lifelong friends after the war, seeing each other socially as often as twice a week in Chicago. As surgeon's steward, Ruger was entitled to early discharge. William (Bill) Young is pictured next to William Park in figure 5, the photograph of *Essex* gunners. His war service did not begin aboard *Essex;* he had manned a Parrot gun aboard USS *Cayuga* in the capture of Forts Jackson and St. Philip in the Battle of New Orleans, under withering fire from both forts and harrying by three Confederate steamers. Young's actions won him the Medal of Honor, which was awarded on April 3, 1863. Though given an early discharge, as noted here, he promised his mates he would return to the gunboat after forty days' leave, and, as good as his word, he rejoined the *Essex* crew on February 6, 1864.

So last week he received five months wages and one month's leave to go to New Orleans. When he arrived there he made inquiries and found that his intended had got tired of waiting. she had married some other man and gone to New York. Last night he returned here and this morning told the men belonging to his Company all about it, gave them forty dollars to have a spree with. he then went outside placed the muzzle of his Enfield under his chin, pulled the trigger with his toe and blowed his brains out. They buried him this evening in the cemetery (in Consecrated ground).[88]

88. It is unusual for Park to recount a personal story like this, especially one involving someone other than a messmate or shipmate. The narrative, though stark and unadorned, is novelistic in its force, right down to the pointed reference to the burial in consecrated ground. The unidentified soldier was a member of the First Louisiana (Union) Volunteers, formed in New Orleans in 1862, mostly from soldiers of the Thirteenth Connecticut who had been sent to police the Crescent City. It was this regiment, under Colonel Richard E. Holcomb, that oversaw construction of Fort Butler, before leaving to take part in the siege of Port Hudson. Thirty members of the First Louisiana, along with Holcomb himself, died at Port Hudson in an assault on Sunday, June 14, after which the remnant returned to its base at Donaldsonville. For more on the regimental history of the First Louisiana Volunteers, see the engaging, self-published memoir of Lieutenant George G. Smith (publication details at note 69 above). Smith does not recount the anecdote Park includes here. Nor does James Henneberry.

1864

January 2nd, 1864

Yesterday being the first of the New Year, came in very cold. It was the coldest day in Louisiana for the last eight years. One of our old veterans died last evening. He was one of the first sailors that the Government sent to St. Louis. his name is Joseph Stanley, Quartermaster, a native of Liverpool, England and one of my messmates. We buried him to day in the City Cemetrey.[1]

1. Joseph Stanley died of typhoid fever. Henneberry says of him that he had earlier fought in the Mexican-American War and had been, in peacetime, a "whaler on the Northern seas" before entering service for the Union in 1861. Messmates had special obligation to one another in times of crisis, sickness, and death. If death occurred during battle and there was no nearby cemetery or opportunity to get to one, burial was often hasty—the body wrapped in a blanket or the sailor's ship hammock and laid wherever a grave could be readily dug, often close to the bank of the river (never, as in the seagoing navy, in the water itself). Frank L. Church, a marine aboard USS *Cricket* in service in the Red River campaign, describes removing the remains of an acquaintance from a grave along the riverbank—concerned that "high water would wash the body out"—and reinterring them in a cemetery in Alexandria (*Civil War Marine: A Diary of the Red River Expedition, 1864,* ed. James P. Jones and Edward F. Keuchel [Honolulu: University Press of the Pacific, 2003], 53). In a case such as Park describes here, during a lull in fighting, a coffin was likely prepared and draped with a flag, then removed from the boat with great solemnity. A service would have been said as the sailor was laid to rest; if the ship's captain had a religious disposition, he might read a Christian burial rite, but formalities were often minimal. A headboard with the sailor's name was made by his mates and placed at the gravesite. Messmates were also expected to send news of the death and personal effects home to the sailor's family. For an eyewitness description of a naval burial carried out in the Mississippi Squadron, see the April 12, 1864, letter of Symmes E. Browne in *From the Fresh-Water Navy: 1861–64: The Letters of Acting Master's Mate Henry R. Browne and Acting Ensign Symmes E. Browne,* ed. John D. Milligan (Annapolis: United States Naval Institute, 1970), 259.

January 6th

Since last date we have had very cold weather. Last night it snowed. The ground is covered. It is the first snow that has been seen here for twelve years. This morning the Tin Clad *Albert Robb* arrived from Cairo. She brought down the Fleet Paymaster and money to pay the Fleet. This evening she left for New Orleans.

January 8th

Yesterday morning the *Riel* went up the river taking the *Ben Franklin* in tow. The *General Lyons* arrived from Cairo. She brought us a Mail, and eleven thousand feet of Lumber. She left in the evening. This morning the tow boat, *Ike Hammitt* came down. She brought us a Barge load of Coal. She left here in the afternoon takeing one of the empty barges up with her.

January 23rd

Since last date three tin clads passed here bound to New Orleans to reinforce Farragutts fleet. The crews of the boats went up to Cairo on the *Robb* leaveing the boats to be manned by Farraggut's men. Yesterday the *New National* arrived with a mail. She left this morning, on her passage down she had her smoek stacks blown overboard. She had rigged jury ones[2] made out of lumber which answered the purpose very well.

February 22nd

Nothing of importance has occurred since last date. The mail boats arrive regularly twice each month. Yesterday the small steamer *St. Mary's* came down from Cairo, completely rebuilt and made into a gunboat carrying one 24 pounder, howitzer and commanded by acting master D. P. Rosenmiller, formerly acting Second Master on board the *Essex* when Captain Porter had command.[3] Her name is also changed to the *Alexandria.* To day being Washington's birth day we dressed ship and fired a national salute.

2. "Jury rigged" (improvised) as distinct from "jerry rigged," which has a more pejorative sense—implying shoddy workmanship.

3. Rosenmiller had been singled out for particular praise by Captain William D. Porter with respect to the confrontation with *Arkansas* in a letter dated August 6, 1862, a copy of which Park kept with his diary (see appendix 2). Porter observes that *Essex* "had only forty men on duty at the time of our going into action. My first master, R. K. Riley was sick in hospital, and

March 6th

Yesterday evening two brigades of cavalry arrived here from New Orleans. They numbered about 6,000. They encamped in Town all night and started this morning for Red River and Texas. The tin clad *Signal* came down this morning from the Admiral with orders for us to proceed up red river. We started at 11 o'clock, the *Signal* taking us in tow.

March 8th

Yesterday we passed the monitor *Neosho,* laying at Morganzia bend,[4] and we arrived here at Red River about 11 P.M. We found the Fleet laying here 16 boats in all. The admiral had his flag on the *Black Hawk.*

March 11th

Yesterday afternoon Admiral Porter came on board and inspected the vessel and crew. Today the Admiral had all hands from the Fleet on shore reviewing them. We made quite an imposing appearance and numbered about fifteen hundred men. Ellets, marine brigade of boats, and twelve transports arrived here from above, they were all loaded with troops. In the evening two transports arrived from New Orleans with troops.

March 12th

This morning all the Fleet got under way and proceeded up Red River. The following is the names of boats. *Laffayette, Choctaw, Eastport, Essex, Benton, Pittsburgh, Mound City, Louisville, Carondelet, Chillicothe, Ozark, Osage,* and *Neosho,* the three latter boats are monitor's, with revolving turrets, and the three first mentioned boats are rams, and all the above mentioned boats are heavy iron clads, and I think they are the finest fleet of iron clads afloat in the world at the present time.[5] Besides the ram *Price,*[6] the Flag ship *Black*

---

his place was supplied by Second Master David Porter Rosenmiller, who conducted himself to my entire satisfaction." Rosenmiller was a cousin to the Porter brothers.

4. Located twenty miles below the confluence of the Mississippi and Red Rivers, Morganzia Bend was a staging area for Union forces along the Lower Mississippi in 1864.

5. This is the first and only time that Park records a strong sense of personal pride in the naval fleet of which he has been so long a member.

6. That is, *General Price,* formerly part of the Confederate River Defense Fleet, captured at the Battle of Memphis.

Hawk, the tin clad *Washita*[7] which alone mounts 40 guns, and several other tin clads whose names I do not know accompanied us. When we reached the Atchafayala[8] river the fleet separated, part of the boats going down that river,[9] and the remainder of us kept on up the red, and at dark we tied up to the bank about 35 miles from the mouth.

March 14th

Yesterday morning we started at daylight and passed the Black river. We made very poor progress during the day, on account of the narrow channel, and the short bends of the river. at some of the bends the boats had to get out lines ashore to assist them to turn.[10] Just at dark we passed a four gun battery which was abandoned, the embracing for two of the guns were newly cut. We tied up about a mile above the battery. This morning got under way again and got along about the same speed as yesterday until about 10 o'clock, when the leading boats came to a stand still where the river was blockaded about 7 miles below Fort De Russey[11] by driving spiles[12] across the river. The spiles were driven in clusters about 12 feet apart, and connected by stringers of heavy

7. Park may be forgiven for his misspelling of *Ouachita,* the largest of the Union tinclads. She had been the Confederate steamer *Louisville* before her capture in July 1863 and her subsequent makeover for Federal use.

8. That is, Atchafalaya—a 130-mile tributary of the Mississippi, flowing from near the confluence of the Red and Mississippi Rivers to the Gulf of Mexico.

9. Those headed downriver were to assist in the landing of Smith's force at Simmesport, from which point they were to march overland to Alexandria to rendezvous with Banks.

10. Whether intentionally or not, Park sounds a note of foreboding about conditions along the Red River, where the water was unseasonably shallow and was to prove in some places to be unnavigable by the Federal fleet, with dire consequences for the mission.

11. Fort DeRussy, named for Colonel Lewis G. DeRussy of Natchitoches, who oversaw construction of the earliest fortifications at the site in November 1862.

12. "Spiles" is an archaic term (cf. "piles") used by Park and several other contemporary witnesses in describing the river obstruction designed to prevent the Union gunboats from reaching the fort, or at least to slow their progress sufficiently to warn those holding the fort of their approach. The fact that it was beyond the reach of the guns of Fort DeRussy, however, meant that the effort to dismantle it proceeded without harassing fire. A detailed diagram of the "Confederate dam" is reproduced in Steven M. Mayeux, *Earthen Walls, Iron Men: Fort DeRussy, Louisiana, and the Defense of Red River* (Knoxville: University of Tennessee Press, 2007), 132.

timber on the top, a second line of spiles was driven about 12 feet below the clusters and heavy timbers above the spiles and floated the logs down so that they formed a raft that extended about 200 yards above the spiles. The ram *Eastport* and tin clad *Hindman* were at work all day clearing a passage; about sundown they succeded in getting through all the monitors. Our crew went on board *Price* and went to work on the spiles clearing a passage so that the transports can get through. About 10 o'clock a tug returned from the *Eastport* stating that the Fort had surrendered to our troops, who arrived in the rear of the Fort, as the gunboats came up the front. The boats only fired two shots at it, when they hauled down the flag.

March 16th

On the night of the 14th the Admiral arrived, with the other Iron Clads and transports. The soldiers that came in the transports were landed in the Atchafalaya and had marched across the country to Fort De Russey. On the morning of the 15th all the gunboats and transports passed through the blockade, leaving the *Essex* and *Price* to clear the remainder of the spiles away. About 4 o'clock in the afternoon the admiral sent a dispatch down telling us to come up to the Fort. At dark we tied up to the bank, astern of the *Benton* about ½ a mile below the Fort. The remainder of the Fleet had started up the river for Alexandria. This morning we got under way and proceeded up to the Fort accompanied by the *Benton.* Three of the Marine Brigade boats, and four transports were laying here. After breakfast the soldiers commenced leveling the earthworks, and all our men were sent on shore to dismount the guns, and brick up the carriage. There was 250 men captured here, and 10 guns. Our soldiers lost 10 killed and 30 wounded. Fort De Russey is the strongest and best fortification that I have seen in rebeldom but fortunately it was not completed. The water batteries consisted of one casemated iron battery of 3 guns and two barbell batteries, one mounting 3 guns and the others, one 8 pound rife. The casemated battery was built of oak timber two feet thick, and covered with two tiers of railroad iron, the whole leaning at an angle of 35 degrees to glance the shot off. The main fort was situated on a piece of rising ground about half a mile from the river, and was connected with the water batteries by a covered way. It was laid out in the form of a star, with bombproofs for the garrison, and if it had been completed, one thousand men could hold it against 10 thousand.[13] In the afternoon the tinclads *Cricket* and *Hindman* came down the river. they report that General Franklin's division of Banks army had captured Alexandria after skirmishing with the rebel troops through the streets, and that our boats were in chase of the rebel rams. The *Cricket* went on down the river and the *Hindman* stopped and took the Prisoners down with her. Ten of the Prisoners took the oath of allegiance and enlisted in some of the regiments here. In the evening we crossed the river to try our 100 pounder rifles on the iron battery at 700 yards distance. We fired five shots, but none of them penetrated through. Wherever they struck the bars of iron went flying over the top of the battery. Some of the shots splintered the wood work inside but nothing to hurt. All the shots were broken into a dozen different pieces, and penetrated about eighteen inches into the wood work.

March 17th

Last night preparations were made to blow up the magazine of the main, or upper Fort, and all the troops were ordered to withdraw to a safe distance. Two guns that were captured there were also loaded and a train of powder laid to them so that they should burst at the same time. At 10 o'clock the magazine exploded, and the guns went off at the same time, making a louder report than even the magazine did. The explosion sent the heavy casemate timbers, and dirt, to the distance of six hundered yards, breaking the trees down the same as if we had been firing grape and canister amongst them. Some of the dirt and falling timber killed one soldier and wounded seven, and the piece of the gun that burst killed 2 men and wounded one. In the afternoon we filled up our magazine with the powder from the magazine belonging to the water batteries. The Most of the Barrels were marked for Farragut's Squadron and I think probably they had been captured at Galveston. In the evening the *Benton* went up the river.

March 18th

This morning we blew up the remaining magazine, and again tried our guns on the battery at 400 yards distance but none of our shots penetrated inside. The *Benton* came down the river and tied up to the bank.

13. Steve Mayeux includes a range of similarly complimentary assessments from Union personnel getting their first look at the river fortress (ibid., 189–92). For Park, less given to hyperbole than most, this is a surprisingly strong statement.

March 20th

This morning all the Soldiers started up the river leaving the *Essex* and *Benton* to guard the place.[14] The Planters is coming in by scores to take the oath of allegiance, and all are, or pretend to be, Union men.[15] There are two soldiers Officers left here to collect and organize the negroes into military companies, and they have armed and sent bands of these negroes into the country to bring in more and they are plundering peaceable citizens, especially the houses where they find only women and children, but I understand that Capt. Townsend has taken steps to put a stop to this disgraceful affair.[16]

14. As at Port Hudson, *Essex* is here charged with the responsibility of guard duty along the river—securing and/or holding Union positions in hostile territory. In this instance, she (and *Benton*) had the better end of the bargain from the fleet engaged in the disastrous expedition up the Red River toward Alexandria and Shreveport (see Gary D. Joiner, *One Damn Blunder from Beginning to End: The Red River Campaign of 1864* [Lanham, MD: Rowman and Littlefield, 2003]). See also *Little to Eat and Thin Mud to Drink: Letters, Diaries, and Memoirs from the Red River Campaigns, 1863–1864*, ed. Gary D. Joiner (Knoxville: University of Tennessee Press, 2007); and Ludwell H. Johnson III, "A Campaign That Failed," *The South Besieged*, vol. 5 of *The Image of War: 1861–1865*, ed. William C. Davis, 6 vols. (Garden City, NY: Doubleday, 1983), 346–77.

15. As the tide of the war was turning decisively in the west, defection to the Federal ranks became more common. Though the numbers vary in contemporary accounts, Park's estimate of "scores," rising to "hundreds" by the end of the month, is likely dependable. His disclaimer about the actual allegiance of the signers of the oath is not without foundation. For one thing, contemporary accounts make clear that "all persons owning property were compelled to take the oath to save it from being foraged" (M. R. Ailenroc, *The White Castle of Louisiana* [1903; repr., Baton Rouge: Louisiana Library Association, 1986], 60). According to the diary of "Southern Unionist" Dennis E. Haynes, "rebels . . . did not regard the oath as binding on their consciences . . . for, when Banks evacuated Alexandria they all went back to the rebels. Not the last nor least important among them was Louis Texada, who was the 'life and blood of the conspiracy' in that section" (*A Thrilling Narrative: The Memoir of a Southern Unionist*, ed. Arthur W. Bergeron Jr. [Fayetteville: University of Arkansas Press, 2006], 55). The fact that much of Alexandria was burned to the ground by Union forces as they left on May 13 may have accounted for some rethinking of loyalties on the part of many in that city. Marine officer Frank L. Church, who had enjoyed lavish hospitality from some of the belles in Alexandria during his stay there, callously recounts "bidding them a last good bye" as they tried frantically to salvage personal belongings from their burning homes (Church, *Civil War Marine*, 56).

16. Though there is more than a hint of racial bias in Park's account, it is clear that black troops had ample precedent for "plundering peaceful citizens" in the behavior of rank-and-file

March 24th

Since last date several transports loaded with troops belonging to Bank's army passed here bound up the river. About two thousand bales of Cotton and a large quantity of railroad iron has been sent to Cairo as a prize to the fleet, and I understand there is plenty more waiting for transportation. Two deserters from General Walkers army[17] came on board and said that when they left he was making tracts[18] for Texas. They belonged to an independent company of heavy artillery and had been stationed here, since they began to build the Fort. I was surprised to see the numbers of men who were coming in by hundreds to take the oath of allegiance, and I asked one of the deserters the reasons that the rebels did not conscript in the Parish. He said they formed themselves into companies and resisted the draft and when pressed too hard retreated into the swamp and kept up a guerilla warfare with Walker and his friends as the citizens term them.[19]

April 3rd

Since the last date several boats passed up loaded with troops. Last week the guerillas captured and burnt the Steamboat *La Crosse* about 20 miles above here. She was on an expedition with speculation to buy up cotton. They lost 100,000 dollars by the operation. The *Benton* was ordered up there the

---

Union forces. For women left alone on plantations, who were famously haughty in the face of white Union depredations (e.g., defiantly singing "The Bonnie Blue Flag" as their property burned), raids by bands of armed former slaves, some of whom apparently felt entitled to victimize their erstwhile masters, were psychologically traumatic.

17. John George Walker, commander of the "Greyhound Division" of the Confederacy—so named because of its long, rapid marches—had served in the Army of Northern Virginia with distinction early in the war, before his transfer to the Trans-Mississippi Department in early 1863. Under Walker's leadership, his men marched nine hundred miles and fought three major battles in ten weeks between March and May 1864. His personal memoirs, written in exile shortly after the war, have recently been edited by Richard Lowe: *Greyhound Commander: Confederate General John G. Walker's History of the Civil War West of the Mississippi* (Baton Rouge: Louisiana State University Press, 2013). See also J. P. Blessington, *The Campaigns of Walker's Texas Division, By a Private Soldier* (New York: Lange, Little and Co., 1875).

18. That is, "making tracks." Walker's division was made up entirely of soldiers from Texas.

19. This conversation, as Park recounts it, offers a concise account of the paramilitary presence along the river—men committed to defending the "Southland" on their own terms, without the obligations and strictures of professional military service.

next day, leaving for us to guard about 150 bales of cotton they had brought in from the surrounding country.[20] To day the *Lafayette Choctaw* and *Washita* passed down on an expedition to go up the Black river and they report that all the fleet had passed the rapids, and were on the way to Shreveport. During the forenoon the tow boat *Ike Haggett* came down with a barge load of cotton; and after taking on board fifty nine bales for us, started for Cairo. Several influential citizens has asked permission to raise one regiment of cavalry and one of infantry to protect themselves, and they say there is 2,500 conscripts that has escaped from the rebel army and are willing to join the home guard.

April 8th

Yesterday the *General Lyons* brought up the mail, and proceeded on up to Alexandria, where she left the mail and stores for the Fleet, on board the *Black Hawk,* and came down here this forenoon and took on all the guns there were captured here, also the remainder of the cotton that the *Benton* left under our charge. In the evening she started for Cairo.

April 16th

During the last week, several roumours has been brought down by passing boats that Bank's has had a fight at a place called Grand Ecore, and he got pretty

20. Acquisition of cotton during the Red River campaign became something of a scandal, and both complicated and compromised Federal military objectives. Northern speculators accompanied the fleet, and boats like *Essex* were often used to guard and transport cotton. General Benjamin Butler and his brother Andrew were widely suspected of profiteering in the cotton trade, and other well-placed Federal officers, including Nathaniel Banks, were implicated as well. David Dixon Porter cites Captain William S. Burns on this account, with respect to the Red River campaign: "We all saw an immense amount of bagging and roping upon the steamer *Black Hawk* (General Banks's headquarters boat) when it arrived at Alexandria. . . . And during our occupancy of Alexandria . . . I myself saw steamers loaded with cotton and sent down the river under the protection of the hospital flag" (Porter, *Naval History of the Civil War,* 547). In addition to the legal but dubious cotton "trade" authorized by the Lincoln administration, seizure of cotton under various pretexts as war booty by both naval and land forces was ubiquitous. David Dixon Porter himself confiscated cotton from warehouses in Alexandria, his men stenciling "C.S.A." on the bales before marking them "U.S.N."—prompting the cynical observation that the initials stood for "Cotton Stealing Association of the United States Navy" (see Ludwell H. Johnson, *Red River Campaign: Politics and Cotton in the Civil War* [Kent, OH: Kent State University Press, 1999]).

badly whipt in the first day's fight but recovered his losses in the next two day's fighting. We have got no reliable news of the fight yet. Several boats has passed here loaded with wounded men and one boat loaded with rebel Prisoners. A band of bushwhackers has been committing depredations on the inhabitans round this section last week, and on the evening of the 14th a company of local citizens came down to the boat to procure arms, which we gave them. They then started out to hunt up the bushwhackers, accompanied by Captain Lee, and 20 of his niggers, that he had raised here.[21] Yesterday the expedition returned having captured five of the band, with their horses and accoutraments, also killing one of their number and wounding one. The prisoners were brought on board of the *Essex* for safe keeping. This morning we took on board all the shot and shell that was captured here ready for a move but I have not heard where we are going yet. In the evening the *Benton* came down the river and tied up for the night. She brought the news down that the rebels had tried to board to[22] of our gunboats up the river, The *Neosho* and *Lexington.* They were laying tied up to the bank when the rebs made a rush on board but were handsomely repulsed. The *Lexington* opened fire with her guns and small arms, killing and wounding 60 rebels. The *Neosho* got her hot water hose to play on them that was on her decks whilst she opened with grape and canister from her 11 inch guns upon them on shore. After she had repulsed them 230 dead men was found on her decks besides what had jumped overboard.[23]

April 17th

This morning the *Benton* went down the river. At 10 o'clock We got under way and proceeded down the river. We passed two boats going up loaded with troops. In the evening the Officers shot two allagators.[24]

21. "Captain Lee" is tentatively identified by Steven Mayeux as Abner N. Lee of the Seventy-First U.S. Colored Troops, a "one-man Freedmen's Bureau . . . in charge of all activities relating to contrabands in the area" (see Mayeux, *Earthen Walls, Iron Men,* 211–12).

22. That is, "two."

23. The carnage reported here is staggering, and casualty numbers may be somewhat inflated. Confederate losses during one particularly audacious attack on the gunboats, at Blair's Landing on April 12, included Confederate Brigadier General Thomas Green, who recklessly (and drunkenly) charged the boats on horseback, only to have his rebel yell snuffed by a cannon shot from the Federal fleet.

24. This is Park's first mention of alligators, but they were frequently seen and shot by officers and sailors along the southern Mississippi waterways, and sometimes even made their way

April 18th

This morning we reached the mouth of the river.[25] We sent the prisoners on board of the ram *General Bragg,* to be sent to New Orleans. The steamboat *Lancaster No. 4* came alongside and took us in tow up the Mississippi river.

April 20th

Last night we arrived at Natchez.[26] To day we coaled ship. The *Choctaw* and *Lafayette* came down the river and after coaling up proceeded on down. this evening the *Benton* came down and anchored.

April 22nd

This morning the Steamboat *Brilliant* took us in tow. At 12 o'clock we came to a place where one of her passengers had 150,000 dollars worth of cotton laying. As soon as we got in sight of the place, a party of guerillas set fire to it, and by the time we reached it the most of it was consumed. We got our steam pumps to work on it and managed to save some 15 bags that had not been touched. The *New National* passed us at Waterproof on her way up to Cairo. Our boat leakes so that we have to keep two steam Syphon pumps going night and day.

April 24th

Yesterday we passed the remains of the *Indianola,* off Jeff Davis's plantation. She is ready to be launched as soon as the river rises.[27] We arrived at Vicks-

---

into personal sketchbooks (see Henry O. Gusley, *The Southern Journey of a Civil War Marine: The Illustrated Note-book of Henry O. Gusley,* ed. Edward T. Cotham Jr. [Austin: University of Texas Press, 2006], 61).

25. That is, the junction of the Red River and the Mississippi.

26. *Essex* has not been back to Natchez since September 1862, when, in response to a small arms attack by locals, she fired on and destroyed much of the lower part of the city; Natchez surrendered to *Essex*'s Captain William Porter the same week. Henneberry, in his own entry for April 20, mentions the evident unease of many locals with the ironclad's return: "the citizens eyed us like so many demons."

27. The Union ironclad *Indianola* was captured by Confederates on February 24, 1863, and then famously scuttled by them on March 14, when a large "dummy" ironclad floated downriver toward them and they mistakenly feared that she was about to be recaptured (see Park's entry for March 2, 1863, and accompanying note). The wreckage of *Indianola* lay just off

burg last night. This morning the Tin clad *No. 11* came down from Yazoo City with the crew of the Tin clad *Petrel* on board. The *Petrel* had been captured by the rebels two miles above the city whilst she was at the bank, wooding. All the crew had escaped except the captain and Pilot who remained behind and set fire to the boat.[28]

April 27th

We left Vicksburg on the evening of the 25th in tow of the steamboat *Ike Davis* for Sheppwith's Landing at which place we arrived this morning and commenced taking in coal. In the evening we started up the river for White River.

April 30th

This morning we arrived at the mouth of White River and commenced taking in Coal. On the passage up, the tow boat *Brown* passed us bound up. Her Captain reports that the army is falling back to Alexandria and the Fleet has returned to the head of the rapids waiting for the river to rise.[29] He also reports that the

---

Hurricane Plantation, which belonged to Jefferson Davis's older brother Joseph but had long been abandoned, burned, and looted. The ironclad was not in fact refloated until January 1865.

28. *Petrel* was reportedly one of the "favorite tinclads" in the brown water navy, and her loss was a source of chagrin and embarrassment to David Dixon Porter, especially since so many officers and crew fled the ship rather than staying with Captain Thomas McElroy, pilot Kimble Ware, and the seventeen-year old quartermaster John Nibbe, whom Park does not mention. The latter was awarded the Congressional Medal of Honor for his gallantry in attempting to save *Petrel,* the citation reading in part: "When all the others had deserted the flag, Nibbe assisted in getting the wounded off the guard and proceeded to get ready to fire the ship despite the escaping steam from the boilers at which time he was surrounded on all sides by the rebels and forced to surrender."

29. When Porter's flotilla returned from engagements upriver near Shreveport to the falls at Alexandria on April 28, the river's depth was catastrophically low at 3 feet 4 inches, and "waiting for the water to rise" was futile. The dire situation was alleviated by an army engineer, Lieutenant Colonel Joseph Bailey, whose prewar experience as a lumberman in Wisconsin included construction of river dams; he famously boasted to Banks, "I wish I was as sure of heaven as I am that I can save the fleet." Though the idea of damming the river was deemed impracticable by many, no other solutions were forthcoming, and work soon commenced on Bailey's Dam (ultimately a series of dams), which permitted the fleet to float to safety below the falls by mid-May. Congress formally thanked Bailey and promoted him to brigadier general. In

rebels are again in possession of Fort De Russey and that they opened a heavy fire of musketry on the *Brown* as she passed, killing one man.

May 4th

On the morning of the 1st of May we left White River and arrived here at Memphis this morning. The tin clad *Kenwood* arrived here shortly after us. She was from Red River and had Captain Phelps on board, the Captain of the *Eastport.* He reports that the *Eastport* was sunk, and whilst trying to raise her, with the assistance of the two submarine boats *Champions No. 2* & 5 The rebel sharpshooters and artillery opened fire on them, killing a large number of her crew and sinking the two *Champions* also disabeling two tin Clads that was protecting them. They had finally to abandon the *Eastport* and blow her up.[30]

May 7th

Yesterday and to day We have been punting ashore all the ammunition that was captured at Fort De Russey.

Admiral Porter's words, though "the proposition looked like madness, and the best engineers ridiculed it," Bailey "saved the Union a valuable fleet, worth nearly two million dollars, and deprived the enemy of a triumph which would have emboldened them to carry on this war a year or two longer." For a brief history, with diagrams, maps, and photos, see Steven D. Smith and George J. Castille III, *Bailey's Dam* (Baton Rouge: Department of Culture, Recreation and Tourism, 1986); and Shelby Foote, *The Civil War: A Narrative* (New York: Random House, 1974), 3:15–85. See also Park's entry for May 9.

30. A former Confederate vessel, *Eastport* (first mentioned by Park on March 12) had been captured and put into Federal service as an ironclad ram in August 1862; she was the largest ironclad in the Mississippi Squadron. While taking part in the Red River Campaign, she hit a rebel torpedo just below Grand Ecore on April 15 and was towed downstream, badly damaged. She grounded repeatedly in the shallow water, and despite the efforts of Captain Phelps and his crew, along with tinclads *Cricket, Fort Hindman,* and *Juliet,* and pump boats *New Champion* and *Champion No. 5,* she was eventually destroyed near Montgomery to prevent her capture. The other vessels were then attacked relentlessly as they tried to escape downriver. The fate of *New Champion,* sometimes listed as *Champion No. 3*—though Park, along with marine officer Frank L. Church, in his *Diary of the Red River Expedition,* calls her *Champion No. 2*—was especially horrific, as her captain, engineers, and over 150 black refugees seeking safe passage to the "land of freedom" were killed when her boiler was pierced; Confederate Colonel Joseph Lancaster Brent called it "probably the most fatal single shot fired during the war."

May 9th

The *General Lyons* arrived this morning from Red River. She reports that the rebels had captured two tin clads and destroyed them;[31] also that the Admiral was damming the river below the falls to enable him to get the gunboats down that were above.

May 14th

Last night the two turreted Monitor *Winebago* passed down bound for red river. For the last week the newspapers has been full of accounts of the fighting in Virginia and Georgia and from all accounts the Union army's are successful at both places. General Grant, with the army of the Potomac is driving Lee back on to Richmond, whilst Butler with a large army has landed on the South side of the James river, and cut the railroad communications with Richmond and keeping Beauregard from reinforceing Lee. Sherman in Georgia has driven Johnstones army through Tunnel Hill and Dalton.

May 16th

This morning the double turreted Monitor, *Chickawaw,* passed down. In the afternoon the *New National* passed down with the Mail for the fleet.

May 20th

This evening the tin clad *Cricket* arrived with dispatches from the Admiral. She reports that all the fleet had got down over the falls and had arrived at the mouth of the river.

May 24th

This afternoon the Flag Ship *Black Hawk* passed up with Admiral Porter on board.[32]

31. *Tinclad No. 8,* also known as *Signal* and *Tinclad No. 25, Covington,* had been ordered downstream on May 5 to protect the transport *John Warner,* loaded with cotton and more than two hundred members of the Fifty-Sixth Ohio Infantry, heading home on furlough. They were ambushed near Dunn's Bayou. None of the three vessels survived the day. Most of *Covington*'s crew escaped back to Alexandria, but the men aboard *Signal* and *Warner* were almost all killed, wounded, or captured.

32. Henneberry adds a sly observation that Porter is "on his way to Washington as fast as he can go, to beat if possible Gen. Banks who is also on his way there"—each to press his own version

May 29th

The Iron Clad *Carondelet* arrived here to day from red river. She had to take all the iron of her sides and throw six of her guns overboard before she could get over the falls at Alexandria. All the other boats had to do the same.[33] She reports that the Monitor *Osage* got on the bar at Helena and broke her back. They are taking the iron and turret, guns and ammunition off her.

June 10th

This morning the *Carondelet* went up the river. During the forenoon General A.J. Smith's division of the 17th Army Corps arrived from below. In the afternoon three soldiers, belonging to the Second New Jersey Cavalry, were executed in Fort Pickering for robbery, rape, and murder.[34]

June 12th

Yesterday some of the stragglers arrived here from Sturgis army. They report that they met Forrest at Guntown Mississippi and were defeated with heavy loss, loseing all their artillery and wagon trains. By all accounts it was a complete "skeddadle" the first battle of Bull run wasn't a patch on it. General Sturgis was one of the first to arrive at Memphis.[35] This morning General Smith's division went out to Collierville to look after Forrest.

---

of events in the failed expedition. Disaffection with Banks's leadership following the Red River debacle was nearly universal among sailors and officers, according to Symmes Browne, Acting Ensign on Union tinclad *Forest Rose* (Browne and Browne, *From the Fresh-Water Navy,* 271).

33. In a footnote to the good news of the fleet's being rescued from above Alexandria by Bailey's Dam, Park's account here captures some of the immense loss to the gunboats in the Red River Campaign—all of which now need to be refitted with iron and remounted with guns.

34. The crimes of robbery and rape (not murder) were committed by three privates, Jacob Snover, John Callahan, and Thomas Johnson, in a drunken spree while on picket duty. Following their court-martial, they were executed by firing squad "in the presence of 10,000 soldiers and many thousand citizens" of Memphis (Lyman B. Pierce, *History of the Second Iowa Cavalry* [Burlington, IA: Hawk-eye Steam Book and Job Printing, 1865], 97). According to another account: "The whole command was marched past them, as they lay mangled and bleeding, a terrible warning to wrong-doers" (*History of the Ninth Regiment Illinois Cavalry Volunteers* [Chicago: Donohue and Henneberry, 1888], 431–32). Whether or not any of the sailors were present, the events obviously had a sobering effect on the naval crews anchored offshore.

35. At the Battle of Brice's Crossroads, Federal troops under Brigadier General Samuel D. Sturgis were soundly defeated by a much smaller force led by Major General Nathan Bedford

July

I do not think I shall keep a journal any longer, as there is nothing worth recording. This month Smith's forces met Forrest's at Tupelo and defeated them with heavy loss. Forrest lost some two thousand killed and wounded, our loss about three hundered and fifty. On the 21st of August Forrest made a raid into the City of Memphis and after stopping about half an hour was repulsed with the loss of about two hundered and fifty men, our loss amounting to about the same number.[36] The old *Essex* is still laying here repairing and on the 19th of September I took my farewell look at her, and left for Cairo on the Steamer *Bell Memphis,* where I received my discharge, and on the 26th of September I arrived in Chicago just three years and one day since I joined the service.

Farewell old Journal
I am very Respectfully
Your obedient servant
William L. Park

Forrest. The humiliation of the survivors and the ignominy of Sturgis's own retreat is evident in Park's account. As a result of the fiasco, Sturgis was demoted and saw no further service in the Civil War.

36. The Second Battle of Memphis (the first being the naval fight in June 1862) was an audacious strike by Forrest into the Union-held city with the intent of freeing Southern prisoners from the Irving Block Prison and kidnapping three Union generals. Although he failed in those objectives, he managed to seize large quantities of supplies, including horses, and to embarrass General Cadwallader C. Washburn (with whom he had had a very testy correspondence earlier in the summer), who fled a downtown hotel to Fort Pickering wearing only his nightshirt.

Afterword

The Wake of War

WILLIAM LITTLE PARK (D. 1909)

William Park was twenty-seven when he mustered out in late September 1864. Though he does not mention it in his diary, he received a welcome bonus shortly before his formal discharge. In recognition of the fateful confrontation with *Arkansas* following the Battle of Baton Rouge, all members of the *Essex* crew who had been part of the action were given a portion of a sizable (though long-delayed) cash bounty.[1] How the money was divvied up is unclear: the ship was operating with a skeleton crew that day, as many officers and seamen were too sick for duty. Regulations concerning distribution of prize money were contentious and often interpreted expediently. But however large or small, the bounty was doubtless a welcome parting gift as Park reentered civilian life.

It is unclear why William chose Chicago; his extended family was living either in Scotland or in Canada, and his only previous association with the city was as his site of enlistment. But inasmuch as service in the Union navy had forged his allegiance to the United States, it had also effected his naturalization[2] and established him on American pension roles. He was to live in the

1. Congress authorized a payment of twenty-five thousand dollars in prize money in June 1864 (see *Dictionary of American Naval Fighting Ships* (Department of the Navy), "William D. Porter," www.history.navy.mil/danfs/w8/william_d_porter.htm). Fourth Master D. P. Rosenmiller is known to have received six hundred dollars.

2. A bill in 1862 allowed those who served in the United States military and had at least one year of residency to petition for citizenship; foreign-born combatants like William Park who fought for the Union in the Civil War were thus eligible to become American citizens following service.

United States for the rest of his life. His Chicago mates, James Henneberry and William "Hank" Ruger, the former of whom mustered out at the same time, likely convinced him that Chicago would be a good place to settle down and to find employment. Ruger was a close enough friend that he and Park saw each other with great frequency in the immediate aftermath of their service on *Essex*.[3] Another former shipmate, Nicholas J. McCarty, was also in Chicago. One of the unfortunate victims of the Fort Henry boiler explosion on February 6, 1862, he had been "sent to Mound City Hospital dreadfully scalded and burnt" but somehow survived and recovered. He, too, was to socialize with Park after the war.

William was not well cut out for a desk job or city routines. His first instinct was to go back on the Lakes during shipping season, where there was plenty of work on commercial vessels for an experienced tar like himself. After three years on the ironclads, his return to Great Lakes boats—hauling grain, iron ore, coal, or lumber—must have seemed relatively painless; his hardened body and well-honed skills would have made the work come easily, especially without the threat of incoming mortar shells or guerilla sharpshooters to contend with. The Lakes themselves, however, with their frequent violent storms, were more than dangerous enough, and working the ships was not for the faint of heart. There were 421 marine disasters in the 1865 shipping season and 621 in 1866; a single four-day gale in 1869 took down ninety-eight ships.

By his own account, William "sailed on the lakes for two seasons and did nothing all winter." His months of unemployment in the winters of 1864, 1865, and 1866 doubtless included time spent with his *Essex* cronies and recounting stories, reading such official records as were available in published form, and copying some of these documents by hand as appendices to his own personal journal. He also began courting his future wife—who probably had more than a little to do with coaxing him away from work on the Lakes.

Agnes Gillespie (b. 1843) was almost literally the "girl next door"; her family, like William's, was from Dumfriesshire, Scotland. She was born in Applegarth, about twelve miles from the farm owned by William's parents. At the time of the 1861 Scottish census, as William was enlisting for service on the Union inland navy, she was nineteen and living at home with her parents and six siblings; her father, David Gillespie, was farming 240 acres in

3. See preface, note 5.

Highlaw, St. Mungo's parish (still in Dumfriesshire), with his two eldest sons, John and Thomas. Sometime in the next few years, the family uprooted and settled in Chicago, where David Gillespie went to work in the meatpacking industry, possibly in the Union Stock Yard, which had been built primarily by "Scots, Scottish Americans, and Ulster Scots, and was a magnet for Scottish immigrants."[4]

It is impossible to know whether William had been acquainted with Agnes's family in Scotland or how they connected in postwar Chicago. But expatriate Caledonians tend always to seek each out. Chicago had, by the time William made his home there, a large Scottish population and a well-established United Scottish Societies of Chicago, including notably a Saint Andrew Society that hosted annual Robert Burns celebrations and other similar social mixers. And, though his wartime diary gives no evidence of religious temperament or interests, William may also have attended Presbyterian Church functions with an eye to friendship and potential courtship. Agnes's parents were founding members of the Chicago Scotch Presbyterian Church, which in 1867 had built an edifice on the corner of Adams and Sangamon Streets and called as its first pastor a Scottish-born divine with the wonderfully predictable name of Rev. Dr. Robert Burns.[5] Less than a month after *this* Robbie Burns arrived in Chicago, he united William Little Park and Agnes Gillespie in holy matrimony.[6]

William and Agnes lived with her parents on Throop Street in the early years of their marriage. In 1870, they were still part of the Gillespie household, along with two small children, George and Carrie, neither of whom survived early childhood.[7] William opened a butcher shop with his father-in-law,

4. June Skinner Sawyers, "Scots," *The Electronic Encyclopedia of Chicago* (Chicago: Chicago Historical Society, 2005).

5. Robert Ferrier Burns, D.D., a native of Paisley, Scotland, and son of "the father of Canadian Presbyterianism" (Robert Burns Sr.) came to Chicago after serving churches in Kingston and St. Catharines, Ontario. He was an eloquent pulpit orator and a learned "old country" divine; he was also, with Dwight L. Moody, active in the work of the Young Men's Christian Association (YMCA) in Chicago. In the three years of his Chicago tenure, the congregation grew from the 46 original members to 319.

6. April 23, 1867, according to Cook County marriage records, though William records the date as May 22, 1867, in a pension application in 1898—likely simply a lapse of memory.

7. The other members of the household listed in the July 1870 census are Agnes's parents, David and Sarah Gillespie, and her siblings George (21), James (18), and Harry (16). The two

David Gillespie; Park & Gillespie Meatmarket on West Madison Street was William's place of employment for the next fifteen years, although in his disability claim he acknowledges being less than fully able for the hours and the demands of the business and says he often only "did light work around the store." He was afflicted with several chronic ailments stemming from his service on the gunboats: severe hearing loss, almost complete in his left ear, which commenced at the time of his bout of typhoid fever and was doubtless exacerbated by acoustic trauma from the constant shattering of explosives to which he was subject as a gunner for more than two years thereafter; frequent acute gastritis and digestive disturbance; chronic diarrhea, and severe and often bleeding "piles" (hemorrhoids) that sometimes incapacitated him and kept him in bed for days at a time.

Exposure to "bad water" and "ill cooked food" is given by Park and the shipmates who provide affidavits on his behalf as the likely cause for the onset of violent dysentery and fever that landed him in the Mound City Hospital in December 1861.[8] According to Ruger, William Park "was a good ship mate and would never complain or go to a Doctor"—but he never fully regained his health after January 1862. Park himself adds that "the breaking up of his constitution" was made more extreme when, shortly after being released from hospital and sent back into service, he spent a harrowing, sleepless night with his *Pittsburg* crewmates bailing the grounded boat with buckets while up to his waist in freezing water.[9]

William's father-in-law and business partner, David Gillespie, died in 1881. Not long afterward, in search of better health and new opportunities, William moved his family—now including four children (David, b. 1873; Mary, b.

---

small Park children (aged 2 years and 9 months) counted here are never mentioned by William in later records. One could also wish for some record of the Parks' experience at the time of the Great Chicago Fire in October 1871, which destroyed more than twenty thousand houses and left more than one hundred thousand Chicagoans homeless; their own home, church, and business were fortunately outside the burn zone—though the butcher shop in the 400 block of West Madison only barely so.

8. "Bad water" was indeed a major contributing factor to rampant illness of all kinds on the boats, as shore latrines and detritus (and human and animal corpses) contaminated river water from which soldiers and sailors drank.

9. See the diary entry for February 14, 1862. The description here is given in a statement dated September 12, 1889, as part of Park's successful claim for increased war-related disability pension.

1876; Charles, b. 1878; and Jessie, b. 1880)—to a 160-acre parcel of tallgrass prairie on Lake Marsh near Castlewood, Hamlin County, in Dakota Territory (South Dakota). The lure of free land on which to homestead—the same incentive that had brought Laura Ingalls's family to De Smet, South Dakota, a few years earlier—proved irresistible to William. It seems an unlikely and daunting locale for an old salt like himself, and neighbors in South Dakota clearly doubted his fitness for rural life.[10] Although the change in location initially did him some good, William's health "gave way again" after two years, and he was laid up for several months in the autumn of 1886, unable to get out of bed. One can only imagine what life was like for Agnes and the children in such circumstances. South Dakota, with its sparse population, windblown terrain, frigid winters, and drought-prone summers must have taxed their endurance even when William was able to work. It is easy to read in Laura Ingalls Wilder's unvarnished account of life as a newlywed farmer's wife in the late 1880s, just thirty miles away (*The First Four* Years),[11] something of what the Parks must have faced.

In 1888, William and Agnes returned with their children to Chicago. Within months, William applied for disability income, attesting that his health, which was ruined as a result of service in the Union navy, prevented him from supporting his family. He was fifty-two. A modest pension increase was indeed approved, and William never worked again. Fortunately, his children were beginning to make their own way in the world. His son David found work with Crane, a thriving Chicago-based company started as a one-man brass and bell foundry in 1855 but, by 1890, an industrial powerhouse with more

10. Two local farmers later attested, in affidavits supporting Park's request for a pension increase, that he appeared "sickly" and was chronically "unable to do a day's work."

11. The manuscript of *The First Four Years* was found among the papers of Laura's daughter, Rose Wilder Lane, after her death in 1968 and published in its original unedited form by Harper and Row in 1971. Debt, hailstorms, parching winds, crop failure, a house fire, and diphtheria stalked the Wilders in the early years of their marriage (1885–89) and prompted their eventual move from South Dakota to Mansfield, Missouri. See also Wilder's *On the Way Home* (New York: Harper and Row, 1962), which chronicles the family's departure from the Dakotas: "For seven years there had been too little rain. The prairies were dust. Day after day, summer after summer, the scorching winds blew the dust and the sun was brassy in a yellow sky. Crop after crop failed. Again and again the barren land must be mortgaged, for taxes and food and next year's seed. The agony of hope ended when there was no harvest and no more credit, no money to pay interest and taxes; the banker took the land. Then the bank failed."

than 1,500 employees. David was to stay with Crane for his entire working life, climbing the corporate ranks; his younger brother Charles later worked for the company as well.

William's long-suffering wife, Agnes, died on May 25, 1892, after which, widowed and unemployed, poor, and frail of health, William lived with various of his children—all of whom married and continued to reside in the Chicago area—until his own death seventeen years later, on October 7, 1909. David made the funeral arrangements, and the family laid him to rest in quiet dignity next to Agnes at Graceland Cemetery. William left no will and had no worldly goods to pass on to his children beyond the memories of his Civil War service aboard the Mississippi ironclads, painstakingly recounted in a Louisiana schoolgirl's notebook and then later revised into a more reflective memoir.

The latter text, almost certainly written after Park returned to Chicago from the Dakotas in 1888, was bound into a smooth-grained black-leather volume, its cover stamped with a gilded title: "W. L. Park's journal."[12] It was likely at that point, having rewritten and expanded his account of his *Essex* service, that William passed on the original, bilingual text published here—containing also Celeste Repp's "Compositions françaises" from St. Mary's Academy in Baton Rouge—to his Canadian relatives. Perhaps he thought that the French materials, which were undecipherable and inconsequential to him, would be of some local interest in Quebec.

MATILDA VICTOR (D. 1891)

What Matilda Victor called her "life of martyrdom" following upon her youthful conversion to the Catholic faith[13] was exacerbated by the political

12. After William died, his son Charles kept it for a time, affixing in it a small 1924 newspaper clipping about remnants of *Essex* having been salvaged in the Ohio River. The volume eventually went to Charles's niece, Virginia A. Park. It was Virginia, William's long-lived, unmarried granddaughter and last living descendent, from whom Chicago's Newberry Library acquired the memoir in 2006. I am indebted to the staff of the Newberry for providing me with a copy of the text of "W. L. Park's journal," permitting me thus to compare the two versions of Park's wartime experience aboard *Essex* (see appendix 3). Along with the leather-bound memoir, Virginia donated to the Newberry an undated daguerreotype portrait of her grandfather (figure 3), which is used with permission here.

13. She described it thus in her letter to Orestes Brownson, August 22, 1859 (see introduction, note 26).

turmoil of secession, occupation, bombardment, and battle in her adopted city. By the autumn of 1861, virtually all the men on whom she had depended for material and spiritual support in Baton Rouge were dead or gone to battlefields in Virginia and Maryland. Her problems with shrinking enrollments, inadequate staff, and lack of funds were of little interest to anyone, and it took every ounce of her considerable resourcefulness to survive from month to month. Though she attempted to keep her school going in the early stages of the war and even hosted a benefit for local Confederate Volunteers in January 1862, it was all for naught. The fabric of her community was irreparably rent. On April 25, 1862, a day before New Orleans fell to the Federals, the Confederate state government abandoned Baton Rouge; two weeks later, Union forces took possession of the arsenal and barracks without firing a shot. As an eyewitness remembered it:

> One magnificent morning in early summer the whole river . . . was suddenly, as if by magic, ablaze with the grandeur of Federal gunboats and transports with flags and bright-colored streamers flying from every peak, their decks thronged with brilliantly uniformed officers. We stood upon the veranda, with streaming eyes and bursting hearts, the gay strains of "Yankee Doodle" as they floated o'er the waters filling our souls with bitterness unspeakable, and watched the victorious pageant, until . . . it anchored amid blare of trumpet and beat of drum beside the deserted landing of our dear little city. The enemy was there![14]

The town's population at this point consisted largely of noncombatants: women and children, the elderly and disabled, slaves and free blacks, Northern sympathizers, those who were unfit or unwilling for military service, and those who had returned from service maimed or sick. None of these posed a threat to Federal troops, and an uneasy truce prevailed for a time between occupiers and occupied. Even a fiery young woman like Sarah Morgan was prepared to cooperate with "honorable" enemies, however bitterly she resented their presence.[15]

14. Eliza McHatton Ripley, *From Flag to Flag: A Woman's Adventures and Experiences in the South during the War, in Mexico, and in Cuba* (New York: Appleton and Co., 1889), 24.

15. The military officer in charge, General Thomas Williams (figure 9), unlike General Benjamin Butler in New Orleans—famously labeled "the Beast" by Southern partisans—earned considerable respect and cooperation from citizens of Baton Rouge, as he seemed concerned to protect their rights and property. He was in fact extremely demanding of his troops, a stickler

Self-styled local "guerillas," however, answerable to no military organization or established rules of engagement and filled with rowdy bravado, regularly harassed Union gunboats from shore batteries. On May 27, 1862, a rowboat carrying navy personnel ashore to get laundry done in Baton Rouge was fired on by a group of these irregulars. Admiral Farragut was incensed and decided to "send a message" in the form of a sustained bombardment of the city. One civilian was killed, several others wounded, and many buildings were damaged or destroyed. St. Joseph Catholic Church, the construction of which had so taxed Frs. Lavay and Hubert, but which now stood as a neogothic landmark in the center of town, suffered greatly under the Union shells;[16] so, too, did St. Mary's Academy.

Whether she had previously nailed her own colors to the mast, Matilda Victor chose sides that day. She fled from her home and her damaged school straight to the Union fleet, where she declared herself a loyal citizen of the United States and made good her escape. According to a postwar letter written on her behalf by Admiral Farragut, "she was driven out of Baton Rouge by my guns when my boat was fired upon by the guerrillas. She sought refuge on board my ship, and I took her down to New Orleans, with her sister and her companion, a French lady."[17] Matilda and her two associates were the "three Northern females" mentioned in Farragut's letter to Gideon Welles,

---

for military discipline and protection of noncombatants—which caused resentment among his men but eased the worst fears of the city's inhabitants. Sarah Morgan refers to him several times as "a dear old gentleman" and a "good man," whose kindness and generosity prompted Sarah to "admire the enemy" (Morgan, *The Civil War Diary of a Southern Woman* [New York: Simon and Schuster/Touchstone, 1992], e.g., 99, 107, 109, 143). "Under Gen. Williams' rule," she says, "I was perfectly satisfied that whatever was done, was done through necessity, and under orders from headquarters, beyond his control; we all liked him" (143). Williams's death in the Battle of Baton Rouge was regarded as tragic by many locals (and also suspicious, as persistent early rumors circulated that "friendly fire" was the cause); none of the officers who came after him achieved anything like the same level of trust.

16. St. Joseph's iconic steeple had not been completed by 1862 because of lack of funds. It was the foreshortened tower, which rose a little above the roofline of the edifice, that Farragut's shells found. Several months later, as a result of the damage, a large section of the roof, vault, and back wall of the sanctuary collapsed, making the building unusable.

17. This letter, dated September 22, 1865, is addressed simply to "those who may have it in their power to assist her in any way to recover her property or to make a living." Farragut had written an earlier letter, dated January 3, 1865, asserting that "Miss Victor and her two assistants

dated May 30: "I brought down [to New Orleans] three Northern females, who had been teaching school there and had become odious simply because they were Northerners" (*ORN*, 1.18.520).

It is unclear which of Matilda's sisters would have been with her at St. Mary's—possibly unmarried Florence, visiting from Sandusky, or Gertrude, who had married British-born William Hawkesworth, a civil engineer, in 1863 and was living in New Orleans in the mid-1860s.[18] A less likely, but nonetheless intriguing, possibility is that it was, rather, Matilda's *sister-in-law* Metta, whose credentials with the Union officers would have been unimpeachable and very helpful to Matilda.[19] At any rate, Matilda seems to have sheltered in New Orleans briefly and then returned to Baton Rouge, concerned about her property and belongings. She had by then made another strategic decision. According to a letter dated August 23, 1862, from Lieutenant Colonel Henry H. Elliott, First Louisiana United States [Union] Volunteers:

> The school [St. Mary's Academy] having been interrupted in consequence of the presence of Federal troops, and all the scholars being withdrawn by their parents (all sympathizers with secession), Miss Victor was thrown suddenly out of employment, and, of course, her income stopped; not only that, but her debtors either dishonestly refused to pay bills for tuition or tendered the money in Confederate notes. Immediately after General Williams landed, Miss Victor called on him, and through me tendered the use of her academy [as a hospital] for soldiers, and also offered her services as nurse.[20]

fled to us in a great state of terror [and] that she is and always has been, as far as I am capable of judging, a strong Union woman." In a postscript, he adds tellingly that "Miss Victor's brothers are all in the service of the Union, and her oldest brother is writing *The History of the Rebellion*—Orville Victor." Both notes may be found in House Report No. 3346 of the 49th Cong., 1st Sess., House of Representatives, *Mathilda Victor*, in *Congressional Edition*, vol. 2445 (Washington, DC: U.S. Government Printing Office, 1886); hereafter this House Report is cited as *MV* (1886).

18. Gertrude (née Victor) and William Hawkesworth's firstborn child, Alan Spencer Hawkesworth, was born in New Orleans on August 10, 1867; the family moved for a time to the United Kingdom after the war.

19. Orville Victor's wife, Metta Victoria Fuller Victor, was a prolific writer, whose abolitionist sentiments were notably showcased in her best-selling Beadle novel, *Maum Guinea and Her Plantation "Children"*—published a decade after *Uncle Tom's Cabin* and nearly as popular (see the introduction).

20. *MV* (1886), 4.

Matilda herself later recounted that after Baton Rouge was occupied, she admitted to her dormitory a number of sick and wounded men for care and treatment. This building "contained about forty rooms and was admirably adapted for use as a hospital." Indeed, it was "a large and delightful place fully furnished and provided with all necessary comforts." She went on to assert that "her loyalty was well known to the officers of the United States Army and Navy" and that she freely volunteered the use of her facility, since the need for a hospital "was urgent and pressing."[21] Additionally, "she rendered every possible service in the care of the sick and wounded soldiers of the Union Army in her buildings, where she [had] bedding, bed clothes, cooking utensils, dishes, &c, for the comfort of at least 150 persons, and that she spared no labor or care in providing for the wants and restoration to health of the Union soldiers."[22]

Matilda seems to have stayed on as volunteer nurse and liaison through the relatively uneventful summer months of 1862. One assumes she was there, ensconced with soldiers and officers and a small housekeeping staff, when,

21. Williams's army had spent several weeks upriver in an unsuccessful attempt to dig a bypass canal near Vicksburg, to cut the city off from the Mississippi and "make it an inland town"; the squalid conditions, "malarious atmosphere," and extreme heat were such that hundreds fell ill. "Nearly ½ of my whole force is on the sick list," wrote Williams to his wife on July 20 ("Letters of General Thomas Williams, 1862," *American Historical Review* 14, no. 2 [1909]: 324). The next day he reported, "I'm preparing to send all the sick down the river to Baton Rouge, some 1100!" (ibid.) By midsummer, the Union camp in Baton Rouge was more of an infirmary than military encampment. Sarah Morgan observes that "it is like a graveyard in its quiet at times," with the sick arriving daily and the undertakers unable to keep up with the need for coffins (Morgan, *Civil War Diary,* 181). Meanwhile, aboard the Union gunboats, the situation was equally dire. In his notation for August 5 (the day Breckinridge tried to retake Baton Rouge), Park says that "very near all the Ships Company is on board the Hospital Boat with Swamp Fever." In the immediate aftermath of the battle, Park's shipmates James Henneberry and Hank Ruger were both hospitalized in Baton Rouge, very likely in Matilda Victor's school-turned-hospital (see, in the introduction, the discussion titled "How Did Celeste's Notebook Find Its Way into William Park's Hands?").

22. Senate Report No. 1096, 48th Cong., 2d Sess., United States Senate (To accompany bill S. 2117, "For the relief of Mathilda Victor," January 28, 1885), 3. Hereafter, this Senate Report will be referred to as *MV* (1885). Interestingly, a cross-town educational academy for young men in Baton Rouge, Magruder's Collegiate Institute, became a Confederate hospital facility after the Battle of Baton Rouge; its role is as conspicuous as St. Mary's Academy's is obscure to present memory (see *The Battle of Baton Rouge and Related Historic Civil War Sites* tourist leaflet: www.youngsanders.org/CivilWarinBatonRougeTourBrochure-3pg.pdf).

in the predawn hours of August 5, Confederate General John Breckinridge launched a surprise attempt to retake the city, in what came to be called the Battle of Baton Rouge. The entire Union encampment, and indeed the whole town, became suddenly a battlefield. Terrified citizens were "roused from their beds by firing and fighting; rushing half-clad from houses being riddled with shot and shell . . . through streets filled with men fighting hand to hand."[23]

Events seemed initially to favor a Confederate victory, but Union gunboats proved decisive. An officer from USS *Kineo* came ashore and took up position on the tower of the Capitol building, from which elevation he could both observe the battle lines and signal where the vessels should aim their shells.[24] When the Confederate ram *Arkansas,* which Breckinridge had counted on to neutralize the Union ironclads, developed engine trouble five miles upriver, was fired on by *Essex,* and then scuttled,[25] Breckinridge's hopes to retake the city were dashed.

How long Matilda may have stayed on to house and care for sick and wounded men in blue is uncertain. Her situation must have seemed increasingly untenable in a city where all of her erstwhile acquaintances were "sympathizers with secession" and increasingly hardened in their anti-Yankee sentiments. In the wake of the brief but devastating Battle of Baton Rouge, in which casualties numbered in the hundreds on both sides, a third of the city was destroyed by United States troops. Major General Benjamin Butler ("the Beast") actually ordered the entire place burned to the ground, but cooler heads prevailed, arguing on behalf of orphans and widows and others whose suffering had already greatly exceeded any culpability attached to simple habitation in an "insurrectionary" hometown. In mid-August, however, when the Union army elected to withdraw from the city, insult and injury were added to the general misery: more homes and property were destroyed, including the fences and outbuildings, and Matilda's cottage on the St. Mary's Academy site, "by order of Colonel Payne [i.e., Halbert E. Paine] . . . who was then in

23. Ripley, *From Flag to Flag.*

24. *Harper's Weekly,* September 6, 1862.

25. The events are described in Park's diary and recounted briefly in William Porter's farewell speech. The "official" version of events was hotly disputed in the following days by participants and observers on all sides. Park's is a straightforward account; the notes following his entry for August 6, 1862, include some of the contradictory claims.

command of the United States forces at this post."[26] Anything deemed likely to afford shelter to returning Confederate forces or anything that obstructed the view of the ironclad gunners was reduced to rubble (see figure 11). Union soldiers then went on a wanton spree of looting and destruction before boarding their transports for New Orleans.[27]

At that point, it seems, Matilda had had enough. Though it is unclear when she shook the dust off her feet, the Academy property, between late August and December 1862, stood vacant for all but about three weeks. Since she was identified now as a "truly loyal and patriotic lady" and "fast and unflinching friend of the [United States] Government,"[28] Miss Victor's bridges to the community she had served and people she had loved were burned; she had no abiding home in Baton Rouge; indeed, she would not long have any abiding city in the South.[29]

26. *MV* (1885), 6. Ironically, Paine was apparently among those who had persuaded Butler not to carry out his intention to raze the city. For Paine's recollections of his sojourn in Baton Rouge, see *A Wisconsin Yankee in the Confederate Bayou Country: The Civil War Reminiscences of a Union General,* ed. Samuel C. Hyde Jr. (Baton Rouge: Louisiana State University Press, 2009), chap. 6. A detailed list of houses "north of North Street" destroyed by Federal troops under Paine's orders was published in the *Baton Rouge Weekly Gazette and Comet,* October 22, 1862; it includes that of "Mrs. [*sic*] Victor."

27. The vandalism at the Morgan home was especially scandalous, leaving not only the family but also other occupants of the area "heartsick and indignant" (see Sarah Morgan's *Civil War Diary,* 233–36; 235n82. Such gratuitous destruction of personal property by occupying Federal forces overturned any goodwill that had been previously won during General Williams's tenure. Paine's troops also removed a cherished statue of George Washington from the rotunda of the State Capitol and took it with them, an act regarded locally as an "outrageous act of spoliation."

28. *MV* (1886), 7.

29. She apparently stayed in New Orleans off and on until the spring of 1864, when, in consideration of her loyalty to the United States and her loss of home and livelihood, she was provided free travel to New York (see Banks, *Nathaniel P. Banks Letter Book: 1863–1864,* MSS. 2326, p. 9, Louisiana and Lower Mississippi Valley Collections, LSU Libraries, Baton Rouge, 9). Matilda evidently felt safe in New Orleans under Union occupation, which lasted for the duration of the war and well into Reconstruction; she would have had safe haven with her sister Gertrude and her family (see note 18, above). The claim that she was in Baton Rouge "persecuted and reviled by the enemies of the country, menaced with violence and death" may have been exaggerated, but she had doubtless become something of a pariah there. From New York, where she may have stayed for a time with her brother Orville and sister-in-law Metta, she settled in Lansing, Michigan.

She was therefore unlikely to have seen it (and she was not consulted in advance)[30] when General Nathaniel Banks, in reoccupying Baton Rouge, designated the empty Academy buildings as a "refuge for 'contrabands' for a period of more than one year."[31] Once that term ended, the property was vacated once more and "left exposed to vandalism" by squatters and occasional habitation by United States troops, all of which resulted in damage "to the extent of almost total destruction." In one final indignity, a Union cavalry regiment moved in during the spring and summer of 1864 and used the buildings for stabling horses.[32]

Matilda began to gather testimony and support for her damages claim almost immediately after Baton Rouge was occupied. Her list of supporters and character witnesses constitutes an impressive Who's Who of Federal army and navy officers—Rear Admiral David Farragut; Lieutenant Colonel Henry H. Elliott, First Louisiana Volunteers (Union); Brigadier General W. P. Benton; Colonel Edward Martindale, Eighty-Third Regiment United States Colored Infantry; Brigadier General Fitz Henry Warren; Major General Benjamin Butler; Major General Nathaniel Banks. Banks himself ordered a military commission in March 1864 "to determine the amount of damages and rent due Miss Mathilda Victor"; more than a dozen witnesses, both military and civilian, were called to give testimony. But establishing that she was owed compensation (upward of twenty thousand dollars by one reckoning) and actually receiving compensation were two very different matters, as she was to learn to her sorrow over the course of twenty years. The fine art of buck-passing was demonstrated by every political body to which she appealed, despite the merits of her case: "her flourishing school scattered and broken

30. Her claims and affidavits make clear that the only use she offered or intended for the Academy property was as a field hospital for sick and wounded troops, and that she was promised appropriate rent for such use.

31. *MV* (1886), 6. See figures 15 and 16.

32. This last use of the St. Mary's property was attested by Colonel Edward Martindale of the Eighty-Third Regiment, U.S. Colored Infantry, who avers that "he was well acquainted with Matilda Victor, late a loyal resident of said city [i.e., Baton Rouge]," whose "constancy under losses and sufferings to which she has been exposed in consequence of her remarkable loyalty commend her to great consideration on the part of the Government, and to practical and speedy relief" (*MV* [1886], 4).

up, her house and home and only means of support ruined and destroyed by her own Government."[33]

Matilda moved to Lansing, Michigan, and began to forge a new identity. Her days of trying to run a small private academy were over, but it is hard to imagine her giving up her vocation as a teacher; she might have been drawn to Lansing by Abigail Rogers and her extremely ambitious and academically rigorous Michigan Female College, established in 1855. The college did not long survive the death of its founder in 1869 but would still have been in its full flower when Matilda arrived. It would certainly have suited her intellectual and religious temperament, and her Catholicism would not have been a hindrance to her teaching there.[34] There was in Lansing a flourishing constituency of strong, like-minded women, and Matilda was, after her interminable frustrations in Baton Rouge, ready for activism. She found a home among local suffragists who were engaged in a vigorous and well-organized initiative to secure the elective franchise for women in Michigan, and became for a time corresponding secretary for the Michigan Woman Suffrage Association.[35] In

33. Ibid., 2.

34. According to the school's brochure, "The study of the Holy Scriptures will form a regular part of the whole Course, both Preparatory and Collegiate." A classically oriented and demanding curriculum with firm biblical moorings, overseen by competent women (rather than the poorly trained nuns about whom she had complained to Orestes Brownson) would have been precisely Matilda's idea of a proper female education.

35. Catholic bishops and clergy were generally outspoken in their opposition to women's suffrage, arguing that it posed a threat to the family. Matilda had no intention of marrying and no vocation for the religious life; she was, she felt, being denied reasonable compensation by her government. For her, the right of women to participate in the political process was incontestably just. Among younger contemporary Catholics who entered into the suffrage debate in the late years of the nineteenth century were Schuyler Neilson Warren, an ardent suffragist and member of the Philothea Society of New York, and the bluestocking essayist Agnes Repplier of Philadelphia. Repplier's moral seriousness, nourished by Catholic intellectual tradition, prompted both a commitment to political justice and a judicious caution against feminist utopianism; enfranchised women would neither end war nor cloak society in a kindly blanket, she argued. Indeed, "emancipation implies the sacrifice of immunity, the acceptance of obligation. It heralds the reign of sober and disillusioning experience" ("Woman Enthroned," *Atlantic Monthly,* March 1918, 308; see also her essay "Women and War," in *Counter-Currents* [Boston: Houghton Mifflin, 1916]). Repplier and Victor both lived in Philadelphia in the 1880s and may well have known each other through Catholic and/or literary circles such as the Browning Society or Contemporary Club.

that role she wrote a rather audacious letter to Mark Twain in 1872, proposing that he write an original drama "to make money for the state organization purposes, &, at the same time to present the question [of women's suffrage] to the people in a popular form." She indicated that he would be paid whatever seemed appropriate, and she even had the temerity to provide for him dramatis personae that she thought would serve the cause.[36] Alas, he turned her down. Undaunted, she kept up a tireless effort to build support for a ballot initiative throughout the state:

> Those who were engaged in the canvass had enthusiastic meetings everywhere. They not only filled all their regular appointments, but spoke in the prisons, asylums; even the deaf and dumb were refreshed with the gospel of woman suffrage. . . . Everything that could be done was done by the friends of the amendment throughout the State; meetings held and tracts on every phase of the question scattered in all the most obscure settlements; inspiring songs sung, earnest prayers offered . . . women everywhere . . . persuading voters to cast their ballots for temperance, moral purity and good order, to be secured only by giving the right of suffrage to their mothers, wives and daughters.[37]

36. "A minister of the [Justin Dewey] Fulton or Robert Laird Collyer pattern *rabidly* opposed—a negro—a dutchman & an Irishman, also opposed. A saloon keeper & a young & green graduate of "Yale" or some other college excluding women, also opposed—a reformed drunkard, favorably inclined—a strong minded woman—all the better if an old maid, a strong advocate of the movement—a gay young miss on the rampage after a husband, very much opposed—an old farmer—a regular ol broadhorn very bitter—a young popinjay just shedding his pin-feathers, opposed. Mixing & mingling these characters with a due proportion of friends & advocates will, I think, give as a drama that will be of much service to us." This correspondence, dated April 18, 1871, can be found in *Mark Twain's Letters,* vol. 5, *1872–1873,* ed. Lin Salamo and Harriet Elinor Smith (Berkeley: University of California Press, 1997), 80–81. Notably, the clerical antagonists to women's suffrage she includes here do not here include a Catholic priest: there is no evidence to suggest that Matilda's suffragist convictions were concomitant with an estrangement from her adopted faith.

37. Elizabeth Cady Stanton, Susan Brownell Anthony, Matilda Joslyn Gage, et al., *History of Woman Suffrage,* vol. 3, *1876–1885* (New York: Fowler and Wells, 1886), 522. Matilda Victor is here mentioned by name among the public advocates and activists in Michigan. Meanwhile, Matilda's sister-in-law Frances Fuller Victor (estranged by 1870 from Henry Victor) was simultaneously secretary of the Oregon State Woman Suffrage Association and a member of its executive committee. If Matilda and Frances maintained a correspondence, it has not survived. An intellectual biography of Frances Fuller Victor is currently being prepared by Dr. Sheri Bartlett Browne at Tennessee State University; see her "A Lovely but Unpredictable

Matilda was evidently not shy about taking the message out on the lecture circuit. She spoke to the Woman Franchise Association in Chicago on May 3, 1870—to a disappointingly slim audience.[38] A few months later she was in Lindsey, Ohio, a step away from her hometown of Sandusky, to give a public address on the question of female enfranchisement. A response by an attendee, published in the *Fremont (OH) Weekly Journal* over the initials "J.A.M." and dated 7 October 1870, indicates something of the challenge Matilda and other suffragists faced, when even ostensibly laudatory comments were laced with condescension:

> On the evening of September 28th, the citizens of Lindsey [Ohio] were favored with a lecture on "Woman's Rights and Her Duties." The speaker, Miss Matilda Victor, did herself credit, as also the cause she advocates. In manner and appearance she represents the perfect lady. The address was able and interesting, and, in many respects equal to lectures delivered by members of the male sex. The subject matter of the discourse was presented in an intelligible and logical style, being replete with pleasantries and amusing incidents, calculated to illustrate more forcibly and practicably the arguments presented. To be engaged in advocating and publicly promulgating the doctrine of so unpopular a cause, requires considerable nerve, patience, and perseverance to labor successfully, and it must certainly be a considerable sacrifice to endure the sneers of its opponents, who ridicule and abuse in every possible way its teachers, and apply to them the sobriquet of "strong minded woman" and other similar epithets.

Meanwhile, the Committee on Claims of the Fortieth Congress (1867–69), during the presidency of Andrew Johnson, had taken up Matilda Victor's petition for damages. The committee debated, questioned, submitted a report (No. 199), accompanied by a bill to authorize payment (S. 875), which was "read and passed to a second reading," and then "before an final action was reached thereon the Congress expired." The Forty-First Congress, meeting during the presidency of Ulysses S. Grant, "withdrew the papers in the case from the files of the Senate, and recommitted them for examination and further report." And then, "after mature consideration, find[ing] no reason

River: Frances Fuller Victor's Early Life and Writing," *Oregon Historical Quarterly* 112 (Spring 2011): 8–33; and Jim Martin, *A Bit of a Blue: The Life and Work of Frances Fuller Victor* (Salem, OR: Deep Well, 1992).

38. Reported in *Harrisburg Telegraph,* May 4, 1870, 2.

to change their former conclusions . . . adopt[ed] their former report"—but failed to resolve the claim.[39] Three presidents later, the Forty-Eighth Congress looked at the same petition and was still unable to come to a satisfactory resolution. In fact, the findings of the Senate Committee on Claims in that instance (January 28, 1885, during the administration of Chester Arthur), following upon a Board of Survey convened in September 1883, expressed skepticism that Matilda was due any compensation at all, beyond the single payment of $1,500 she had received from the Quartermaster's Department in 1862 for rental of St. Mary's Academy as a hospital facility. Their reasoning: (1) since the destruction carried out under the order of Colonel Paine was "under urgent and imperative military necessity," it was therefore lawful, and the government had no liability; (2) since the wholesale destruction of buildings, grounds, and property by soldiers and contrabands (much less horses) amounted to "unlawful acts," the United States was under no obligation to make good the loss; (3) the outstanding rent she claimed (for use of the Academy under military command over nearly three years) was not justified since she showed no contract; (4) moreover, the rent she asked for seemed "liberal" for a property "rendered comparatively useless for school purposes" (by the destructive uses to which it was put under Union command). And, in one last bit of sophistry, (5) "The claimant's property was situated within a State whose citizens were in open insurrection against the United States. . . . And while it appears that the use of her property was tendered to the officers in command of the United States forces, it also appears that her school had been broken up by a state of actual war [indeed, by Farragut's gunboats!], and she had been compelled to flee from Baton Rouge by fear of personal violence. Her previous consent was not necessary to the occupation of her property under such circumstances." The committee recommended against passage of the bill.[40]

39. It may have been exasperation that led her at this point to write to Benjamin Bently, asking for consideration by the Southern Claims Commission. She received only a curt and dismissive note, dated January 7, 1874, indicating that "Your claim, insofar as destruction is concerned, is not within the jurisdiction of the Southern Claims Commission. . . . [It] does not take cognizance of property destroyed in the war." In any case, he added, the deadline for application had passed. The original of this correspondence is held in the archives of Wellesley College (OCLC no. 70813460).

40. *MV* (1885), 6–8.

The Forty-Ninth Congress (1886), under Grover Cleveland, reconsidered the petition and came to a decidedly different and more favorable conclusion, finding that every argument set out by the previous committee was wrongheaded and prejudicial and failed to acknowledge the obvious harm and suffering to which the United States government had subjected this patriotic, loyal, and patient citizen. It recommended a payment of ten thousand dollars as "full and complete satisfaction of any and all claims," noting that the sum was arbitrary and insufficient but that Matilda herself, "consistently with her past life, is willing to accept it and contribute the balance due her to her country."[41] Matilda Victor was nearly sixty years old. Her claim had taken more than two decades to resolve, and her compensation was by any reckoning a fraction of what she was owed.

She moved from Lansing, Michigan, to Philadelphia sometime in the late 1870s or early 1880s after several ringing failures of the Michigan suffrage initiative.[42] She listed herself as "authoress" and "publisher" in city directories and census records, but whether she was composing suffragist tracts or educational treatises or edifying fiction, no writings in her name are extant; perhaps she chose, as her sisters-in-law, Metta and Frances, often did, to write under a pseudonym.[43]

One would like to think that Matilda spent her last years in relative comfort, and her last day, Christmas 1891, in the company of friends and the enjoyment of her religion. She was in Baltimore. Perhaps she attended Christmas Mass in the neoclassical grandeur of the Baltimore Cathedral and heard the gospel tidings recounted by Archbishop James Gibbons. If so, one would like to think that there was consolation for her that day in the Body and Blood. For in one final irony of her complex and conflicted life, after her passing on December 26, 1891, her remains were returned to Sandusky, Ohio, and interred, without funeral rite or obituary, at Oakland Cemetery—all traces

41. *MV* (1886), 9.

42. She is also known to have returned to Sandusky for the funeral of her mother, Gertrude Nash Victor, on February 19, 1882.

43. Metta Victor wrote under at least nine pen names (see "Pseudonyms of Various Beadle Authors" in "House of Beadle & Adams Online/The Authors and Their Novels," www.ulib.niu.edu/badndp/part4_appen_pseud.html). One wonders if Matilda might have written pseudonymously for Beadle herself, using her family connections there.

of her Catholic identity and all memory of her restless activism buried with her in the unconsecrated ground.

DARIUS HUBERT, S.J. (D. 1893)

Fr. Darius Hubert was alone among the Jesuit Confederate chaplains to return to the South after the war. Joseph Prachensky, after a two-year chaplaincy with the Third Alabama, became a prison chaplain at Ward's Island, New York, for twenty years, after which he taught at Fordham College; Hippolyte Gache (Tenth Louisiana) served academic posts at Loyola, Georgetown, and Fordham. As Gache's editor and translator, Cornelius Buckley, S.J., observes, "the future for the Catholic Church seemed part of the spoils that belonged to the victor."[44]

Fr. Hubert, however, went home to New Orleans, to the Jesuit Church of the Immaculate Conception on Baronne Street. He aspired to nothing more comfortable or prestigious than an ongoing apostolate among brave young men grown quickly old and brokenhearted families to whom sons, husbands, and fathers had not returned.[45] What he found was a community engulfed in intense political, social, and racial turmoil; the Crescent City afforded anything but a respite for its weary returning chaplain. The purveyors and supporters of Reconstruction and those who opposed it waged often bloody battles on city streets. Extreme tensions in a society coming to uneasy terms

44. Peter Louis-Hippolyte Gache, S.J., *Frenchman, Chaplain, Rebel: The Civil War Letters of Pere Louis-Hippolyte Gache, S.J., 10th Louisiana Infantry,* ed. and trans. Cornelius M. Buckley, S.J. (Tuscaloosa: University of Alabama Press, 1981), 233.

45. Casualty numbers among Southern combatants are almost unfathomable. Between 75 and 85 percent of white Southern men of military age served the Confederacy. Of these, "between one in five and one in three . . . died during the war. . . . The odds of a soldier in Lee's Army of Northern Virginia surviving the war alive without serious injury and without being captured were probably about one in five" (W. Fitzhugh Brundage, "Redeeming a Failed Revolution: Confederate Memory," in *In the Cause of Liberty: How the Civil War Redefined American Ideals,* ed. William J. Cooper Jr., and John M. McCardell Jr. [Baton Rouge: Louisiana State University Press, 2009], 127). In Sarah Morgan's doleful words: "Last Saturday, the 29th of April [1865], seven hundred and fifty paroled Louisianans from Lee's army were brought here—the sole survivors of ten regiments who left four years ago so full of hope and determination." By then, her own brothers, George and Gibbes, who served with the First and Seventh Louisiana regiments respectively, had "long been lying in their graves" (Morgan, *Civil War Diary,* 440).

with defeat on the battlefield and a shattered economy at home[46] were ratcheted up by the continuing occupation of Federal forces and carpetbaggers, and by emancipation and suffrage of former slaves coupled with disenfranchisement of ex-Confederates through the Ironclad Oath. Many who had been raised to think of the African Americans under their custody in familiar, even familial terms, were unsettled by the newly empowered strangers in their midst, especially those incited to hostility against former masters. Overall, a seething resentment of "interference" with the Southern way of life and of Northern hypocrisy and moralizing produced a fearsome backlash: among them were the Black Codes—enforcing many of the conditions of servitude by another name—and the rise of vigilantism and political assassination. For Fr. Hubert, who had prayed at the secession of "dear Louisiana" and spent four long years with those fighting ardently for the survival of the Confederacy, pastoral obligations now included not only acceptance of political defeat and conciliation between erstwhile battlefield enemies but also the active fostering of racial harmony between those whose roles had been suddenly redefined.[47] The counsel of peace at the heart of the Gospel was not an easy sell in New Orleans in the wake of war and the bitter experience of Reconstruction.

When yellow fever—the deadly plague with which he was so familiar from his years in Baton Rouge—descended on Savannah in the autumn of 1876, and on Vicksburg, Yazoo City, and Jackson in 1878, Fr. Hubert left his

46. For a succinct description of postwar Louisiana, in which "over one half of the former wealth of the state had been swept away," see the final chapter of John D. Winters, *The Civil War in Louisiana* (Baton Rouge: Louisiana State University Press, 1963), 418–29.

47. New Orleans Catholics, for decades prior to the war, worshiped side by side, irrespective of race; slaves as well as free blacks attended Mass. In 1845, a visitor to St. Louis Cathedral commented: "Never had I seen such a mixture of conditions and colors . . . white children and black, with every shade between, knelt side by side. In the house of prayers they made no distinction of rank and color. The most ardent abolitionist could not have desired more perfect equality" (quoted in James B. Bennett, *Religion and the Rise of Jim Crow in New Orleans* [Princeton: Princeton University Press, 2005], 143). Well into Reconstruction and beyond, Catholic churches in the Crescent City fostered racial inclusion to an unusual degree. In the words of Joseph Hartzell, a Methodist Episcopal clergyman who visited a Catholic service in 1874: "Lips of every shade, by hundreds, press with devout kisses the same crucifixes, and fingers of as great variety in color, are dipped in the holy water" ("Civil Rights in the Churches," quoted ibid., 136). As Bennett observes, "inclusion did not mean equality," however, and racial segregation of churches began to take hold in the 1890s—a complex and seemingly inexorable response to political winds.

priestly duties in New Orleans for several months to minister to the sick and to comfort the dying.[48] That was, at least, a straightforward obligation of charity and one to which he had always readily and gladly subscribed.[49] And then, as Reconstruction eased and Confederate veterans began to gather all over the South to remember their service of Dixie and to pay homage to their fallen friends, Darius Hubert was often there—sometimes as an honored guest and featured speaker but always, it seems, to offer prayers.[50] His identification with "his boys" was entire, and their reverence for him was frank and unabashed: he was the uncontested choice for chaplain of the Louisiana Division of the AANV (Association of the Army of Northern Virginia) when it formed in the early 1870s, and he became, "by unanimous election of his comrades," the chaplain of all veterans of the Virginia campaign. For many years after the war, three large portraits hung side by side in the Confederate Memorial Hall in New Orleans where the veterans met: those of Robert E. Lee, Stonewall Jackson, and Fr. Darius Hubert.

Here, as in so many other ways, Darius Hubert unsettles expectations, proving in the breadth of his affections and depth of his loyalties to defy the categories we still attempt to construct around the irreducible complexities of the Civil War and its aftermath, particularly in the South. A flurry of recent literature deconstructing the Lost Cause (variously denouncing its problematic sentimentality and sanctimony, its hagiographical view of Confederate generals and leaders, its rationalization of military failure in terms

48. The 1878 pestilence arrived first in New Orleans itself in the spring and summer. Fr. Hubert would have been active in providing local assistance first, then essentially "followed" the yellow plague up the river, where help was especially needed. In both Jackson and Vicksburg, he would have been subject to examination by a quarantine doctor before being permitted to enter the city. His history of repeated exposure to the disease would probably have been taken to mean that he was "acclimated" (immune) and unlikely either to succumb or to be a carrier; yellow fever was still assumed, until the 1880s, to be transmitted by human contact.

49. The City of Savannah cast a beautiful gold medal to thank Fr. Hubert for his assistance during the pestilence, a gesture that meant enough to him to be mentioned in a single-paragraph autobiographical account of his life that he dictated at the time of his final illness. He wore the medal (along with an Army of Northern Virginia service medal) when he sat for a portrait by French-born New Orleans painter Alexandre Alaux (figure 17) in the 1880s.

50. That Fr. Hubert's public prayers were so often recorded and commented on is striking. He inclined neither to the formulas of liturgical common prayer nor to the oratory of civic piety but to an expression of heartfelt compassion and compelling personal devotion.

of spiritual virtue and moral superiority, its nascent—or naked—racism) is united in its claim that the view of the Confederacy as a Christian vanguard, propounded in such books as *Christ in the Camp* and *A Narrative of the Great Revival Which Prevailed in the Southern Armies* and kept alive in churches as well as military reunions in the South, was essentially a Protestant evangelical phenomenon: Catholics were (happily, in the view of such authors) generally exempt.[51] But in Fr. Darius Hubert, the Christian character of the men who led the Confederacy—specifically Jefferson Davis, Robert E. Lee, and Stonewall Jackson—found one of its most eloquent spokesmen. He loved those of whom he spoke; he had known all of them personally. He revered their moral character, their self-sacrifice and steadfast courage, and their dignity in the face of an eventual providential determination (for how else could they conceive of it?) against them. When, on May 10, 1881, a monument and statue of Stonewall Jackson was dedicated at the Metairie Cemetery in New Orleans, with Jefferson Davis among the dignitaries present, it was

51. Among the titles: Charles Reagan Wilson, *Baptized in Blood: The Religion of the Lost Cause, 1865–1920* (Athens: University of Georgia Press, 2009); Paul Harvey and Edward J. Blum, *The Color of Christ: The Son of God and the Saga of Race in America* (Chapel Hill: University of North Carolina Press, 2012); Donald G. Mathews, *Religion in the Old South* (Chicago: University of Chicago Press, 1977); Robert J. Miller, *Both Prayed to the Same God: Religion and Faith in the American Civil War* (Lanham, MD: Lexington/Rowman and Littlefield, 2007). Even Southern apologists, intent on "correcting the errors of Yankee history," repeat the general theme that the North was home to Catholics and the South to Protestants and that that divide, as much as any other, defined the conflict (e.g., Lochlain Seabrook, *Everything You Were Taught about the Civil War Is Wrong: Ask a Southerner* [Franklin, TN: Sea Raven, 2010], 48–50). But contemporary records indicate that Catholic chaplains in Lee's army, particularly in the wake of the bloodiest days of the war (fall of 1863), both encouraged and felt the effects of revival, with unusually large crowds at Mass and great numbers of soldiers seeking the confessional. There was a remarkably ecumenical spirit in the camp, explicitly fostered and encouraged by Lee and Jackson. After the war, the best-loved poems of the Lost Cause (e.g., "The Conquered Banner") were written by the Irish Catholic priest and poet Fr. Abram Ryan. Ryan, always something of a maverick, was as restless and melodramatic as Fr. Hubert was self-effacing and peaceable. Some records put Ryan fleetingly on the battlefields of northern Virginia as an intermittent freelance chaplain, especially with Irish troops. Ryan and Hubert may have met each other in Savannah, Georgia, ministering among the victims of yellow fever in 1876, and chances are good that they crossed paths on occasions of public memorial as well. For more on Ryan, see Donald Robert Beagle and Bryan Albin Giemza, *Poet of the Lost Cause: A Life of Father Ryan* (Knoxville: University of Tennessee Press, 2008).

Fr. Hubert who gave both invocation and benediction, the latter of which included the trenchant line: "Thou knowest, O Lord, that when Thou didst decide that the Confederacy should not succeed, Thou hadst first to remove thy servant, Stonewall Jackson."[52] There may be no better single expression of the paradoxical blend of passionate allegiance and spiritual acquiescence at the heart of the Lost Cause.[53]

For Darius Hubert, this was not rhetoric, nor was it politics. He was reconciled to the (re)union of North and South in one great nation because God had evidently ordained it. He betrayed neither bitterness nor obstinacy in the face of it, and specifically decried any perpetuation of "sectional animosity" in the wake of war, praying at a memorial dedication in 1880 that all present strive "to preserve inviolate the blessings of peace" so that "the bonds of fraternal affection and sympathy [may] be cemented and strengthened between the peoples of this great Republic."[54] He strove for racial accord.[55] For him nonetheless, remembrance of the fallen is the obligation

52. *Southern Historical Society Papers* 19 (1891): 156; cf. ibid. 9 (1881): 212–18.

53. The strong sense of spiritual destiny that prevailed in the South, even and especially after defeat on the battlefield, both mimics and turns on its head the earlier Puritan understanding of the New England settlements as constituting a Chosen People, a New Israel under special providential protection and with a specific mission or "errand" in the New World. The pragmatic secularism that took hold in the nineteenth century in this erstwhile "New England Canaan" was in some ways a natural, though ironic, outgrowth of Puritan theology. The spiritual identity that cloaked the agrarian South was of a different character—less revolutionary, less bent on conquest, more genteel and settled and protective of its distinctive culture and manners. Although most Southerners were inclined to ethical complacency concerning human bondage, they were appalled by the crass materialism and "godless" commercialism of the North.

54. Prayer of Fr. Hubert at the unveiling and dedication of the Washington Artillery Monument at the Metairie Cemetery, New Orleans, February 22, 1880; this remarkable prayer was printed entire on the front page of the February 23, 1880, *New Orleans Times-Picayune.*

55. It is important to note that all three of the leaders whom Darius Hubert revered while in military service and later memorialized make poor poster images for racial oppression, especially in their personal relations. Robert E. Lee, who opposed human bondage and freed all the slaves he inherited from his wife's estate in 1862, was nonetheless devotedly accompanied by one of them, William Mack Lee, as his body servant and confidant, throughout the war. "Mack" later wrote of his former master, "there was never one born of a woman greater than Robert E. Lee." Stonewall Jackson established a Sabbath School for slaves and free blacks in Lexington in 1855, providing literacy and religious instruction. A contemporary observer commented that "his servants reverenced and loved him." The son of enslaved parents who were members of

of every generation: "the gratitude of love is a good and perfect gift. It is not only the cause, but also the measure of a nation's greatness."[56]

Concerning Robert E. Lee, the general of whom Stonewall Jackson himself once said "he is the only man that I would follow blindfold," Fr. Hubert offered a memorable panegyric:

> His was a calm, self-possessed dignity, the like of which I have not seen in other men. When, with the grace of manner which distinguished him, he accepted his new responsibilities, "trusting in Almighty God, the voice of approving conscience, and the aid of my fellow-citizens," he was the picture of the ideal patriot marked as one to be forever remembered by all Americans. . . . A perfect gentleman of a State long renowned for its chivalry, he was just, gentle, generous, childlike in the simplicity of his character. His amiability of disposition, deep sympathy with those in sorrow and pain, his nice sense of personal honor, and genial courtesy endeared him to all his friends. I shall

---

Jackson's "colored school," Lylburn Liggins Downing commissioned a stained glass window in Jackson's honor at his African American Fifth Avenue Presbyterian Church in Roanoke in 1905. Jefferson Davis was likewise revered by many who served him at Brierfield, some of whom, according to contemporary newspaper accounts, not only sent personal gifts to him in Biloxi during the 1880s but traveled great distances to attend his funeral in 1889, lamenting the death of "Mars Jeff," their "good, kind master." If Lost Cause historians can be faulted for romanticizing the Old South, their critics can perhaps be faulted for occasional reactionary cynicism. Both accounts, especially when tainted by ideology or historical grievance, tend to selectively overpaint messy facts. An astute recent study that addresses the issue of conflicting memories and opposing versions of the Civil War narrative is Caroline E. Janney, *Remembering the Civil War: Reunion and the Limits of Reconciliation* (Chapel Hill: University of North Carolina Press, 2013), esp. chaps. 5 and 7. Another admirably even-handed treatment of the issues surrounding Civil War memory—especially as it concerns black slaves, freemen, and soldiers—is Christopher Waldrep, *Vicksburg's Long Shadow: The Civil War Legacy of Race and Remembrance* (New York: Rowman and Littlefield, 2005). Earlier but still indispensable volumes are Elizabeth Fox-Genovese's *Within the Plantation Household: Black and White Women of the Old South* (Chapel Hill: University of North Carolina Press, 1988), and her husband Eugene Genovese's *Roll, Jordan, Roll: The World the Slaves Made* (New York: Vintage, 1976); cf. their cowritten volumes: *Slavery in White and Black: Class and Race in the Southern Slaveholders' New World Order* (Cambridge: Cambridge University Press, 2008); and *The Mind of the Master Class: History and Faith in the Southern Slaveholders' Worldview* (Cambridge: Cambridge University Press, 2005).

56. From the "Invocation by Rev. Father Hubert," in *Dedication of the Tomb of the Army of Northern Virginia, Louisiana Division, and Unveiling of Statue of Stonewall Jackson at Metairie Cemetery, New Orleans, May 10th, 1881* (New Orleans: M. F. Dunn and Bro., 1881), 6–7.

> never forget his sweet, winning smile, and his clear, honest eyes, that seemed to look into your heart while they searched your brain. He is stamped upon my memory as being apart and superior to all others—a man with whom few of whom I have ever read are worthy to be classed.[57]

After the old chieftain himself, Jefferson Davis, died on December 6, 1889, more than 150,000 mourners, "all conditions of whites, blacks, ex-Confederates, ex-Federals, and even Indians and Chinamen," came by to pay their respects as his body lay in state in the City Hall of New Orleans; Darius Hubert was among the very last to do so before the casket was closed, at noon on December 11: "So quietly, it was impossible to say when he entered, Father Hubert came for a last visit to the great man he loved. Mr. Lewis [A. J. Lewis, president of the Army of Tennessee] at once surrendered his position, and with his gentle countenance deeply moved the aged priest prayed long and fervently over the still, white face beneath the clear glass covering. Gradually the look of pain wore away and was replaced by a glow of joy."[58] Fr. Hubert followed with other clergy as the draped casket was carried by a military honor guard out into the brilliant sunlight and set on the exterior portico of the building, where a massive crowd had gathered. There, Scriptures were read, the solemn funeral liturgy spoken, and the Episcopal bishop of Louisiana, John Nicholas Galleher, gave a well-turned but somewhat stilted eulogy. A formal benediction was pronounced by Rev. Ebenezer Thompson of Biloxi, Mississippi. And then, according to the reporter for the *Times-Democrat,* "came the most affecting portion of the entire service":

> Rev. Father Hubert, of the Jesuit Church, stood once more beside the beloved remains. The priest's sensitive face was eloquent with overwhelming emotion. His gentle voice trembled with suppressed sorrow, and there were few dry eyes as he prayed with almost passionate fervor: "Oh God! Loving and compas-

57. Emmanuel de la Morinière, S.J., "Chivalry," in *The Louisiana Book: Selections from the Literature of the State,* ed. Thomas M'Caleb et al. (New Orleans: R. F. Straughan, 1894; repr., New Orleans: Cornerstone, 2012), 178–79.

58. J. William Jones, *The Davis Memorial Volume: Or, Our Dead President Jefferson Davis, and the World's Tribute to His Memory* (Richmond, VA: B. F. Johnson, 1890), 527–28. The account is drawn from the "very full, accurate, and deeply interesting" eyewitness report published in the *New Orleans Times-Democrat* of events surrounding the funeral. An earlier visitation by Fr. Hubert to the remains is noted in the *New York Times,* December 9, 1889, under the heading "Crowds View the Body."

> sionate Father, in the name of my broken-hearted comrades, I beseech Thee to behold us in our bereavement, from whom Thou has taken one who was to us a chief, a leader, and a noble and constant exemplar. Thou knowest how in time of his power he ever took care that his soldiers should have with them Thy ministers, to cheer, to warn, to teach them how to fight and die for the right. See him now at the bar of Thy judgment, at the throne of Thy mercy-seat, and to him let justice and mercy be shown. And may we one day with him love and bless and praise Thee forever more, through our Lord Jesus Christ. Amen."[59]

From there, Davis was borne through the streets of New Orleans to Metairie Cemetery and laid to rest in the tomb of the Army of Northern Virginia, under the Jackson monument where Fr. Hubert had prayed so fervently in 1881.

The aged priest, long dogged with sickness and frailty, was himself forced to scale back his active ministry in 1890. In 1891, while hearing confessions at the Baronne Street church, he suffered a stroke. He was taken from New Orleans to the St. Stanislaus Novitiate in Macon, Georgia, where it was hoped that his health would improve with a change of climate and a quieter and less demanding public role. Confined to a wheelchair, he was daily rolled about the campus, enjoying conversation with teachers and mentoring young men concerning the spiritual duties that they were preparing themselves to assume. To the end, "there was no theme next to the Gospel that he so delighted in discussing as reminiscences of the Civil War. He was one of the truest, bravest and most zealous defenders of the Lost Cause."[60] Though, in consequence of his frailty, he offered to resign his position as chaplain of the Army of North-

59. Jones, *The Davis Memorial Volume*, 530–32. Some newspaper accounts have "heartbroken" for "broken-hearted." It is unsurprising that as the immediate memory of events faded, the mistaken assertion that Darius Hubert "preached the eulogy" at the funeral of Jefferson Davis crept into a number of sources. The error occurs, for example, in Frank M. Uter's *A History of the Catholic Church in Baton* Rouge (Baton Rouge: St. Joseph Catholic Church, 1992); and in Gache, *Frenchman, Chaplain, Rebel*, 230, which attributes as source the third volume of Hudson Strode's biography of Jefferson Davis, *Jefferson Davis: Tragic Hero. The Last Twenty-Five Years, 1864–1889* (New York: Harcourt Brace, 1964). Strode, however, correctly has Hubert praying rather than preaching. It is clear from contemporary reports of the funeral that Fr. Hubert's prayer, emotionally charged and unscripted, perfectly expressed the collective grief, love, and admiration of the assembled crowds for the Confederacy's first and only president, and was better remembered than the eulogy.

60. "Father Hubert's Death: The Last Days of His Life at St. Stanislaus College, in Macon," *New Orleans Daily Picayune*, June 17, 1893.

ern Virginia, the veterans refused him, prompting an affectionate letter: "I am most thankful to my dear comrades to keep me with them as long as I live, and if at any time I can be with them, they will see me at my post. . . . When you call the rolls, think of me and say in your heart, 'That poor fellow is absent through mere necessity, but we hope not forever.'"[61] He gently reassured the veterans, in several letters, that he was not in a hurry to follow old Stonewall, to "cross over the river and rest under the shade of the trees"; nonetheless, he expressed the hope that "if you hear that the commander-in-chief has called me to the grand reunion above," he would be remembered with affection, adding tenderly, "Blessing all, from my heart."

Fr. Darius Hubert died in Macon on June 14, 1893, a month shy of his seventieth birthday, having filled up his biblically allotted "threescore and ten" years with a long obedience of extraordinary pastoral care—to schoolgirls and soldiers, novices and generals, among many others. His last words, as recounted by those at his bedside, were, "I did my best." After a Requiem Mass at St. Stanislaus College, he was buried under the old Confederate breastworks, grass-covered and dotted with flowers, within the very trenches that had been dug to check Sherman's march.[62]

In New Orleans, two large, standing-room-only public memorials were held—a solemn Requiem Mass at the Jesuit Church in which Fr. Hubert had ministered for so many years and a veterans' Mass Meeting at Memorial Hall, at which two of the speakers were local Protestant pastors, fellow chaplains, and intimate friends.[63] The old priest's remains were later moved from Georgia to the Jesuit cemetery at Spring Hill College near Mobile, Alabama, where, in the elegiac words of Terence King, S.J.: "in the green gloom of pines

61. "Father Hubert: Some of the Last Letters Written by the Beloved Soldier-Priest," *New Orleans Daily Picayune,* June 18, 1893.

62. Albert Biever, S.J., "A Devoted Chaplain: Father Herbert [*sic*] and How He Served the Cause," *Richmond Dispatch,* December 21, 1902, 14.

63. Rev. Dr. Thomas R. Markham, Lafayette Presbyterian Church, and Rev. A. G. Bakewell, Trinity Chapel (Episcopal). Markham was chaplain to the Confederate Veterans Association of the Army of Tennessee; he and Hubert attended veterans' reunions together throughout the 1870s and 1880s. Fr. Hubert's unaffected and cheerful devotion across denominational lines was noted in almost every published remembrance of him (see "Father Herbert [*sic*] and How He Served the Cause," 14). A handwritten reminiscence composed by a fellow Jesuit, Fr. John Logan, shortly after Fr. Hubert's death (held in the Archives of the New Orleans Province, Society of Jesus, Loyola New Orleans University), recounts the way in which the extraordinary

. . . within sound of the rushing river . . . in the holy silence of our God's acre, one of the Civil War Chaplains, Father Darius Hubert, sleeps unto the day of universal reveille and the coming of *signifier sanctus Michael.*"[64]

CELESTE (SISTER MARY EUPHRASIA) REPP (D. 1914)

Celeste Repp was sixteen when St. Mary's Academy closed in the spring of 1862 amid the upheavals of war, her formal education thus coming to an abrupt close. Bereft of both parents, she probably moved back, initially, to the boardinghouse of her seventy-eight-year-old grandmother and guardian, Augustine Mears. "Madame Mears Hotel" was popular with diners as well as lodgers in Baton Rouge despite its proprietor's advanced age.[65] When William Howard Russell, the distinguished special correspondent for *The Times* (London), traveled to the American South "to see with my own eyes how affairs stand there," he dined at "Mrs. Meers" in Baton Rouge on June 11, 1861, with Judge William Avery and Frederick Daniel Conrad, both wealthy local planters.[66]

Celeste had a number of well-placed relatives, including her uncles Judge

---

esteem in which Fr. Hubert was held in New Orleans and across the South, "without distinction of rank or creed," ennobled the reputation of Catholics generally and Jesuits specifically, in a time when "the young have unfortunately not always found much to attract or admire in our local priesthood." While some of the Confederate veterans avowed that, had he not been called to the priesthood, Hubert could have been a Forrest or Jackson, Logan says he had all the makings of an apostle. In the case of Darius Hubert, such disparate accolades were not as contradictory as they seem.

64. "Letters of Civil War Chaplains," *Woodstock Letters* 43, no. 1 (1914): 24. "*Signifier sanctus Michael*" = "the standard-bearer, holy Michael" [the archangel], words from the Requiem Mass. A 1929 Mobile newspaper recounts that on Memorial Day of that year Fr. Hubert's grave was decorated by local students, among whom were "grandsons of Confederate soldiers to whom Fr. Hubert ministered during the War Between the States." For these young men, family stories of Darius Hubert were still fresh. For those who followed, living memories soon dimmed.

65. An affectionate remembrance of Augustine Mears, with a description of her property, was published many years after her death in the *Baton Rouge State Times Advocate,* February 19, 1915. Its author, John McGrath, had as a young apprentice at the adjacent printing office of the *Gazette,* relished stealing pecans from Madame Mears's yard.

66. *William Howard Russell's Civil War: Private Diary and Letters, 1861–1862,* ed. Martin Crawford (Athens: University of Georgia Press, 1992), 72. The notes clearly identify "Mrs. Meers" [*sic*] as Augustine Mears, Celeste's maternal grandmother. Conditions that prevailed following Union occupation and especially after the Battle of Baton Rouge (August 5, 1862) were much less sanguine than those reflected in Russell's memoir. Augustine may well have been

John Junius Burk and physician Augustus Hunter Mears and her cousin-by-adoption Andrew Stewart Herron. Had she so desired, she could certainly have found a suitable marriage partner and a comfortable niche in postbellum Baton Rouge society.[67] But the devout spirituality and concern for the less fortunate that had been kindled in her as a child and that animated her "Compositions françaises" of 1859–60 inclined her toward another kind of life. On August 3, 1868, Celeste was received into the order of the Sisters of Mercy at Vicksburg, Mississippi; she made her perpetual vows three years later, on July 10, 1871, donning the black veil and the name Sister Mary Euphrasia.[68]

A nun's life is, by design, "hid in Christ with God," and little of Celeste's biography as a Sister of Mercy can be found in public records or in the sparse

---

driven out of the city with her dependents to seek refuge with relatives or friends. The family grande dame lived to see hostilities end, however, and to return home. On November 3, 1866, having buried two husbands, three of her six children, and numerous grandchildren, and having provided material and spiritual support to her large family through the best and worst of times, this resourceful and resilient soul at last found rest. Augustine Verret Millet Mears was eighty-two.

67. Celeste's sister Alice is presumed to have married, but no information has emerged about her whereabouts after the war. Her other sisters, Marie Augustine and Junia, had died in 1850 and 1863 respectively. John Jr. had died on his third birthday in 1851. Brothers Henry (b. 1850) and William (b. 1853), too young to fight for the Confederacy, were spared being soldiers. When their grandmother Augustine died in 1866, they were taken in by their uncle, Pierre ("Pete") Millet, the town wharfmaster. Henry worked at a local foundry and continued to be active at St. Joseph Church; on January 1, 1878, after ringing the bell for New Year's Mass, he collapsed and died in the priest's residence; he was twenty-eight. William struck out for Texas as a young man, settling in the hamlet of Mexia in Limestone County and then moving to Galveston, where he worked for a dry goods retailer. On October 12, 1881, he married into a Prussian Jewish family living in Galveston. He and his wife, Henrietta (née Goettinger), had two sons, Henry (b. 1882) and William Jr. (b. 1885) and two daughters, Marguerite (b. 1890) and Julia (b. 1894). The family moved, fortuitously, just prior to the Galveston hurricane in 1900, to Sault Ste. Marie, Michigan, but later returned to Texas, settling in Dallas. The degree to which Celeste kept up with any of her siblings after she became a Sister of Mercy is unknown; in 1885 she donated the family property in Baton Rouge (which seems to have reverted to her after her brother Henry's death) to her young nephew, William's son Henry D. Repp.

68. The person whose name Celeste took was Euphrasia of Constantinople, a fourth-century nun venerated as a saint in both the Roman Catholic and Eastern Orthodox rites. Celeste may also have intended a connection to Sister Mary Euphrasia Pelletier, founder of the Sisters of Our Lady of Charity of the Good Shepherd in France, who died on April 24, 1868, just months before Celeste entered the Mercy convent.

collected memoirs of the Vicksburg house.[69] We can be sure that, notwithstanding her spiritual preparedness, it was a challenging transition for her. The city she came to in the early years of Reconstruction was, like Fr. Hubert's New Orleans, racially divided, impoverished, and often violent. It had long been a center of gambling, prostitution, and crime; now it was simmering with social and political enmity. It was also physically scarred by army encampment and naval bombardment. The bitter legacy of General Ulysses S. Grant's forty-seven-day siege, which had reduced Vicksburg's inhabitants to living in caves and tunnels and foraging for rats to eat, was exacerbated by prolonged Federal occupation.[70] Mississippi had been the second state to secede; it would be the second to last to return to the Union. Under both presidential and congressional Reconstruction, many locals remained defiantly "unreconstructed." However intent the Sisters were on positive and generous ministry, they had a great deal to overcome—not least, initially, the rehabilitation of their facilities after long and destructive use by Major General Henry W. Slocum and his forces.

The reputation of the Mercy Sisters as nurses for both Union and Confederate combatants during the Civil War was impressive enough that it prompted appreciative comment by both Jefferson Davis and Abraham Lincoln. President Lincoln famously commissioned an iconic image of a Sister of Mercy tending to a wounded soldier in Vicksburg (see figure 19; a similar image is included in the three-panel mural dedicated to the Sisters on the Vicksburg waterfront). Throughout the war, in whatever makeshift quarters were made available to them, the nuns dressed wounds, fed patients, helped soldiers write letters to loved ones, read Scripture, prayed, and offered spiritual consolation and instruction to those who sought it. They were steadfast in duty

69. Notably, these include Sister Mary Paulinus Oakes, R.S.M., ed., *Angels of Mercy: An Eyewitness Account of the Civil War and Yellow Fever* (Baltimore: Cathedral Foundation Press, 1998); *Sisters of Mercy: Spirituality in America 1843–1900*, ed. Kathleen Healy, RSM (New York: Paulist Press, 1992); and Mother Mary Bernard, *The Story of the Sisters of Mercy in Mississippi, 1860–1930* (New York: Kennedy, 1931).

70. In her contemporary account, Sister Ignatius Sumner records that on their return to their mother house after the war, the Sisters "passed through a desolated and destroyed region, everywhere, as far as Vicksburg, showing the marks of relentless and savage destruction" (Oakes, *Angels of Mercy*, 28).

and courageous amid typhoid and smallpox epidemics that prompted others to flee. They refused payment for their services.

In the immediate wake of war, there were only ten Mercy Sisters left in Vicksburg—a small and exhausted band who had been scattered and harried for four years, nursing Confederate soldiers variously in Monroe, Louisiana; Mississippi Springs, Jackson, and Oxford, Mississippi; and Shelby Springs, Alabama. Those who were there to see it reported that when the nuns returned to Vicksburg, their habits and veils were in tatters, their feet bound in rabbit skins, their bodies emaciated from near-starvation. According to the diary of one of the Sisters, they had at times survived on unsalted cornbread, sage tea, and sweet potato "coffee." They soon reopened their school, St. Francis Xavier Academy (Vicksburg's first educational institution), the primary apostolate to which they had been called in 1861 by Father F. X. Leray. They also provided services of various kinds to the poor and marginalized, especially among the immigrants that huddled in shanties along the muddy Mississippi riverfront. They nursed the sick. They conducted catechism classes for black children. Celeste was among the few Sisters added to the community during Reconstruction, and she shortly took up duties as a teacher at St. Francis Xavier. Her former headmistress in Baton Rouge, Matilda Victor, always so exasperated that responsibility for Catholic education rested entirely in the hands of (mostly foreign) nuns rather than able lay teachers, would perhaps have been gratified that—veil or no—Celeste, a native-born, Academy-educated young woman, had become a teacher.

Despite their slender numbers, the Vicksburg Sisters of Mercy expanded their outreach in 1870, opening new branch houses in both Jackson and Pass Christian. Sister Euphrasia Repp was actively involved in both missions.

Yellow fever, the old enemy that had stalked Celeste's childhood, devastated the ranks of the Catholic faithful in Baton Rouge, and claimed the life of her mother, Amelina Repp, in 1855, returned with a vengeance to communities along the Mississippi River in the late summer of 1878. In Vicksburg, where contemporary correspondence recounts people "dying like sheep," the Mercy superior, Mother Mary de Sales Brown, took over the City Hospital, with her Sisters nursing as many as three hundred patients a day. Six nuns died during the epidemic (along with sixteen doctors), prompting a poetic tribute by local resident Ellen K. Hebron:

A host of pitying Angels
    are camped around the town,
Their busy wings are flitting by
    When daylight goeth down,
On thousand Mercy-errands
    All through the lonely night
To sick and weary still they go
    Upon their mission bright.

O! you who tend the afflicted
    With your doubly grateful care;
O! you who cheer the dying
    With your ministry of prayer;
O! you who stand beside them
    With patient, willing hand,
You all shall be rewarded
    In the far off better land.[71]

Sister Euphrasia was not in Vicksburg when the dreaded scourge hit there; had she been, she might well have encountered again her childhood priest, beloved "Pere Hubert," who came from New Orleans to assist in the crisis. She had, instead, been quarantined by the epidemic in the small coastal town of Pass Christian as the pestilence moved its way up the Mississippi valley.[72] She and Sister Patricia Fox, prevented from leaving for their motherhouse, labored valiantly to serve the local population under extremely difficult conditions. Once quarantines were in place, businesses shuttered and commerce came to a standstill; even essential supplies were difficult to come by. The parish priest of the Pass at that time, Father Henry Georget, was stricken with fever himself, though not fatally, leaving the two Mercy nuns on the front lines tending the sick with a few local nurses. Total cases in Pass Christian numbered 201 (the town's population was only 1,250); there were 27

71. *Vicksburg [MS] Weekly Herald,* October 4, 1878, reprinted in *Sisters of Mercy,* 296–98.

72. Travel between Pass Christian and Vicksburg—which had previously entailed taking a passenger boat to New Orleans and then embarking on a steamboat upriver—was complicated in 1878 by the fact that the Mississippi River, on April 26, 1876, had changed course and left Vicksburg high and dry, a river port without a river. It was not until 1902 that the Army Corps of Engineers completed a diversion of the Yazoo River that brought a riverfront back to the city.

fatalities.[73] Fifty years later, Bishop John Edward Gunn would memorialize the two women's tireless devotion under extreme duress: "It seemed providential that Sister Euphrasia and Sister Patricia were quarantined here during those trying times. . . . Stories are yet current of the heroism of these two Angels of Mercy during the scourge of yellow fever."[74]

Pass Christian was home to Sister Euphrasia for many of her later years of ministry. She lived in a small, austere convent and, in a two-room schoolhouse, provided both catechetical instruction and the rudiments of a liberal arts education (including literature, mathematics, painting, and music) for black children. Having grown up in a slaveholding community and family, she dedicated herself to serving people of color. Her childhood recognition that "We should always be charitable towards the poor because God loves them" had deepened into a vocation of devoted ministry across racial lines. One finds a rare reference to her by name in the annals of St. Philomena Parish concerning her tenure in what came to be called St. Joseph's Colored School at the Pass: "The devoted Sisters did splendid work during all those years, the last of whom were Sister Mary Euphrasia and Sister Mary Catherine. Their names were held in benediction among the colored people for many years after." There are several extant programs from concerts and "grand entertainments" by the children of St. Joseph's Colored School and St. Paul Church in the 1880s and 1890s that bear considerable resemblance to the annual entertainments Celeste would have been part of under Matilda Victor's tutelage at St. Mary's Academy in Baton Rouge—the same mix of instrumental and choral music, poetry and drama, sacred and secular performance pieces, in both English and French. It is easy to imagine Sister Euphrasia, a seasoned teacher with an unusually privileged educational formation, having oversight in putting together such events.[75]

73. Ten Christian Brothers in Pass Christian died of the fever during the late summer and early fall. Thirty miles away, the family of Jefferson Davis mourned the loss of another victim of the epidemic, his twenty-one-year old son and namesake; ironically, Jeff Jr. was felled by yellow fever in Memphis, having moved there only a few months earlier.

74. *Diamond Jubilee, 1851–1926*, commemorative booklet for St. Paul's Parish, Pass Christian, MS (1926), 48.

75. Two such programs have been reprinted in *Jubilee III: 1847–1997*, a sesquicentennial memorial booklet celebrating St. Paul Catholic Church in Pass Christian, prepared by Dan Ellis and later reissued as a self-published paperback *St. Paul: Pass Christian* (2011), 7, 29. Another

Sister Euphrasia Repp outlived most of her peers in the Vicksburg motherhouse as well as her former headmistress and her priest from Baton Rouge; she died on July 18, 1914, as the clouds of another war were looming.[76] Her remains rest under a simple white stone cross in the Sisters of Mercy section of the historic sloping Cedar Hill Cemetery in Vicksburg. From there, according to the certain hope she expressed at thirteen, with fervent youthful devotion, they will be "raised on the last day, more beautiful than ever."[77]

---

can be seen in the St. Philomena section of the website for "Schools of Pass Christian" (http://school.passchristian.net/negro_catholic_school_pass_christian.htm). St. Paul Catholic Church in the Pass had, at this time, both black and white members; a separate black Catholic church was not built until 1911.

76. A brief, and regrettably generic, notice on the front page of the *Vicksburg Evening Post* for that day reads: "Sister M. Euphrasia Repp, aged 68 years, died today in Memphis. She had been in the convent here 50 years. The funeral takes place at the convent Sunday afternoon at 5 o'clock. Rev. Father Mallin officiating. The sister was a most exemplary woman, had led a self-sacrificing and useful life, and richly merits all the rewards of the faithful in the hereafter."

77. See Celeste's poem, "Description d'une Jardin en Printemps," the first of her "Compositions françaises," above.

APPENDIX 1

William Porter's Farewell Speech to the Crew of USS *Essex*

Commodore W. D. Porter, Address to the Crew of the Essex *at New Orleans, September 9, 1862**

Men of the *Essex:*

We have now been associated together on board this vessel very near one year, and during that period you have been successfully engaged with the Enemy in six hard-fought battles. Your first achievement was with four of the craven Rebel gun-boats of vastly superior force, in Lucas Bend, all of which were disabled and driven below the batteries of Columbus. Your next achievement was at Fort Henry where you led the way and by your prowess and valor caused the surrender of that stronghold in the short space of one hour and ten minutes. At the time the *Essex* attacked Fort Henry she could scarcely be called an Iron clad boat. The ports were large and unprotected, and the Boilers exposed, and although fourteen were wounded to death and 24 wounded by steam and scalding waters, you were ready at your guns for action before the surrender of the fort. This Battle was one of the most important of the war, for up to that time our forces could scarcely say they had gained a victory. You by your valor, turned the tide of defeat and gave confidence to the country.

* Both William Park and James Henneberry kept a verbatim copy of the speech given by William D. Porter to the *Essex* crew before he took leave of the ship. (Henneberry's is inadvertently misdated to September 1864.) Park's was recorded on three loose pages (one of which is missing), apparently torn from another lined notebook and folded into his journal, rather than written directly onto the journal pages themselves, as were all other records he copied after the war. The first two extant pages of Park's version are given here, followed by the brief final paragraph, recorded in Henneberry's journal.

For a short period the ship was under external repairs and a large portion of this crew participated in the victories of Donaldson, Columbus, Island No. 10, Fort Pillow, and Memphis. When your old and tried ship became fully equipped you joined her at Cairo, and with your old and tried associates entered on a new field of operations. Vicksburg felt your prowess, and while your country lasts you will be gratefully remembered for your daring and courage at that time. The crowning effort of your courage is yet to be related.

For months the rebels had been building with great care a gun boat and ram up the Yazoo River. This vessel, when finished, successfully encountered and cut up three of the fleet, passed in safety two powerful fleets and took shelter under the batteries of Vicksburg. Here she stood the fire of a large fleet and escaped unhurt. The *Essex* ran past this heavy fort and attacked her. This, too, she stood without much injury. You were next battling away at the enemy before Baton Rouge. On the 6th of August you fought this noted *Arkansas* and after an action of half an hour destroyed this formidable vessel for which act you have received, through the Honorable Secretary of the Navy, the thanks of the Country and the Department. I have now to speak of one more of your feats of courage and chronicle again your valor; it is the attack on and successfully passing a battery of 35 guns at Port Hudson.[1]

Having now detailed your gallant conduct it becomes my painful task to bid you that painful word, Good-bye, and I sincerely hope you may prove the old Iron sided *Essex* as good a ship under your present commander as you did under the (old)

W. D. Porter

1. At this point, Park's copy of the Porter speech ends; the final page, with the last paragraph of the speech, is lost.

APPENDIX 2

Additional Naval Records and Correspondence Copied into the Park Journal

William Park's inclusion of official documents—gathered retrospectively and copied into his journal—is, somewhat surprisingly, limited to 1862, when *Essex* was under the command of William D. Porter. These include documents pertaining to: the engagement at Lucas Bend; the first encounter of *Essex* with the Confederate ram *Arkansas* off Vicksburg; the destruction of *Arkansas* near Baton Rouge; the bombardment of Bayou Sara and Natchez by *Essex;* and the successful passage of *Anglo-American,* under *Essex* officer R. K. Riley, past the batteries of Port Hudson. There are also two records related to *Pittsburg,* the vessel to which Park was transferred during the spring of 1862. These include the successful attack on Fort Donelson and the running of the batteries at Island No. 10. Though his principle of selection is unclear, one assumes these are events of particular significance or pride in Park's memory of that first year; his omission of the Battle of Fort Henry, given its horrors—especially the loss of his friend Andrew Waterman and other shipmates—is perhaps understandable.

These records follow immediately after the conclusion of Park's journal, with one blank page intervening; the titles are all as they appear in his text.

Copy of Official Reports to Secretary of the Navy U.S. Gunboat Essex, *Jan. 13th 1862*

Sir: On the morning of the 11th General McClernand sent on board this vessel, and informed me that the enemy were moving up the river from Columbus with several vessels, towing up a battery. I immediately signaled Lieutenant Commanding Paulding of the *St. Louis* to get under weigh and prepare for action. A very thick fog coming on, we were compelled to steam slowly down the river, but about 10 o'clock or a little after, it rose, and showed us a large steamer at the head of Lucas Bend. We heard her whistle the moment we were seen by them. Shortly after whistling she was joined by another large and a small steamer. We pursued our course steadily down the river, and when within long range the large steamer fired a heavy shell gun, which struck the sand bar between us, and ricocheted within about two hundred yards of this vessel and burst. We at this time did not return the fire, but continued our course down in order to near the vessel. By this time the large steamer was joined by her consorts, and they opened a brisk fire upon us. I now hailed Lieutenant Commanding Paulding, and directed him to try one of his rifle cannons. He instantly fired, and sent his shots completely over the enemy. I then opened from my bow guns, and the action became brisk on both sides for about twenty minutes, the enemy firing by broadsides. This running fight continued until he reached the shelter of his batteries on the Iron bank above Columbus. We continued the action and drove him behind their batteries in a crippled condition, as we could distinctly see our shell explode on his decks. The action lasted over an hour, and terminated, as I think, in a complete defeat of the enemy's boats, superior in size and number of guns to the *Essex* and *St. Louis.* The fire of the *St. Louis* was precise, and the shots told well. The officers and men of this vessel behaved with firmness—Mr. Riley, our First Master, carrying out all my orders strictly, while the officers of the gun divisions, Messrs. Lanning and Ferry paid particular attention to the pointing of their respective guns. Mr. Brittain, my aid, paid all attention to my orders and conveyed them correctly and with alacrity.[1] In fact, all the officers and men on board behaved like veterans.

I have the honor to be, etc.

W. D. Porter, Commander

TO A. H. FOOTE

1. Sixteen-year-old S. B. Britton, Porter's master's mate, was killed less than a month later at Fort Henry by the cannon shot that pierced the ship's middle boiler; his was the first fatality aboard *Essex* in that incident and the only one caused directly by enemy fire rather than scalding or drowning. He is memorialized in the patriotic poem "Boy Britton," written shortly after the event

Extract from Commodore Foote's report of attack on Fort Donelson Flag Ship St. Louis. *February 15th 1862*

Sir: I have the honor to report to the department that, at the urgent request of Major General Halleck and General Grant, who regarded the movement as a military necessity, although not, in my opinion, properly prepared, I made an attack on Fort Donelson yesterday, the 14th instant, at 3 o'clock P.M. with four ironclads and two wooden gunboats, the *St. Louis, Carondelet, Louisville,* and *Pittsburgh,* and the *Taylor* and *Conestoga:* after a severe fight of an hour and a half, being in the latter part of the action less than four hundred yards from the fort, the wheel of this vessel, by a shot through the pilot house, was carried away; the tiller ropes of the *Louisville* were also disabled by a shot, which rendered the two boats wholly unmanageable, and they drifted down the river, the relieving tackles not being able to steer or control them in the rapid current. The two remaining boats, the *Pittsburgh* and *Carondelet,* were also greatly damaged between wind and water, and soon followed us as the enemy rapidly renewed the fire as we drifted helplessly down the river. This vessel, the *St. Louis,* alone received fifty-nine shots, four of them between wind and water; one in the pilot house, mortally wounding the pilot; and others requiring some time to put her in repair. There were fifty-four killed and wounded in this attack, which, notwithstanding our disadvantages, we have every reason to suppose would, in fifteen minutes more, could the action have been continued, have resulted in the capture of the two forts bearing upon us. The enemy's fire had materially slackened, and he was running from his batteries, when the two gunboats helplessly drifted down the river from disabled steering apparatus, as the relieving tackles could not control the helm in the strong current, when the fleeing enemy returned to their guns and again boldly reopened fire upon us from the river batteries which we had silenced.

The enemy must have brought over twenty heavy guns to bear upon our boats from the water batteries and the main fort on the side of the hill, while we could only return the fire with twelve bow guns from the four boats. One

---

by Forceythe Willson and anthologized in *Exercises in Elocution,* ed. A. T. Randall (Albany, NY: Parsons, 1868), 47–50.

rifle gun aboard the *Carondelet* burst during the action. The officers and men in this hotly contested but unequal fight behaved with the greatest gallantry and determination, all deploring the accident which rendered two gunboats suddenly helpless in the narrow river and swift current.

Very respectfully, your
obedient servant,
A. H. Foote

TO HON. GIDEON WELLES

(Copy) Navy department, April 12th 1862

Sir: The department desires you to convey to Commander Henry Walke and the officers and men of the *Carondelet,* also to Acting First Master Hoel of the *Cincinnati,* who volunteered for the occasion, its thanks for the gallant and successful service rendered in running the *Carondelet* past the rebel batteries on the night of the 4th instant. It was a daring and heroic act, well executed, and deserving of special recognition.

Commendation is also to be extended to the officers and crew of the *Pittsburgh,* who in like manner on the night of 6th instant performed a similar service. These fearless acts dismayed the enemy, enabled the army under General Pope to cross the Mississippi and eventuated the surrender to yourself of Island No. 10, and finally in the capture, by General Pope, of the forts on the Tennessee shore, and the retreating rebels under General Mackall.

I would also, in this connection, render the acknowledgements which are justly due the officers and crew of the several boats who, in conjunction with the detachment of the Forty-Second Illinois regiment, under Colonel Roberts, captured the first rebel battery and spiked the guns on Island No. 10 on the night of the 1st instant. Such services are duly appreciated by the department, which extends its thanks to all who participated in the achievements.

I am, respectfully, your obedient servant,

Gideon Welles

TO A. H. FOOTE

U.S. Gunboat Essex. *Below Vicksburg, July 22nd 1862*

Sir: I have the honor to inform you of the arrival of this ship below Vicksburg, Mississippi, and that we lost one man killed and two wounded.

I delivered several shots into the rebel ram *Arkansas,* as I believe, with effect. I endeavored to strike her, but, as we approached they let go her bow lines and the current drifted her stern on. The consequence was this vessel only grazed her side, and ran, with great force, high on the bank, where she lay at least ten minutes, subject to a terrible fire from the shore batteries.

I am very respectfully, your obedient servant,

W. D. Porter, Commander

TO: CAPTAIN C. H. DAVIS

U.S. Gunboat Essex
Off Baton Rouge August 6th 1862

Sir: On the evening of the 4th instant I was informed by General Williams that the rebels, in considerable force, under General Breckinridge, were moving on this place. The rebel ram *Arkansas,* with two gunboats the *Webb* and *Music,* were also in the vicinity of the city to support the attack of the rebel army. I made such a disposition of the naval force under my command as I thought would give the most aid to our small [force] on shore. In the morning of the 5th instant, at 1 o'clock, the enemy made an attack on our land force and drove in the left wing of our army, killing General Williams. Our men retreating, I opened fire with shot and shell over them on the advancing enemy, and turned them back. It was the intention of the enemy to make a simultaneous attack by land and water; but the fire from the *Essex* and the other gunboats driving the enemy back, evidently disconcerted their plans. Though not making her appearance, I had information of the vicinity of the ram *Arkansas;* and this morning I determined to steam up the river and attack her, and, if possible, prevent her rendering further assistance to the land forces she was cooperating with. At 10 a.m. I came in sight of her, at about the distance of half a mile, and immediately opened fire. After an action of about twenty minutes I succeeded in setting fire to her, and at meridian she blew up with a tremendous explosion. The *Arkansas* had a crew of 180, and mounted ten guns (six 8 inch and four 50 pound rifles). This vessel the *Essex* mounts seven guns, and had only forty men on duty at the time of our going into action. My First Master R. K. Riley was sick in hospital, and his place was supplied by Second Master David Porter Rosenmiller, who conducted himself to my entire satisfaction.

I have the honor to be, very respectfully, your obedient servant,

W. D. Porter

TO: HON. GIDEON WELLES, SECRETARY OF THE NAVY

On Gunboat Essex
Off Baton Rouge, August 6th 1862

Sir: This morning, at 8 o'clock, I steamed up the river and at 10 o'clock attacked the rebel ram *Arkansas* and blew her up. There is not now a fragment of her left.

Very respectfully, your obedient servant,

W. D. Porter
Commanding Division of
Flotilla in Western Waters

TO: REAR ADMIRAL D. G. FARRAGUT

Destruction of the ram Arkansas
Flag Ship Hartford, *Aug. 7th 1862*

Sir: It is one of the happiest moments of my life that I am enabled to inform the department of the destruction of the ram *Arkansas;* not because I held the ironclad in such terror, but because the community did.

On the 4th instant, I sent the *Tennessee* up to Baton Rouge with provisions for Commander Porter and the gunboats stationed at that place. On the night of the 5th she returned with the information that the enemy had made a combined attack upon Baton Rouge by the ram and two gunboats, the *Webb* and *Music,* and calling for assistance. At daylight the *Hartford* was under way for this place, with orders for the other vessels to follow me as fast as possible. I arrived here today at 12 am, in company with the *Brooklyn, Westfield, Clifton, Jackson,* and *Sciota.* I had sent the *Cayuga* up before me, agreeably to a request of General Butler, in consequence of the guerillas firing into some of his transports. On my arrival I was informed by Commander W. D. Porter that yesterday morning at 1 o'clock the enemy's forces, under General Breckinridge, attacked General Williams, drove in his pickets, etc. General Williams, having had ample warning, was all prepared for him. The fight was continued with great energy on both sides until 10 a.m. by which time the enemy had been driven back two or three miles, but unfortunately, the gallant General Williams, while cheering on his men, received a Minie ball through his heart. As soon as the enemy was repulsed, Commander Porter, with the gunboats, went up the stream after the ram *Arkansas,* which was laying about five miles above, apparently afraid to take her share in the conflict according to the preconcerted plan. As he came within gunshot he opened on her, and probably soon disabled some of her machinery or steering apparatus, for she became unmanageable, continuing, however, to fire her guns at the *Essex.*

Commander Porter says he took advantage of her presenting a weak point towards him, and loaded with incendiary shells. After his first discharge of this projectile, a gush of fire came out of her side and from that moment it was discovered that she was on fire, which he continued his exertions to prevent from being extinguished. They backed her ashore and made a line fast, which soon burnt, and she swung off into the river, where she continued to burn until she blew up with a tremendous explosion, thus ending the career of the last ironclad ram of the Mississippi. There were many persons on the banks of the river witnessing the fight, in which they anticipated a triumph for Secessia; but on the return of the *Essex* not a soul was to be seen.

I will [leave] a sufficient force of gunboats here to support the army, and will return tomorrow to New Orleans, and depart immediately for Ship Island, with a light heart that I have left no bugbear to torment the communities of the Mississippi in my absence.

Very respectfully, your

obedient servant,
D. G. Farragut
Flag Officer Commanding Western Gulf Blockading Squadron

TO HON. GIDEON WELLES
SECRETARY OF THE NAVY, WASHINGTON, D.C.

Admiral Farragut gives rebel reports of the Arkansas
Flag Ship Hartford
New Orleans, August 10th 1862

Sir: since forwarding the reports, we have picked up a number of prisoners from the ram *Arkansas,* all of whom I have catechised very closely. They agree very well respecting her exit from the Yazoo, and her passing the fleets; they also agree as to the number of killed or wounded on each of these occasions, making in all eighteen killed and a large number of wounded. At Vicksburg they plated the deck with iron, and fortified her with cotton inside. She then came down in command of Lieutenant H. K. Stevens (Brown having been taken sick at Vicksburg) with the intention of making a combined attack with General Breckinridge upon Baton Rouge; but her port engine broke down. They repaired it in the course of the day, and went out to meet the *Essex* the next morning, when they saw her coming up, but the starboard engine gave way, and they ran her ashore, she being perfectly unmanageable.

They say that when the gunboats were seen coming up, and the *Essex* commenced firing, the captain set the ram on fire and told the crew to run ashore. They also state that the gunboats *Webb* and *Music* were sent for to tow her up the river, but they did not arrive, and neither of them had been seen. This is the statement, all of which is respectfully submitted by your obedient servant,

D. G. Farragut

[TO] HON. GIDEON WELLES

United States Gunboat Essex
Off New Orleans, September 9, 1862

Sir: I have the honor to report that, on the 23[d] ultimo having remained off the city of Baton Rouge two days after its evacuation by our troops, I proceeded up the river to reconnoiter reported batteries in progress at Port Hudson, Louisiana, and also coal my vessel at Bayou Sara, the only place I could obtain any, save New Orleans. Arriving there, I found the town entirely deserted, and the coal burning. Sending a boat's crew on shore, they were fired at by guerillas from the houses in heavy force. My men drove them out, and burnt the buildings in the lower part of the town to prevent such being used to protect the enemy. These guerillas had a few days previously fired at and wounded several of the crew of the United States Gunboat *Sumpter.* On the 24th I was necessitated to send the wooden gunboat *Anglo-American,* which I had fitted out and armed, to New Orleans for coal, and I again dropped down the river and awaited her return off Port Hudson. I could discover no guns at this place, but earthworks were in progress, and whilst destroying these I had the misfortune to burst my 10 inch gun. The *Anglo-American* not arriving I returned to Bayou Sara, where we were again fired at from buildings left, on which I ordered those remaining to be destroyed.

The *Anglo-American* joined me on the 29th, and reported three batteries as having opened on her whilst passing Port Hudson. She received seventy-three shots in her en passant. I had received intimation that the rebel gunboat *Webb* was at Natchez, to which city she had conveyed transports with supplies from the Red River. I followed to that city, but found they had sought the protection of the Vicksburg guns. At Natchez a boat's crew from the *Essex* were sent on shore to procure some ice for my sick, when they were wantonly attacked by over two hundred armed citizens, wounding the officer in command, and killing one and wounding five seamen. I immediately opened fire on the town and set a considerable number of the houses from whence they were firing on us on fire. After bombarding the place for an hour, the mayor unconditionally surrendered the city.

I followed the rebel gunboat *Webb* to the batteries at Vicksburg, under the guns of which she, with two transports, lay. Heavy ordnance batteries, extending three miles further down the river than during the siege in July, prevented my nearer approach to these boats. Having exchanged some shots, and ascertained that the upper fleet was not in the vicinity of the town, being short of provisions, my battery weakened by the loss of two guns burst, and also short of ammunition, I determined to steam down the river to New Orleans for supplies, and if possible ascertain the strength of the Port Hudson batteries. On the 7th instant, at 4:15 a.m., we were off that place and, on coming within range, the enemy opened on us a vigorous fire with heavy siege guns. The *Essex* was struck with heavy shot fourteen times. As nearly as I can judge, the enemy had in position from thirty-five to forty guns of 10 inch, 9 inch, and 8 inch caliber, in three batteries commanding the river to the extent of five miles. A 68 pound, 32 pound, and also a 10 inch shot lodged in the *Essex,* but without material damage. We were under fire an hour and three-quarters, during which time the guns were worked well and incessantly, and I have reason to believe the enemy was considerably damaged. Mr. J. Harry Wyatt, acting fourth master, and my secretary, had command of the forward battery, and his conduct met my entire approbation. A land force will be necessary to complete the destruction of this fort, which, if allowed to again be restored, would seriously interrupt the free navigation of the Lower Mississippi.

Very respectfully, your
obedient servant,
W. D. Porter
Commodore United States Navy

[TO] HON. GIDEON WELLES
SECRETARY OF THE NAVY, WASHINGTON, D.C.

P.S. In the various encounters I have had since leaving St. Louis on the last cruise (July 6), the *Essex* has been struck by heavy shot perceptibly one hundred and twenty-eight times—glancing shot have left no record; three have broken the iron, and but one through, and that at a distance of a few feet from the battery delivering it.

W.D.P.

United States Gunboat Anglo-American
Off Bayou Sara, Louisiana, Aug. 29, 1862

Sir: In pursuance of your order, I proceeded down stream on the 14th instant, for New Orleans, arriving there on the morning of the 25th. We loaded up with coal, and left that city at 3:15 P.M. on Thursday, the 28th instant. Nothing of importance occurred until I approached Port Hudson. I noticed earthworks had been thrown up on the bluffs as well as the water line, but no guns being in sight, I kept on for about a mile, when another line of earthworks was discovered, as well as indications of rifle-pits. I immediately ordered my rifle 50 pounder to be fired. At this moment the enemy opened on the boat. My rifle gun unfortunately could not be used, as the cartridge had been made wet by a just passed heavy rain. Our howitzer was useless, as no ammunition could be obtained for it at New Orleans. We were now just abreast of the last mentioned earthworks, the enemy's guns playing on us with great rapidity. I could see two 32 pounder cannon and eighteen field-pieces, 6 and 12 pounders. The fire was so heavy on my frail wooden boat that had it not been a matter or urgent necessity to reach you, I should have dropped back, as I had no protection for the machinery, and the fire was so heavy that the firemen were driven from their post.

I determined, from the importance of the case, to push on and rejoin you if possible. I am happy to report we succeeded.

The following casualties occurred: Mr. Parker, pilot, severely wounded in the back from a bursting shell, and James Banes, seaman, slightly wounded by splinter over the eye. We received seventy-three shots—fifteen heavy shots, the balance 12 pounder and grape. One 32 pounder struck the upright brace of the walking beam, breaking it in two.

Very respectfully,
your obedient servant,
R. K. Riley
Commanding Gunboat
Anglo-American

[TO:] COMMANDER W. D. PORTER
COMMANDING NAVAL FORCES BELOW VICKSBURG

APPENDIX 3

William Park's "Abstract Journal" Compared with His Later, Amplified Memoir

The Park journal, as we find it in Celeste's notebook, is characterized by a plainspoken style and often a somewhat ironic voice. It does not editorialize on events, nor does it comment on the foibles or failings of crewmates or officers. It seldom uses personal names. It describes most engagements in minimalist terms. It does not pause over even the carnage on the decks after the Fort Henry disaster beyond an abbreviated, "The scene . . . was sickening. I shall not attempt to describe it." It is for the most part politically dispassionate, describing both Confederate and Union activities with a kind of resolute detachment, or at least with equal irony; the first and only time that Park expresses pride in his long service and something like patriotic feeling is when the Mississippi Squadron, together with ships from the Gulf fleet, masses in preparation for the expedition up the Red River in the spring of 1864. Overall, the journal bespeaks a reserved, dutiful, and skilled warrior who hopes to live through a three-year death game, as he had in Crimea, and get home—wherever home is to be. To his own unvarnished account he later attaches a few additional records relevant to his service aboard *Essex* (see the two previous appendices).

By the time Park decided to write a more expansive and reflective memoir of his wartime experiences, he was an American citizen, settled in the country for which he had fought, and a married father of four. Having entered the service half-heartedly at best, at the urging of his friend Andrew Waterman, he had now a hard-earned identification with the United States. And, like many veterans, he had bonded with local mates over memories and whisky, and had come to feel pride in their shared accomplishments. While the rest of the country seemed convinced that Grant and Sherman and Meade had won the war, the sailors of the inland navy knew better. Or at least they believed that their role had been crucial, indeed indispensable, to the Federal victory. So they pored over published records and officers' memoirs of their various engagements, recounted with one another favorite tales of victories and defeats, bad food and "hard coffee," lucky escapes and fearful loss, sickness, terror, and boredom; in so doing they came slowly to terms, as no one can in the throes of war, with the meaning of it all. "The Rebellion" had been defeated. And Park and his cronies, and those who fought alongside, had helped make that happen.

In his later, undated memoir, which was donated by his granddaughter Virginia Park to the Newberry Library in 2006, Park quotes at length from his own earlier "Abstract Journal" but also relies on published newspaper and magazine stories, as well as the *Official Records* of officers in the brown water navy, which he interweaves, in several places, with his own recollections.[1] Additionally, he makes clear that he has consulted the diaries of some of his mates. He abandons his earlier calendared, day-by-day account for a continuous narrative, the top of each page bearing a simple running head with month and year. The volume does not repeat the title given in the Celeste Repp notebook; there is, in fact, no interior title page; the cover of the black, smooth-grained leather volume is simply stamped in gold lettering with "W. L. Park's journal."[2]

1. This accounts for better spelling in many places, especially of the names of Union vessels.

2. The original Repp/Park journal was evidently accessible through the years to William's young children, who added scribbles and marginalia on many pages, including a poem "to Newton" by daughter Mary in the thrall of first love: "When there is a gloom upon yon valley / And another upon the sea, / Take up these lines, / Oh do remember me." She signed it "a Schoolar, Mary L. Park." William's wife, Agnes, likewise, found the notebook a convenient place to record two recipes for dyes ("Brown" and "Madder Red") while the family was homesteading in South Dakota; they occur on the final page, opposite the inside back cover. The later memoir is, by contrast, nearly pristine. William likely composed it after he came back to Chicago from the failed Dakota experiment in 1888; he sought and received an increase in disability funds in 1889 and was unemployed the rest of his life. Hank Ruger and Nicholas

Though Park contrives to write with some sense of immediacy, even adding a "Preface" that feigns temporal proximity to the action, this is clearly a retrospect of considerable distance and born of substantial reflection on the events themselves. The voice, whenever it departs from quoting the spare narrative of the earlier journal, is one of self-conscious retrospect. Thus: "As most of the officers and crew were green about guns, and everything else concerning the Navy, we cut rather an awkward figure at first, but we soon began to get used to it, and every one seemed to be anxious for a fight, to see what it was like." Notably, at the end of the memoir, he says that midway through the war he was sick and tired of the whole thing and was tempted to throw the journal (this would have been the Repp notebook version) overboard. Thankfully, he changed his mind. And survival prompted a note of gratitude: "I have got through at last and thank God for it." Here again is a voice altered by temporal distance and mature reflection, a very different voice from that recording events in the original text.

Whereas Park's ur-text journal in Celeste's notebook is evidently private, with no pretensions of wider circulation, the author is clearly, in his later memoir, writing for an audience. His "Preface" thus concludes: "As this will be my first attempt to write anything longer than a short letter, nothing very brilliant can be expected, and if any one into whose hands this journal may fall should feel disappointed at not finding it better than it is, the remedy is simple; they need not read it." He concludes the memoir with a tip of the hat to those who have persisted: "So kind readers, if you have had the courage to follow me through this far, I thank you. So farewell!"

In terms of content, there are several striking departures in the later, Newberry text.

First, Park comments, sometimes at length, on the distinct personalities and relative merits of various individuals. He provides a wonderfully telling observation about Flag Officer Andrew Foote during a naval skirmish in mid-April 1862: "The Commodore hoisted his church pennant and went to praying on one end of his vessel, while from the other end he would let fly an occasional shot at the retreating boats." He extols the ship's surgeon on *Essex,* Thomas Rice, as one of the best and most respected in the navy, but observes

---

McCarty both socialized with Park after his return; James Henneberry, who would have been part of the same veterans' circle, died in 1888.

that the paymaster, Joseph H. Lewis, was "cordially hated by the whole ship's company." He winks at William Porter's laudatory report on the coolness and bravery of his young assistant, Master Willie Coates (fourteen years old) off Vicksburg in 1862: "The boy that Porter makes such a fuss about . . . did just the same as any other boy would have done in the same situation. He stowed himself away out of danger until it was all over." He provides several Porter anecdotes that nicely reflect the commander's personality: when Porter was in need of crew for *Essex* in the autumn of 1861, he "pulled up alongside the receiving ship *Maria Denning* . . . and said that he wanted forty of the greatest rascals on board." "We were quickly accommodated," says Park, "with forty careless looking young men who had been 'turned out of irons' for our special benefit. It however soon became apparent that the Captain had chosen the sort of men exactly suitable for him; although at first they were somewhat impatient of restraint they were by no means wanting in courage." Park ultimately offers a remarkably balanced assessment of *Essex*'s first and controversial captain:

> Although his character as a private individual was very far from being spotless or even upright, his reckless daring and utter contempt of danger had made him the idol of the crew, and although he may have deserved blame for sometimes acting too rashly, he certainly merits the gratitude of the loyal part of the country for his service on the Mississippi river. . . . I think it will be conceded by any one not prejudiced against him, or jealous of his growing reputation, that if he was too severe on the rebels along the river bank, he erred on the safe side, and had there been a few more such men as Captain Porter in the Western Navy, the rebels would not so soon have got over the terror with which the sight of a gunboat inspired them during the early part of this war.

No one is given more ink by Park, however, than the commander of USS *Pittsburg*, Egbert Thompson, who comes in for withering and relentless criticism. From the moment William Park is sent aboard *Pittsburg* under orders (while his own ship is being repaired following the Battle of Fort Henry) to the moment he rejoins "the old *Essex*" five months later, Park has not a single good thing to say about Thompson: "He was a drunken, cowardly, mean, small minded little man. I cannot find words to express my abhorrence of such a man, and all his officers were like him, with the exception of Mr. Tennyson the Pilot and Mr. Snyder the third Master." Those few officers for whom Park retained a modicum of respect were driven to disregard normal chain of command in some instances, as were members of the crew, and to assume responsibility for the ship's actions ("our Captain and his subordinates were that drunk that they did not know what they were doing"). Off Fort Pillow in May 1862 *Pittsburg*'s gunners kept up a spirited engagement with the enemy even after Thompson drunkenly ordered them to desist, convinced that they were firing at Union boats. Park's disgust is palpable; the captain had been in bed when Flag Officer Davis had signaled the call to arms, and, though the crew thought this might mean he would go into battle clearheaded for a change, they were mistaken, "for no sooner did he hear the rebel fleet were coming up than he swallowed a pint of whisky at one draught." By the time the battle was raging, Thompson could not, in Park's words, "see a hole through a ladder," let alone differentiate between Confederate and Federal flags. Thompson's reputation for intoxication, incompetence, and cowardice may have been what prompted Davis to leave *Pittsburg* at Fort Pillow rather than having her accompany the fleet to Memphis on June 5–6, 1862. Park, disappointed to miss that action, describes it in detail "as if present" in his Repp notebook journal; in his later memoir he simply includes Davis's official report, noting candidly that "I had not the pleasure to participate in" the Battle of Memphis.

Second, Park offers observations about the quality of various vessels. He condemns all "receiving ships" in the Mississippi squadron as "the dirtiest, most disagreeable, and without exception the most uncomfortable vessels I ever had the misfortunate to put my foot in"; only "Christian resignation" allows him to tolerate them. He regards the Ellet rams, on first sight of them (May 1862), as "the most miserable looking things. . . . They put me in mind of an old log house without a roof." In this case, however, he adds, "appearances are deceptive, for shortly afterwards [i.e., at the Battle of Memphis] they proved themselves more formidable than any of us expected." Comments on individual boats, positive and negative, appear frequently in the text.

Third, he offers a stronger sense of the bonds binding man to man aboard the ships. Though personal names are still few and far between, Park recalls the human toll of the fighting at greater length. Notably, he includes an expansive account of the Fort Henry disaster. After recounting William Porter's version of a "St. Crispin's Day" speech prior to the action, Park inserts an unusual statement, trenchant with the weight of his prior battle experience in

Europe: "I repaired to my station very reluctantly." And the harrowing chaos on the gun deck following the boiler explosion is described in gory detail, including the pleas of the suffering sailors that their mates put them out of their excruciating agony; as Park and others tried to cut off their scalded garments to give them relief, "in most cases the skin was pealing off with the clothes." Elsewhere, Park pauses over the death of several individual shipmates. Thus, concerning William Taylor who fell overboard and drowned above Fort Pillow in July 1862, Park observers that he was "one of our best men" and also an excellent swimmer; the latter fact prompts Park's surmise that he must have struck his head when he fell off the boat, fatally disabling him. The man killed during the running of the batteries at Vicksburg later the same month, though still not identified by name (Henneberry gives the name as Peter White), prompts a melancholy observation: "He was the last of four brothers who have fallen in this war and left their Mother a childless widow. The place where he lays is likely to become the last resting place of many a brave man before the fall of Vicksburg." When his mates buried him, Park adds, "his face and hands still bore the marks of Fort Henry." Of another death on the ship, that of an unpopular former inmate named Morgan following an altercation with a crewmate, Park hints at murder and cover-up: "in the rush to separate [Morgan and the unnamed sailor he quarreled with], some one stabbed Morgan in the stomach, and the wound proved too much for the Doctor. . . . Although he had been stabbed at midday where many must have seen the act committed, it was impossible to form the least idea of who was the perpetrator of the crime."

Fourth, he provides some details of his own involvement in specific operations: being sent to summon the towboat *Reliance* to the aid of the stranded *Mississippi* at Port Hudson (March 1863); firing at a rebel officer at the top of the Citadel at Port Hudson (May 1863) with a 9-inch gun, under orders to "knock him over" ("when the smoke cleared away he was nowhere to be seen and the battery was silenced"). Park also provides a more extensive account of his time ashore manning one of the batteries at Port Hudson and admits that contending with small arms fire from rebel sharpshooters was a whole new experience. "I had to brace my nerves and look as disconcerted as possible. I had got used to the big shots passing, but the rifle bullets was something I had not been used to." After the eventual surrender of that fort, Park recounts spending time chatting with Confederate prisoners; those with whom he had been locked in mortal combat for many months were now mere men like himself, prompting curiosity and even sympathy. Many, he learned, had been prisoners before—some captured at Fort Donelson, others at Shiloh. Virtually all of them, he observes, were tired of the war.

Fifth, he occasionally offers commentary on the political views of the crew. In so doing, he retains still some distance from the general opinion, including the near mutinous outrage on the Union gunboats at news of the Emancipation Proclamation: "We heard for the first time of President Lincoln's emancipation proclamation, and I rather think if old Abe had been on our gun deck when that document was read . . . he would have been able to form a pretty correct idea of how the proclamation was received by the whole Western Flotilla. On this occasion the greater part of our crew came out strong, they cursed Old Abe and the abolitionists generally and wished themselves at home and swore that if they had thought that the war was undertaken to free the niggers they never would have joined the service." A little later, he comments on the more muted (or perhaps more hypocritical) racism of Union soldiers: "No doubt many of our soldiers are in favour of freeing the negroes, but I doubt whether many or any of them are prepared to treat them as equals and recognize them as United States soldiers on the same footing as themselves, and although our soldiers may put up with nigger regiments as a necessary evil, they certainly have a strong dislike to them, and the white officers which belong to them."

For Park himself, racial prejudice was not part of his birthright or upbringing in rural Scotland; slavery had been officially abolished in Britain and most of the British Empire before he was born. And while he reflects some dubiety about relations between black and white Americans being normalized in the short run (the racism of his colleagues on the Union ironclads did not encourage optimism), he seems on a personal level to have been more concerned with the content of a man's character than the color of his skin. Hence his "abhorrence" of Egbert Thompson's spinelessness and default of leadership, and his somewhat equivocal but ultimately positive assessment of William D. Porter's warrior virtues of courage, alacrity, and solidarity with his men. In June 1863 at Port Hudson, Park watched as several white regiments were forced to labor in the hot sun while black soldiers took their leisure in the shade of nearby trees; Park was informed that this was a form of particularly degrading punishment devised by General Nathaniel Banks for cowardice on the part of the white troops a few days earlier (see Park's journal entry for June 18, 1863). "The only fault I found in the arrangement," Park observes, "is that he ought to make the officers shoulder the sand bags as well as the men, for they are a great deal more to blame. If they had been in their proper position that morning I am certain that the men would not have been found wanting, for I never yet saw a body of men that would not follow where any officer led." By which he surely meant, "any officer worthy of the name."

Bibliography

Civil War (General)

Allen, Felicity. *Jefferson Davis, Unconquerable Heart.* Columbia: University of Missouri Press, 1999.

Army and Navy Prayer Book [Confederate]. Richmond: Chas. H. Wynne, 1864. Facsimile ed. Unionville, NY: Royal Fireworks, 2005.

Ash, Stephen V. *When the Yankees Came: Conflict and Chaos in the Occupied South, 1861–1865.* Chapel Hill: University of North Carolina Press, 1995.

Bastian, David F. *Grant's Canal: The Union's Attempt to Bypass Vicksburg.* Shippensburg, PA: White Mane, 1995.

Bell, Andrew McIlwaine. *Mosquito Soldiers: Malaria, Yellow Fever, and the Course of the American Civil War.* Baton Rouge: Louisiana State University Press, 2010.

Buchanan, Lamont. *A Pictorial History of the Confederacy.* New York: Crown, 1951.

Cisco, Walter Brian. *War Crimes against Southern Civilians.* Gretna, LA: Pelican, 2007.

The Civil War: A Visual History: Rare Images and Tales of the War Between the States. New York: Parragon, 2011.

Coddington, Ronald S., ed. *Faces of the Civil War: An Album of Union Soldiers and Their Stories.* Baltimore: Johns Hopkins University Press, 2004.

Davis, William C. *Brothers in Arms: The Lives and Experiences of the Men Who Fought the Civil War—In Their Own Words.* New York: Salamander, 1995.

Davis, William C., and Bell I. Wiley, eds. *The Image of War: 1861–1865.* 6 vols. New York: Doubleday, 1981–84.

Donald, D. *Divided We Fought: A Pictorial History of the War, 1861–1865.* New York: Macmillan, 1956.

Evans, Clement Anselm. *Confederate Military History.* 12 vols. Atlanta: Confederate Publishing, 1899.

Fiske, John. *The Mississippi Valley in the Civil War.* Boston: Houghton Mifflin, 1900.

Foote, Shelby. *The Civil War: A Narrative.* 3 vols. New York: Random House, 1958, 1963, 1974.

Garrison, Webb, and Cheryl Garrison. *The Encyclopedia of Civil War Usage: An Illustrated Compendium of the Everyday Language of Soldiers and Civilians.* Nashville: Castle, 2009.

Guerney, Alfred H., and Henry M. Alden. *Harper's Pictorial History of the Civil War: Contemporary Accounts and Illustrations from the Most Important Magazine of the Time.* 1866. Facsimile ed. New York: Random House, 1996.

Gwynne, S. C. *Rebel Yell: The Violence, Passion, and Redemption of Stonewall Jackson.* New York: Scribner, 2014.

Hacker, J. David. "A Census-Based Count of the Civil War Dead." *Civil War History* 57, no. 4 (2011): 307–48.

Heidler, David Stephen, Jeanne T. Heidler, and David J. Coles. *Encyclopedia of the American Civil War: A Political, Social, and Military History.* New York: Norton, 2002.

Johnson, Robert Underwood, and Clarence Clough Buel, eds. *Battles and Leaders of the Civil War.* New York: Century, 1887. Available online at openlibrary.org.

Jones, J. William. *The Davis Memorial Volume; Or, Our Dead President, Jefferson Davis, and World's Tribute to His Memory.* Richmond, VA: R. F. Johnson and Co., 1890.

Keegan, John. *The American Civil War: A Military History.* New York: Knopf, 2009.

Leslie, Frank. *Leslie's Illustrated Civil War.* Jackson: University Press of Mississippi, 1992.

Miller, Francis Trevelyan. *The Photographic History of the Civil War.* 10 vols. New York: Review of Reviews, 1911. Reprint, New York: Blue and Grey, 1987.

Moore, Frank, ed. *The Rebellion Record: A Diary of American Events.* 12 vols. New York: Van Nostrand, 1861–68.

New York Times Complete Civil War: 1861–1865. Edited by Harold Holzer and Craig L. Symonds. New York: New York Times, 2010.

Rosen, Robert N. *The Jewish Confederates.* Columbia: University of South Carolina Press, 2000.

Schult, Duane. *The Most Glorious Fourth: Vicksburg and Gettysburg, July 4, 1863.* New York: Norton, 2002.

Shaara, Jeff. *Gods and Generals.* New York: Ballantine, 1996.

Strode, Hudson. *Jefferson Davis: Confederate President.* New York: Harcourt, Brace, 1959.

———. *Jefferson Davis: Tragic Hero. The Last Twenty-Five Years, 1864–1889.* New York: Harcourt, Brace, 1964.

Sutherland, Daniel E. *A Savage Conflict: The Decisive Role of Guerrillas in the American Civil War.* Chapel Hill: University of North Carolina Press, 2009.

Taylor, William Banks. *King Cotton and Old Glory: Natchez, Mississippi in the Age of Sectional Controversy and Civil War.* Hattiesburg, MS: Taylor, 1977.

Van Doren Stern, Philip, ed. *The Life and Writings of Abraham Lincoln.* New York: Random House, 1940.

Victor, Orville James. *The American Rebellion: Some Facts and Reflections for the Consideration of the English People.* New York: Beadle and Co., 1861. Reprint, n.p.: Nabu Press, 2011.

———. *The Comprehensive History of the Southern Rebellion and the War for the Union.* 1862. Reprint, Rarebookclub.com, 2012.

———. *The History, Civil, Political, and Military, of the Southern Rebellion.* Reprint, Ann Arbor: University of Michigan Library, 2009.

———. *Incidents and Anecdotes of the War, Together with Life Sketches of Eminent Leaders, and Narratives of the Most Memorable Battles for the Union.* New York: James D. Torrey, n.d.

White, Ronald C. *A. Lincoln: A Biography.* New York: Random House, 2009.

Whites, LeeAnn, and Alecia P. Long, eds. *Occupied Women: Gender, Military Occupation, and the American Civil War.* Baton Rouge: Louisiana State University Press, 2009.

Personal Memoirs and Correspondence

Ailenroc, M. R. [Cornelia Randolph]. *The White Castle of Louisiana.* Little Rock, AR: Morton, 1903. Reprint, Baton Rouge: Louisiana Library Association, 1986.

Bacon, Edward W. *Double Duty in the Civil War: The Letters of Sailor and Soldier Edward W. Bacon.* Edited by George S. Burkhardt. Carbondale: Southern Illinois University Press, 2009.

Banks, Nathaniel Prentiss. Nathaniel P. Banks Letter Book: 1863–1864. MSS. 2326. Louisiana and Lower Mississippi Valley Collections. Louisiana State University Libraries.

———. Nathaniel Prentiss Banks Papers. (1829–1911). MSS 11734. Manuscript Division, Library of Congress.

Blessington J. P. *The Campaigns of Walker's Texas Division, By a Private Soldier.* New York: Lange, Little and Co., 1875.

Brinton, John H. *Personal Memoirs of John H. Brinton, Civil War Surgeon, 1861–1865.* New York: Neale, 1914. Reprint, Carbondale: Southern Illinois University Press, 1996.

Brown, Spencer Kellogg. *His Life in Kansas and His Death as a Spy, 1842–1863, as Disclosed in His Diary,* edited by George Gardner Smith. New York: Appleton, 1903.

Browne, Henry R., and Symmes E. Browne. *From the Fresh-Water Navy: 1861–64: The Letters of Acting Master's Mate Henry R. Browne and Acting Ensign Symmes E. Browne.* Edited by John D. Milligan. Vol. 3 in the Naval Letters Series. Annapolis, MD: United States Naval Institute, 1970.

Browne, Junius Henri. *Four Years in Secessia: Adventures Within and Beyond the Union Lines: Embracing a Great Variety of Facts, Incidents, and Romance of the War.* Detroit: W. H. Davis, 1866.

Caldwell, Charles. Charles H. B. Caldwell Papers. MSS 253. "Port Hudson" series. Williams Research Center. Historic New Orleans Collection.

Chestnut, Mary Boykin. *A Diary from Dixie.* Edited by Ben Ames Williams. New York: Houghton Mifflin, 1949. Reprint, Cambridge: Harvard University Press, 1980.

Church, Frank L. *Civil War Marine: A Diary of the Red River Expedition, 1864.* Edited and annotated by James P. Jones and Edward F. Keuchel. 1975. Reprint, Honolulu: University Press of the Pacific, 2003.

Currie, George E. *Warfare along the Mississippi: The Letters of Lieutenant Colonel George E. Currie.* Edited by Norman E. Clarke Sr. Ann Arbor: Edwards, 1961.

Davis, Jefferson. *The Rise and Fall of the Confederate Government.* 2 vols. New York: D. Appleton and Co., 1881.

De Forest, John William. *A Volunteer's Adventures: A Union Captain's Record of the Civil War.* Edited by James H. Croushore. New Haven, CT: Yale University Press, 1946. Reprint, Baton Rouge: Louisiana State University Press, 1996.

Dewey, George. *Autobiography of George Dewey: Admiral of the Navy.* New York: Scribner, 1913.

Emerson, W. Eric, and Karen Stokes, eds. *Faith, Valor, and Devotion: The Civil War Letters of Willia Porcher DuBose.* Columbia: University of South Carolina Press, 2010.

Farragut, Loyall. *The Life of David Glasgow Farragut, First Admiral of the United States Navy: Embodying His Journal and Letters.* New York: D. Appleton, 1882.

Galligan, Edward M. Shipboard *Essex* Journal, October 1, 1861, to July 27, 1863. Photocopy of typed transcription. Montana Historical Society, Helena.

Gore, Laura Locoul. *Memories of the Old Plantation Home & A Creole Family Album.* Vacherie, LA: Zoë, 2007.

Grant, Ulysses S. *The Personal Memoirs of Ulysses S. Grant.* 2 vols. 1885. Reprint, Old Saybrook, CT: Konecky and Konecky, 1994.

[Griffis, Montgomery P.] *This Jolly Little Gunboat: The USS* Winona *on the Gulf Coast and Mississippi River 1861–1863.* Edited by Patrick E. Purcell. Iowa City: Camp Pope, 2014.

Gusley, Henry O. *The Southern Journey of a Civil War Marine: The Illustrated Note-Book of Henry O. Gusley.* Edited and annotated by Edward T. Cotham Jr. Austin: University of Texas Press, 2006.

Henneberry, James E. Shipboard *Essex* Journal, 1861–1864. Photostat of the original handwritten text. Chicago History Museum Research Center.

"J.M.M." Letter by a member of the 174th New York Regiment, May 2, 1862. New York State Military Museum and Veterans Research Center. http://dmna.state.ny.us/historic/reghist/civil/infantry/174thInf/174thInfCWN.htm.

Joiner, Gary D., ed. *Little to Eat and Thin Mud to Drink: Letters, Diaries, and Memoirs from the Red River Campaigns, 1863–1964.* Knoxville: University of Tennessee Press, 2007.

Jones, James P., and Edward F. Keuchel. *Civil War Marine: A Diary of the Red River Expedition, 1864*. 1975. Reprint, Honolulu: University Press of the Pacific, 2003.

Kleinpeter, George, and Family. Papers. Louisiana and Lower Mississippi Valley Collection. Louisiana State University.

Lee, William Mack. *History of the Life of Rev. Wm. Mack Lee: Body Servant of General Robert E. Lee through the Civil War.* Norfolk, VA: Smith Printing, 1918.

Logan, Fr. John, S.J. Untitled and undated personal remembrance of Fr. Darius Hubert, written shortly after his death in 1893. New Orleans Province Jesuit Archives, Loyola University, New Orleans.

Morgan, Sarah. *The Civil War Diary of Sarah Morgan.* Edited by Charles East. Athens: University of Georgia Press, 1991. Reprinted as *Sarah Morgan: The Civil War Diary of a Southern Woman.* New York: Simon and Schuster/Touchstone, 1992. All citations are to the 1992 edition.

———. "The Hope Estate Ladies" (November 19, 1908). Unpublished manuscript. LSU Libraries Special Collections. An excerpt appears in Leah Wood Jewett, "A Confederate Girl Remembers," *Civil War Book Review* (Winter 2011). www.cwbr.com.

Morrison, John G. "The Civil War Diary of John G. Morrison, 1861–1865." Naval Historical Center Library, Washington Navy Yard. http://dmna.ny.gov/historic/reghist/civil/infantry/30thInf/30thInf_Diary_Morrison.htm.

Oakes, Sister Mary Paulinus, R.S.M., ed. *Angels of Mercy: An Eyewitness Account of the Civil War and Yellow Fever: A Primary Source by Sister Ignatius Sumner.* Baltimore: Cathedral Foundation Press, 1998.

Paine, Halbert Eleazer. *A Wisconsin Yankee in Confederate Bayou Country: The Civil War Reminiscences of a Union General.* Edited by Samuel C. Hyde Jr. Baton Rouge: Louisiana State University Press, 2009.

Park, William Little. "W. L. Park's Journal." Newberry Library, Chicago.

Porter, Admiral David D. *The Naval History of the Civil War.* New York: Sherman Publishing Co., 1886. Reprint, Mineola, NY: Dover, 1998.

Ratchford, J. W. *Some Reminiscences of Persons and Incidents of the Civil War.* Privately printed, 1909. Facsimile ed., Austin, TX: Shoal Creek, 1971.

Read, Charles W. "Reminiscences of the Confederate States Navy." *Southern Historical Society Papers* 1 (1876): 331–62.

Ripley, Eliza McHatton. *From Flag to Flag: A Woman's Adventures and Experience in the South during the War, in Mexico, and in Cuba.* New York: Appleton and Co., 1889.

Russell, William Howard. *William Howard Russell's Civil War: Private Diary and Letters, 1861–1862.* Edited by Martin Crawford. Athens: University of Georgia Press, 1992.

Smith, George Gilbert. *Leaves from a Soldier's Diary: The Personal Record of Lieutenant George G. Smith.* Putnam, CT: George G. Smith, 1906.

Thompson, General M. Jeff. *The Civil War Reminiscences of General M. Jeff Thompson.* Edited by Donald J. Stanton, Goodwin F. Berquist, and Paul C. Bowers. Dayton: Morningside House, 1988.

Walke, Henry. *Naval Scenes and Reminiscences of the Civil War in the United States on the Southern and Western Waters during the Years 1861, 1862, and 1863 with the History of That Period Compared and Corrected from Authentic Sources.* New York: F. R. Reed and Co., 1877.

Walker, John George. *Greyhound Commander: Confederate General John G. Walker's History of the Civil War West of the Mississippi.* Edited by Richard Lowe. Baton Rouge: Louisiana State University Press, 2013.

Watson, William (of Skelmorlie, Scotland). *Life in the Confederate Army: Being the Observations and Experiences of an Alien in the South during the American Civil War.* London: Chapman and Hall, 1887.

Welles, Gideon. *Diary of Gideon Welles, Secretary of the Navy under Lincoln and Johnson.* Edited by Howard K. Beale. 3 vols. New York: Norton, 1960.

Williams, Thomas. "Letters of General Thomas Williams, 1862." *American Historical Review* 14, no. 2 (1909): 304–28.

The Navy War

Anderson, Bern. *By Sea and by River: The Naval History of the Civil War.* New York: Knopf, 1962.

Barry, John M. *Rising Tide: The Great Mississippi Flood of 1927 and How It Changed America.* New York: Simon and Schuster, 1997.

Bennett, Michael J. *Union Jacks: Yankee Sailors in the Civil War.* Chapel Hill: University of North Carolina Press, 2004.

Bragg, Marion. *Historic Names and Places on the Lower Mississippi River.* Vicksburg, MS: Mississippi River Commission, 1977.

Budd, Nicholas F. "The Adaptation of the Vessels of the Western Gunboat Flotilla to the Circumstances of Riverine Warfare during the American Civil War." Masters thesis, U.S. Army Command and General Staff College, 1997.

Cunningham, Edward. *The Port Hudson Campaign: 1862–1863.* 1963. Reprint, Baton Rouge: Louisiana State University Press, 1994.

Deans-Barrett, Catherine. "History of Mound City Marine Ways during the Civil War." *Cairo Evening Citizen,* April 13, 1961.

deKay, James Tertius. Monitor*: The Story of the Legendary Civil War Ironclad and the Man Whose Invention Changed the Course of History.* New York: Ballantine, 1997.

Duffy, James P. *Lincoln's Admiral: The Civil War Campaigns of David Farragut.* Hoboken, NJ: Wiley, 1997.

Dufour, Charles L. *The Night the War Was Lost.* 1960. Lincoln: University of Nebraska Press, 1990.

Edmonds, David C. *The Guns of Port Hudson.* 2 vols. Lafayette, LA: Acadiana, 1983–84.

Fiske, John. *The Mississippi Valley in the Civil War.* Boston: Houghton Mifflin, 1900.

Fowler, William M. *Under Two Flags: The American Navy in the Civil War.* New York: Avon, 1990.

Gift, George W. "The Story of the *Arkansas.*" *Southern Historical Society Papers* 12 (1884): 48–54, 115–19, 163–70, 205–12.

Gosnell, H. Allen. *Guns on the Western Waters: The Story of River Gunboats in the Civil War.* 1949. Reprint, Baton Rouge: Louisiana State University Press, 1993.

Hearn, Chester G. *Ellet's Brigade: The Strangest Outfit of All.* Baton Rouge: Louisiana State University Press, 2006.

Hurst, Robert M., Jr. "Marine Ways at Mound City Played Important Part in the History of This Nation." *Cairo Evening Citizen,* November 2, 1938.

Jackson, Rex T. *James B. Eads: The Civil War Ironclads and His Mississippi.* Westminster, MD: Heritage, 2004.

Johnson, Ludwell. *Red River Campaign: Politics and Cotton in the Civil War.* Kent, OH: Kent State University Press, 1999.

Joiner, Gary D. *Mr. Lincoln's Brown Water Navy: The Mississippi Squadron.* New York: Rowman and Littlefield, 2007.

———. *One Damn Blunder from Beginning to End: The Red River Campaign of 1864.* Lanham, MD: Rowman and Littlefield, 2003.

Konstam, Angus. *Union River Ironclad 1861–65.* Oxford: Osprey, 2002.

Langley, Harold D. "The Sailor's Life." In *Fighting for Time,* vol. 4 of *The Image of War: 1861–1865,* 6 vols., edited by William C. Davis and Bell I. Wiley. New York: Doubleday, 1981–84.

Lester, C. E. "The Gun-Boat *Essex.*" *Harper's New Monthly Magazine,* February 1863, 397–406. Available online at Cornell University's The Making of America site: cdl.library.cornell.edu/moa.

Mahan, Alfred Thayer. *The Gulf and Inland Waters: The Navy in the Civil War.* New York: Scribner's, 1883.

Miller, Francis Trevelyan, ed. *The Navies.* Volume 6 of *The Photographic History of the Civil War.* New York: Castle, 1957.

Milligan, John D. *Gunboats down the Mississippi.* Annapolis: United States Naval Institute, 1965.

Phillips, Dinwiddle B. "Notes on the *Monitor–Merrimac* Fight." *Southern Bivouac* (March 1887). Condensed and reprinted in *Battles and Leaders of the Civil War,* edited by Robert Underwood Johnson and Clarence Clough Buel, 1:712–18. New York: Century, 1887. Available online at openlibrary.org.

Pratt, Fletcher. *Civil War on Western Waters, Illustrated with Maps and Photographs.* New York: Holt, 1956.

Quarstein, John V. *The CSS* Virginia: *Sink Before Surrender.* Charleston: SC: History Press, 2012.

Roca, Steven Louis. "Presence and Precedence: The USS *Red Rover* during the Civil War, 1861–1865." *Civil War History* 44, no. 2 (1998): 91–110.

Scharf, John Thomas. *History of the Confederate States Navy from Its Organization to the Surrender of Its Last Vessel.* New York: Rogers and Sherwood, 1887.

Shea, William L., and Terrence J. Winshel. *Vicksburg Is the Key: The Struggle for the Mississippi River.* Great Campaigns of the Civil War. Lincoln: University of Nebraska Press, 2003.

Smith, Myron J., Jr. *The CSS* Arkansas: *A Confederate Ironclad on Western Waters.* Jefferson, NC: McFarland, 2011.

———. *The Timberclads in the Civil War.* Jefferson, NC: McFarland, 2008.

———. *Tinclads in the Civil War: Union Light-Draught Gunboat Operations on Western Waters, 1862–1865.* Jefferson, NC: McFarland, 2008.

———. *The USS* Carondelet: *A Civil War Ironclad on Western Waters.* Jefferson, NC: McFarland, 2010.

Tucker, Spencer C. *Blue & Gray Navies: The Civil War Afloat.* Annapolis, MD: Naval Institute Press, 2006.

Veit, Chuck. *A Dog before a Soldier: Almost-Lost Episodes in the U.S. Navy's Civil War.* North Attleboro, MA: Veit, 2010.

Williams, Glenn F. "The Many Tasks of Uncle Sam's Webfeet." *America's Civil War Magazine* 15, no. 1 (2002): 22–29

———. "Uncle Sam's Webfeet: The Union Navy in the Civil War. *International Journal of Naval History* 1, no. 1 (2002).

Louisiana (General) and Baton Rouge

Carleton, Mark T. *River Capital: An Illustrated History of Baton Rouge.* Woodland Hills, CA: Windsor, 1981.

Draughon, Ralph, Jr. *Down by the River: A History of the Baton Rouge Riverfront.* New Orleans: U.S. Army Corps of Engineers, New Orleans District, 1998.

East, Charles. *Baton Rouge: A Civil War Album.* Baton Rouge: East, 1977.

Martin, Mark E. *Historic Photos of Baton Rouge.* Nashville: Turner, 2008.

Rodrigue, Sylvia Frank, and Faye Phillips. *Baton Rouge.* Images of America series. Charleston, SC: Arcadia, 2008.

Wall, Bennett H., and John C. Rodrigue, eds. *Louisiana: A History.* 6th ed. Chichester, UK: Wiley, 2014.

The War in Louisiana, Louisiana Troops

Bergeron, Arthur W., Jr. *Guide to Louisiana Confederate Military Units.* Baton Rouge: Louisiana State University Press, 1989.

Booth, Andrew B. *Records of Louisiana Confederate Soldiers and Louisiana Commands.* 3 vols. New Orleans: n.p., 1920.

Dabney, Thomas Ewing. "The Butler Regime in Louisiana." *Louisiana Historical Quarterly* 27 (1944): 487–526.

Dimitry, John. *Confederate Military History of Louisiana.* Pensacola, FL: eBooksOnDisk.com, 2005.

Hearn, Chester G. *When the Devil Came Down to Dixie.* Baton Rouge: Louisiana State University Press, 2000.

Hollandsworth, James G., Jr. *Pretense of Glory: The Life of General Nathaniel P. Banks.* Baton Rouge: Louisiana State University Press, 1998.

Jones, Terry L. *Lee's Tigers: The Louisiana Infantry in the Army of Northern Virginia.* Baton Rouge: Louisiana State University Press, 1987.

Marshall, Jeffrey D. "'Butler's Rotten Breath of Calumny': Major General Benjamin F. Butler and the Censure of the Seventh Vermont Infantry Regiment." *Vermont History* 72 (2004): 23–54.

Mayeux, Steven M. *Earthen Walls, Iron Men: Fort DeRussy, Louisiana, and the Defense of Red River.* Knoxville: University of Tennessee Press, 2007.

Richey, Thomas H. *The Battle of Baton Rouge.* 2nd ed. College Station, TX: Virtual Bookworm.com Publishing, 2005.

Savas, Theodore P., David A. Woodbury, and Gary D. Joiner, eds. *The Red River Campaign: Union and Confederate Leadership and the War in Louisiana.* Shreveport: Parabellum, 2003.

Winters, John D. *The Civil War in Louisiana.* Baton Rouge: Louisiana State University Press, 1963.

Catholics and Catholic Education in the Nineteenth Century

Bernard, Mother Mary, R.S.M. *The Story of the Sisters of Mercy in Mississippi, 1860–1930.* New York: Kenedy, 1931.

Biever, Albert H., S.J. *The Jesuits in New Orleans and the Mississippi Valley: Jubilee Memorial.* New Orleans: Society of Jesus in Louisiana, 1924.

Clancy, Thomas H. "The Antebellum Jesuits of the New Orleans Province, 1837–1861." *Louisiana History* 34, no. 3 (1993): 327–43.

Diamond Jubilee: St. Paul's Parish 1851–1926. A commemorative booklet (51 pages) for St. Paul's Parish, Pass Christian, MS. Pages 43–48 are devoted to the Sisters of Mercy mission in Pass Christian.

Jacobs, Richard M., O.S.A. "U.S. Catholic Schools and the Religious Who Served in Them: Contributions in the 18th and 19th Centuries." *Catholic Education* 1, no. 4 (1998): 364–83.

Gache, Fr. Louis-Hippolyte, S.J. "Our College at Baton Rouge, Louisiana." *Woodstock Letters* 27 (1898): 1–5.

Healy, Kathleen, R.S.M. *Sisters of Mercy: Spirituality in America 1843–1900*. New York: Paulist, 1992.

Hitzman, Rev. Lyle F. "St. Joseph Church, Baton Rouge (1792–1893): The First One Hundred Years." Master's thesis, Notre Dame Seminary, New Orleans, 1973.

Jubilee III: St. Paul Catholic Church 1847–1997. Edited and compiled by Dan Ellis. Pass Christian, MS: St. Paul Catholic Church, 1997.

Kelly, Sister M. Veronica. "A Century of Catholic Education in Baton Rouge, 1847–1947." Master's thesis, Catholic University of America, 1947.

Kenny, Michael, S.J. *Catholic Culture in Alabama: Centenary Story of Spring Hill College 1830–1930*. New York: America, 1931.

Miller, Randall M., and Jon L. Wakelyn. *Catholics in the Old South: Essays on Church and Culture*. Macon, GA: Mercer University Press, 1999.

Mobley, John. "The Academy Movement in Louisiana." *Louisiana Historical Quarterly* 30 (1947): 738–978.

Nugent, Sister Helen Louise. *Sister Louise: Josephine Van Der Schrieck 1813–1886*. Studies in American Church History. Washington, DC: Catholic University of America, 1931.

Oakes, Sister Mary Paulinus. *The Tapestry of Mercy: The History of the St. Louis Regional Community of the Sisters of Mercy of the Americas*. St. Louis: Sisters of Mercy, 2008.

O'Donnell, H. J. "The Lay Teacher in Catholic Education. *Notre Dame Journal of Education* 2 (1971): 84–96.

Platt, R. Eric. *Sacrifice and Survival: Identity, Mission, and Jesuit Higher Education in the American South*. Tuscaloosa: University of Alabama Press, 2014.

Uter, Frank. *A History of the Catholic Church in Baton Rouge*. Baton Rouge: St. Joseph Cathedral, 1992.

Woodstock Letters: A Record of Current Events and Historical Notes Connected with the Colleges and Missions of the Society of Jesus in North and South America. Baltimore, MD: Woodstock College, 1872–1969.

Religious Issues in the Civil War

Carey, Patrick W. "Orestes Brownson and the Civil War." *U.S. Catholic Historian* 31, no. 1 (2013): 1–20.

Faust, Drew G. "Christian Soldiers: The Meaning of Revivalism in the Confederate Army." *Journal of Southern History* 53 (1987): 63–90.

Harman, Troy D. "The Great Revival of 1863: The Effects upon Lee's Army of Northern Virginia." In *The American Civil War in 1863: Programs of the Eighth Annual Gettysburg Seminar,* 105–30. Gettysburg, PA: Gettysburg National Military Park, 2001.

Mathews, Donald G. *Religion in the Old South.* Chicago: University of Chicago Press, 1977.

Miller, Randall M., Harry S. Stout, and Charles Reagan Wilson, eds. *Religion and the American Civil War.* New York: Oxford University Press, 1998.

Miller, Robert J. *Both Prayed to the Same God: Religion and Faith in the American Civil War.* Lanham, MD: Rowman and Littlefield, 2007.

Mitchell, Reid. "Christian Soldiers? Perfecting the Confederacy." In *Religion and the American Civil War,* edited by Randall M. Miller, 297–309. New York: Oxford University Press, 1998.

Noll, Mark A. *The Civil War as a Theological Crisis.* Chapel Hill: University of North Carolina Press, 2006.

Pastor, Lori Renee. "Black Catholicism: Religion and Slavery in Antebellum Louisiana." Master's thesis, University of Dallas, 2003.

Phillips, Jason. *Diehard Rebels: The Confederate Culture of Invincibility.* Athens: University of Georgia Press, 2007.

Rable, George C. *God's Almost Chosen Peoples: A Religious History of the American Civil War.* Chapel Hill: University of North Carolina Press, 2010.

Romero, Sidney J. *Religion in the Rebel Ranks.* Lanham, MD: University Press of America, 1983.

Snay, Mitchell. *Gospel of Disunion: Religion and Separatism in the Antebellum South.* Cambridge: Cambridge University Press, 1993; Chapel Hill: University of North Carolina Press, 1997.

Stern, Andrew Henry. *Southern Crucifix, Southern Cross: Catholic-Protestant Relations in the Old South.* Tuscaloosa: University of Alabama Press, 2012.

Woodworth, Steven E. *While God Is Marching On: The Religious World of Civil War Soldiers.* Lawrence: University Press of Kansas, 2001.

Civil War Chaplains

Beagle, Donald Robert, and Bryan Albin Giemza. *Poet of the Lost Cause: A Life of Father Ryan.* Knoxville: University of Tennessee Press, 2008.

Bennett, William W. *A Narrative of the Great Revival Which Prevailed in the Southern Armies during the Late Civil War Between the States of the Federal Union.* Philadelphia: Claxton, Remsen and Haffelfinger, 1877.

Boswell, E. M. "Rebel Religion." *Civil War Times Illustrated* 11, no. 8 (October 1972): 26–33.

Brinsfield, John Wesley. *The Spirit Divided: Memoirs of Civil War Chaplains—The Confederacy.* Macon, GA: Mercer University Press, 2006.

Brinsfield, John W., William C. Davis, James I. Robertson, and Benjamin Maryniak. *Faith in the Fight: Civil War Chaplains.* Mechanicsburg, PA: Stackpole, 2003.

Daniel, W. Harrison, ed. "Chaplains in the Army of Northern Virginia: A List Compiled in 1864 and 1865 by Robert L. Dabley." *Virginia Magazine of History and Biography* 71, no. 3 (1963): 327–40.

Dollar, Kent T. *Soldiers of the Cross: Confederate Soldier Christians and the Impact of War on Their Faith.* Macon, GA: Mercer University Press, 2005.

Faherty, William Barnaby. *Exile in Erin: A Confederate Chaplain's Story—The Life of Father John B. Bannon.* St. Louis: Missouri Historical Society Press, 2002.

Fuller, A. James. *Chaplain to the Confederacy: Basil Manly and Baptist Life in the Old South.* Baton Rouge: Louisiana State University Press, 2000.

Gache, Peter Louis-Hippolyte, S.J. *Frenchman, Chaplain, Rebel: The Civil War Letters of Peter Louis-Hippolyte Gache, S.J., 10th Louisiana Infantry.* Edited and translated by Cornelius M. Buckley, S.J. Tuscaloosa: University of Alabama Press, 1981.

Germain, Dom Aidan Henry. *Catholic Military and Naval Chaplains, 1776–1917.* 1929. Reprint, Berwyn Heights, MD: Heritage, 2007.

Jones, J. William. *Christ in the Camp: Or, Religion in Lee's Army.* Richmond, VA: B. F. Johnson and Co., 1887.

King, T[erence] S., S.J. "A Confederate Chaplain at Frederick, 1862–64." *Woodstock Letters* 58, no. 3 (1929): 566–78.

———. "Letters of Civil War Chaplains." *Woodstock Letters* 43, no. 1 (1914): 24–34.

———. "Letters of Civil War Chaplains." *Woodstock Letters* 43, no. 2 (1914): 168–80.

Maryniak, Benedict R., and John Wesley Brinsfield, Jr. *The Spirit Divided: Memoirs of Civil War Chaplains—The Union.* Macon, GA: Mercer University Press, 2007.

Romero, Sidney J. "Louisiana Clergy and the Confederate Army." *Louisiana History* 2, no. 3 (1961): 277–300.

Rumberg, H. Rondel, ed. *Chaplain's Handbook* [Confederate]. Enlarged Sesquicentennial ed. Columbia, TN: Sons of Confederate Veterans, 2011.

———. *Stonewall Jackson's Chaplain: Beverly Tucker Lacy.* Spout Spring, VA: Society for Biblical and Southern Studies, 2013.

Sheeran, Rev. James, C.S.S.R. *Confederate Chaplain: A War Journal.* Edited by Joseph T. Durkin, S.J. Milwaukee: Bruce, 1960.

Tucker, Phillip Thomas. *The Confederacy's Fighting Chaplain: Father John B. Bannon.* Tuscaloosa: University of Alabama Press, 1992.

Wiatt, William Edward. *Confederate Chaplain: William Edward Wiatt, An Annotated Diary.* Edited by Alex L. Wiatt. Lynchburg, VA: Howard, 1994.

Slavery, Abolition, and Race

Bennett, James B. *Religion and the Rise of Jim Crow in New Orleans.* Princeton: Princeton University Press, 2005.

Blum, Edward J., and Paul Harvey. *The Color of Christ: The Son of God and the Saga of Race in America.* Chapel Hill: University of North Carolina Press, 2012.

Campbell, Edward D. C., Jr., ed. *Before Freedom Came: African-American Life in the Antebellum South.* Richmond: Museum of the Confederacy and the University Press of Virginia, 1991.

Fox-Genovese, Elizabeth. *Within the Plantation Household: Black and White Women of the Old South.* Chapel Hill: University of North Carolina Press, 1988.

Genovese, Eugene. *Roll, Jordan, Roll: The World the Slaves Made.* New York: Vintage, 1976.

———. *The Slaveholders' Dilemma: Freedom and Progress in Southern Conservative Thought, 1820–1860.* Columbia: University of South Carolina Press, 1992.

Genovese, Eugene, and Elizabeth Fox-Genovese. "The Divine Sanction of Social Order: Religious Foundations of the Southern Slaveholders' World View." *Journal of the American Academy of Religion* 55 (1987): 211–34.

———. *The Mind of the Master Class: History and Faith in the Southern Slaveholders' Worldview.* Cambridge: Cambridge University Press, 2005.

———. "The Religious Ideals of Southern Slave Society." *Georgia Historical Quarterly* 70, no. 1 (1986): 1–16.

———. *Slavery in White and Black: Class and Race in the Southern Slaveholders' New World Order.* Cambridge: Cambridge University Press, 2008.

Phillips, Ulrich Bonnell. *Life and Labor in the Old South.* New York: Little, Brown, 1929. Reprint, Columbia: University of South Carolina Press, 2007.

Richter, William L. "Slavery in Antebellum Baton Rouge, 1820–1860." *Louisiana History* 10 (1969): 125–46.

Siebert, Wilbur Henry. *The Underground Railroad: From Slavery to Freedom.* New York: Macmillan, 1898.

Sloane, Rush R. "The Underground Railroad of the Firelands." *Firelands Pioneer,* n.s., 5 (1888): 28–59.

Woodward, C. Vann. *The Strange Career of Jim Crow.* 1955. Commemorative (third revised) edition, with a new afterword by William S. McFeely. New York: Oxford University Press, 2002.

Aftermath, Assessment, the Lost Cause

Andrews, Sidney. "Three Months among the Reconstructionists." *Atlantic* 17 (1866): 237–46.

Blair, William A. *Cities of the Dead: Contesting the Memory of the Civil War in the South: 1865–1914.* Chapel Hill: University of North Carolina Press, 2004.

Cooper, William J., Jr., and John M. McCardell Jr. *In the Cause of Liberty: How the Civil War Redefined American Ideals.* Baton Rouge: Louisiana State University Press, 2009.

Curran, Robert Emmett. "The Irish and the Lost Cause: Two Voices." *U.S. Catholic Historian* 31, no. 1 (2013): 129–45.

de la Morinière, Emmanuel. "Chivalry." Lecture given at Odd Fellows Hall, New Orleans, April 5, 1893. In *The Louisiana Book: Selections from the Literature of the State,* edited by Thomas M'Caleb, 174–79. New Orleans: R. F. Straughan, 1894. Reprint, New Orleans: Cornerstone, 2012.

Eggleston, George Cary. *A Rebel's Recollections.* A series of essays published in the *Atlantic* in 1874 and subsequently gathered into a single volume of the same name. New York: Hurd and Houghton, 1875.

Foster, Gaines M. *Ghosts of the Confederacy: Defeat, the Lost Cause, and the Emergence of the New South.* New York: Oxford University Press, 1987.

Gallagher, Gary W., and Alan T. Nolan. *The Myth of the Lost Cause and Civil War History.* Bloomington: Indiana University Press, 2000.

Genovese, Eugene. *A Consuming Fire: The Fall of the Confederacy in the Mind of the White Christian South.* Athens: University of Georgia Press, 1998.

Janney, Caroline E. *Remembering the Civil War: Reunion and the Limits of Reconciliation.* Chapel Hill: University of North Carolina Press, 2013.

Neff, John R. *Honoring the Civil War Dead: Commemoration and the Problem of Reconciliation.* Lawrence: University Press of Kansas, 2005.

Pasquier, Michael. "Catholic Southerners, Catholic Soldiers: White Creoles, the Civil War, and the Lost Cause in New Orleans." Master's thesis, Florida State University, 2003.

Phillips, Jason. *Diehard Rebels: The Confederate Culture of Invincibility.* Athens: University of Georgia Press, 2007.

Pollard, Edward Alfred. *The Lost Cause: A New Southern History of the War of the Confederates: Comprising a Full and Authentic Account of the Rise and Progress of the Late Southern Confederacy—The Campaigns, Battles, Incidents, and Adventures of the Most Gigantic Struggle of World History.* New York: E. B. Treat, 1866.

Roland, Charles P. *Reflections on Lee: A Historian's Assessment.* Mechanicburg, PA: Stackpole, 1995.

Ryan, Abram Joseph. *Poems: Patriotic, Religious, Miscellaneous.* Baltimore: J. B. Piet, 1880.

Stout, Harry. *Upon the Altar of the Nation: A Moral History of the American Civil War.* New York: Viking, 2006.

Townes, W. Stuart. *Enduring Legacy: Rhetoric and Ritual of the Lost Cause.* Tuscaloosa: University of Alabama Press, 2012.

Trowbridge, J. T. *The Desolate South, 1865–1866: A Picture of the Battlefields and of the Devastated Confederacy.* Edited by Gordon Carroll. New York: Little, Brown, 1956.

Unger, Irwin, ed. *Essays on the Civil War and Reconstruction.* New York: Holt, Rinehart and Winston, 1970.

Waldrep, Christopher. *Vicksburg's Long Shadow: The Civil War Legacy of Race and Remembrance.* New York: Rowman and Littlefield, 2005.

Whites, LeeAnn, and Alecia P. Long. *Occupied Women: Gender, Military Occupation, and the American Civil War.* Baton Rouge: Louisiana State University Press, 2009.

Wilson, Charles Reagan. *Baptized in Blood: The Religion of the Lost Cause, 1865–1920.* 1980. Athens: University of Georgia Press, 2009.

Other Miscellaneous Works of Relevance to the Repp/Park Journal

Anthony, Susan B., Elizabeth Cady Stanton, and Matilda Joslyn Gage, et al., eds. *History of Woman Suffrage.* 6 vols. Rochester, NY: Susan B. Anthony, 1881–1922.

Bloom, Khaled J. *The Mississippi Valley's Great Yellow Fever Epidemic of 1878.* Baton Rouge: Louisiana State University Press, 1993.

Campbell, Charles, ed. *Some Materials [largely contributed by Junia A. Burk] to Serve for a Brief Memoir of John Daly Burk . . . With a Sketch of the Life and Character of His Only Child, Judge John Junius Burk.* Albany, NY: Joel Munsell, 1868.

Clemens, Samuel. *Mark Twain's Letters.* Vol. 5, *1872–1873.* Edited by Lin Salamo and Harriet Elinor Smith. Berkeley: University of California Press, 1997.

Cotton, Gordon A. *Images of America: Vicksburg.* Charleston, SC: Arcadia, 1999.

Fahs, Alice. *The Imagined Civil War: Popular Literature of the North and South, 1861–1865.* Chapel Hill: University of North Carolina Press, 2001.

Humphreys, Margaret. *Yellow Fever and the South.* Baltimore: Johns Hopkins University Press, 1999.

Johannsen, Albert. *The House of Beadle and Adams and Its Dime and Nickel Novels: The Story of a Vanished Literature.* 2 vols. Norman: University of Oklahoma Press, 1950.

King, Grace Elizabeth. *New Orleans: The Place and the People.* New York: Macmillan, 1895. Reprint, n.p.: General, 2009.

Kirke, Edmund. *Among the Pines: Or, South in Secession-Time.* 1862. Reprint, New York: Haskell House, 1969.

———. *My Southern Friends.* 1863. Reprint, New York: Haskell House, 1869.

Martin, Jim. *A Bit of A Blue: The Life and Work of Frances Fuller Victor.* Salem, OR: Deep Well, 1992.

McCaleb, Thomas. *The Louisiana Book: Selections from the Literature of the State.* New Orleans, 1894. Reprint, New Orleans: Cornerstone, 2012.

"Metta Victoria Fuller Victor." *Nineteenth-Century American Women Writers.* Westport, CT: Greenwood, 1997.

O'Brien, Frank P. *The Beadle Collection of Dime Novels Given to the New York Public Library by Dr. Frank P. O'Brien.* New York: New York Public Library, 1922.

Spencer, Platt Rogers. *Spencerian Key to Practical Penmanship.* New York: Ivison, Phinney, Blakeman and Co., 1866.

Sperry, Kip. *Reading Early American Handwriting.* Baltimore: Genealogical Publishing, 1998.

Stokes, George Stewart. *Agnes Repplier: Lady of Letters.* Philadelphia: University of Pennsylvania Press, 1949.

Thornton, Tamara Plakins. *Handwriting in America: A Cultural History.* New Haven, CT: Yale University Press, 1998.

Victor, Metta Victoria Fuller. *Maum Guinea, and Her Plantation "Children," Or Holiday-Week on a Louisiana Estate.* New York: Irwin P. Beadle and Co., 1861. Reprint, Bedford, MA: Applewood, 1999.

———. *The Unionist's Daughter: A Tale of the Rebellion in Tennessee.* New York: Beadle and Co., 1862. Reprint, Indianapolis: Repressed, 2014.

Contemporary Newspapers and Magazines

Atlantic Monthly
Baton Rouge Daily Advocate
Baton Rouge Daily Comet
Baton Rouge Daily Gazette and Comet
Baton Rouge Gazette
Baton Rouge State Times Advocate
Baton Rouge Weekly Comet
Baton Rouge Weekly Gazette and Comet
Century Magazine
Catholic World
Harper's Weekly
New Orleans Bee (L'Abeille)
New Orleans Daily Picayune
New Orleans Mirror
New Orleans Morning Star and Catholic Messenger
New Orleans Times-Picayune
New York Times
Plaquemine Southern Sentinel
Richmond Daily Dispatch
Richmond Dispatch
Richmond Times
Richmond Times-Dispatch
Southern Bivouac
Vicksburg Daily Herald
Vicksburg Evening Post
Vicksburg Weekly Herald
West Baton Rouge Sugar Planter

Journals/Periodicals

Civil War History

Civil War Times Illustrated

Journal of Southern History

Journal of Southern Religion

Museum of the Confederacy Magazine

North and South

Southern Historical Society Papers

Archives and Government Sources

Census records [Canada] for Pontiac County, Clarendon Township [Province of Quebec].

Census records [Scotland] for Dufriesshire County.

Compiled Service Records of Confederate General and Staff Officers, and Nonregimental Enlisted Men.

Compiled Service Records of Volunteer Union Soldiers.

Compiled Service Records of Union Sailors.

Congressional Serial Set. Washington, DC: U.S. Government Printing Office. Federal Census records for East Baton Rouge Parish and nearby parishes in Louisiana; New Orleans, LA; Chicago, IL; Hamlin County, SD; Little Rock, AK; Lansing, MI; Philadelphia, PA; Sandusky, OH.

Index to Rendezvous Reports during the Civil War, 1861–1865.

Louisiana Historical Association collection. MSS Collection 55. Louisiana Research Collection. Howard-Tilton Memorial Library. Tulane University. New Orleans.

Navy Survivors' Certificates.

United States Naval Enlistment Rendezvous, 1855–1891.

U.S. Civil War Soldiers, 1861–1865. National Park Service.

U.S. Navy Department. *Official Records of the Union and Confederate Navies in the War of the Rebellion.* 30 vols. Washington, DC: U.S. Government Printing Office, 1894–1922. Records specifically concerned with "Naval Forces on Western Waters" are contained in Series 1, vols. 22–27.

U.S. War Department. *The War of the Rebellion: A Compilation of the Official Records of the Union and Confederate Armies.* 130 vols. Washington, DC: U.S. Government Printing Office, 1880–1901.

Other archival collections are noted in the acknowledgments.

Index

Inaccurate spelling in Park's journal or correspondence is corrected in the index. Dates in parentheses following vessel names indicate active service in the Civil War.